VOTER TURNOUT

since 1945

A Global Report

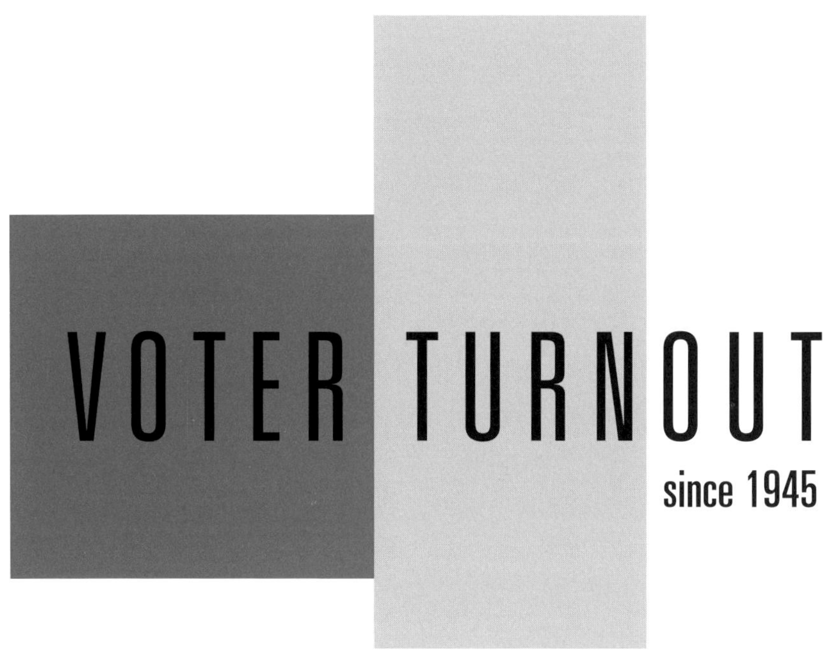

Rafael López Pintor
Maria Gratschew

with

Jamal Adimi, Julie Ballington, Craig Brians,
Sergei Lounev, Dieter Nohlen,
Pippa Norris, Smita Notosusanto, Kate Sullivan,
Edmundo Urrutia

A Global Report

Voter Turnout Since 1945
A Global Report

This is the third book in the voter turnout series, previously entitled *Voter Turnout from 1945 to 1997: a Global Report on Political Participation.*

Design & layout: Holmberg Design AB
Cover Photos: © Theresa Laanela, © Julie Ballington, © Bruce Weaver - AFP
Map design: Martin Ek, adjusted by Holmberg & Holmberg Design AB
Printed and bound by: Bulls Tryckeri, Halmstad
ISBN: 91-89098-61-7

Contents

Figures

VOTER REGISTRATION AND INCLUSIVE DEMOCRACY

GUATEMALA CASE STUDY

RUSSIA CASE STUDY

USA CASE STUDY

YEMEN CASE STUDY

VOTER TURNOUT RATES FROM A COMPARATIVE PERSPECTIVE

WOMEN'S POWER AT THE BALLOT BOX

COMPULSORY VOTING

Preface

This is our third report on voter turnout, based on information collected for the International IDEA Voter Turnout Database - the world's most comprehensive and authoritative collection of statistics tracking participation in electoral processes. It also builds on the work of previous editions, *Voter Turnout from 1945 to 1997: a Global Report on Political Participation.* The Institute plans to publish such a report every two years, each time focusing on a particular theme. This focuses on exercising the franchise through voter registration.

Voter registration is the process by which a person can exercise his or her right to vote. As such, it is a key determinant of electoral participation. History tells us that the removal of barriers to registration is essential to the full exercise of a citizen's political rights. In the first half of the twentieth century the right to vote was extended to many sectors of society; in the second half, as this

Preface

report reveals, the effective use of that right was extended through an unprecedented expansion in the number of registered voters.

Since its inception International IDEA has focused on electoral administration. The collection and analysis of data on methods of voter registration and its effect on voter turnout is thus a natural complement to our other efforts in the electoral field.

The database, which will be updated continuously on International IDEA's website (www.idea.int/turnout), contains an incomparable collection of statistics, gathered from a diverse range of sources around the world. A great number of organizations and individuals made such an unprecedented collection of data possible. First, I would like to extend my appreciation to the electoral management bodies that answered our requests with speed and good humour. Under the supervision of Professor Reg Austin, International IDEA's Elections Team has transformed this project from an occasional publication into a research effort and methodology that form an integral part of our work programme.

Professor Rafael López Pintor of the Universidad Autónoma de Madrid serves as the Senior Research Advisor for the project as well as a lead writer for this publication. His enthusiasm, knowledge and experience have inspired those around him. Special thanks go to Maria Gratschew, whose tenacious research forms the core of this publication, and to Kate Sullivan, whose tireless energy provided us with organizational and substantive support during the final phase of the publication. The project has been realized under the able direction of Patrick Molutsi and Vijay Patidar. Nina Seppäla and Therese Laanela laid the groundwork for the revival of this project. Thank you also to Peter Stephens and Ana Spross for their work in the production of this publication.

In addition, International IDEA wishes to thank the following individuals and organizations for their help in making this study possible: Mathew Batsiua, Inna Baranova, Virginia Beramendi-Heini, Annica Dahlqvist, Staffan Darnolf, Richard Desjardins, Anna Fogelmarck, Mario Henriquez, the Institute for International Education (Stockholm), Denis Kadima, Anna Katz, Wilfried Kindli, Lotta Lann, Charlotta Larsson, Alistair Legge, George Tarkhan-Mouravi, Simon-Pierre Nanitelamio, Mark Payne, Svante Persson, Mate Radics, Ben Reilly, Andrew Reynolds, Richard Rose, Marta Ruedas, Maja Tjernström, Felix Ulloa and Hans-Urs Wili. As this publication and website build on the earlier two editions, we would also like to renew our thanks to those who helped us with the earlier reports.

Bengt Säve-Söderbergh
Secretary-General
Stockholm

Methodology

AIM

The aim of International IDEA's Voter Turnout project is to provide updated and reliable information about voter turnout from around the world. Some trends are highlighted and preliminary conclusions are drawn, but International IDEA does not aim to explain or definitively prove why turnout differs between countries and across regions. The data should be seen as a basis for further research; additional correlations and comparisons can be drawn based on the user's particular needs and interests.

As the project contains the most comprehensive global data on voter turnout since 1945, it will be of great use to all those interested in elections and global political participation whether from a general, a professional or an academic perspective.

CHOOSING THE ELECTIONS

The criteria for including elections in the database are:

- that the elections were held after 1945 but before 30 September 2001;
- that elections were for national political

office in independent nation states. The only exceptions to this rule were those nations which held elections on the eve of their independence from colonial rule, or those small island nations whose sovereignty is limited by "free association" with a larger power (for example, Nigeria in 1959 falls into the first category, and Aruba into the second);

- that there was a degree of competitiveness (that is, more than one party contested the elections, or one party and independents contested the elections, or the election was only contested by independent candidates). This criterion excludes the one-party states of North Korea, China and the Soviet Union, but led to the inclusion of elections such as those in Uganda (where parties were banned) and Egypt in 1976 (where a number of independent candidates ran against the ruling party). Within this "grey area" of competitiveness we have erred on the side of inclusion and, at least where data is available, have included the turnout figures and explanatory variables in the tables for each country; and
- that the franchise was universal. However, for the purposes of comparison we have included the following elections that excluded women from voting: Liechtenstein (pre-1986), Switzerland (pre-1971), Greece (pre-1956), Belgium (1948), Kuwait (1992-1996), Bahrain (1973) and Argentina (1947). In these cases, the voting age population figure only includes men. We have not included elections where the franchise was limited to a very small (and ethnically defined) segment of the population, e.g., South Africa before 1994 and Western Samoa before 1991.

SOURCES

Many researchers have difficulty obtaining information about registration figures and voter turnout rates. International IDEA's extensive network of Election Management Bodies (EMBs) around the world has made it possible for us, in most cases, to use the official data compiled in different countries as our main source of information. When this source has not been available we have used information from government departments, universities or research institutes to find the necessary electoral data.

VARIABLES DEFINED

Voting Age Population

International IDEA has chosen to use not only the reported registration rate to calculate turnout percentages, but also the voting age population (VAP) which includes all citizens above the legal voting age.

We show both indicators for two reasons. First, registration figures can be inaccurate or unavailable, and sometimes voter registers are not used (as in South Africa in 1994). Second, the voting age population figures can provide a clearer picture of participation as they may signal a problem with the voters' register or registration system.

In some countries, the registration rate for a country may exceed the estimated VAP. The explanation for this apparent anomaly usually lies in the inaccuracy of the electoral register. In some countries the register is difficult to keep up to date, and deaths or movements of electors from one district to another are not reflected. Of course, the opposite can also occur: the register can under-represent the true size of the eligible voter pool if, as is often the case, it fails to record the names of new voters who have come of age or migrated to an area. Both of these scenarios represent relatively common problems facing electoral administrators around the world. It is important to emphasize, however, that registration figures are, in most cases, more often updated than population figures.

Literacy, GDP and HDI

The adult literacy rate (1997), human development index (1997), and gross domestic product (GDP) per capita $US 1987 (1997) were taken from the statistical annex of the Human Development Report 1999 (HDR), published by the United Nations Development Programme (UNDP). These were matched with the most recent parliamentary election available in the International IDEA database. There were 153 common countries between the two data sources. The figures were computed as per their subtitle.

The 153 countries common to both the International IDEA and the 1999 HDR databases are: Albania, Algeria, Angola, Antigua and Barbuda, Argentina, Armenia, Australia, Austria, Azerbaijan, Bahamas, Bahrain, Bangladesh, Barbados, Belarus, Belgium, Belize, Benin, Bolivia, Botswana, Brazil, Bulgaria, Burkina Faso, Burundi, Cambodia, Cameroon, Canada, Cape Verde, Central African Republic, Chad, Chile, Colombia, Comoros Islands, Costa Rica, Croatia, Cyprus, Czech Republic, Democratic Republic of Congo, Denmark, Djibouti, Dominica, Dominican Republic, Ecuador, Egypt, El Salvador, Equatorial Guinea, Estonia, Ethiopia, Fiji, Finland, France, Gabon, Gambia, Georgia, Germany, Ghana, Greece, Grenada, Guatemala, Guinea, Guinea-Bissau, Guyana, Haiti, Honduras, Hungary, Iceland, India, Indonesia, Iran, Ireland, Israel, Italy, Jamaica, Japan, Jordan, Kazakhstan, Kenya, Kuwait, Kyrgyzstan, Latvia, Lebanon, Lesotho, Lithuania, Luxembourg, Macedonia, Madagascar, Malawi, Malaysia, Maldives, Mali, Malta, Mauritania, Mauritius, Mexico, Moldova, Mongolia, Morocco, Mozambique, Namibia, Nepal, Netherlands, New Zealand, Nicaragua, Niger, Nigeria, Norway, Pakistan, Panama, Papua New Guinea, Paraguay, Peru, Philippines, Poland, Portugal, Republic of Korea, Romania, Russia, São Tomé and Principe, Senegal, Seychelles, Sierra Leone, Singapore, Slovakia, Slovenia, Solomon Islands, South Africa, Spain, Sri Lanka, St. Kitts and Nevis, St. Lucia, St. Vincent and the Grenadines, Sudan, Suriname, Sweden, Switzerland, Syria, Tajikistan, Tanzania, Thailand, Togo, Trinidad and Tobago, Tunisia, Turkey, Uganda, Ukraine, United Kingdom, United States of America, Uruguay, Uzbekistan, Vanuatu, Venezuela, Yemen, Zambia, Zimbabwe.

Political Participation in New and Old Democracies

Dieter Nohlen

This essay deals with the globalization of democracy, a process that provokes a comparison of the so-called "new" democracies with the established ones. The issue of voter turnout is discussed, followed by a report of selected empirical findings on political participation worldwide using the aggregate data approach. The essay critically evaluates the interpretation of comparative voter turnout data, emphasizing that the central issue is not national or regional differences in voter turnout ratios but the political significance of elections and citizens' political participation in various countries. In this regard, issues such as country-specific social structures and political cultures are addressed, based on the premise that old and new democracies do indeed differ significantly in their understanding of elections and political participation. Even taking into account factors such as institutional arrangements that reduce the effects of macro-historical differences between old and new democracies, problems inherent to new democracies remain utterly important and affect their consolidation. Finally, the essay concludes that the agenda for democracy at the turn of the twenty-first century can be characterized by two options: the diffusion of democracy into the remaining non-democratic corners of the world or the deepening of democracy resulting in consolidation. If so, consolidation, defined as taking steps to increase the significance of political participation by minimizing the importance of factors that undermine its significance, must be at the top of the agenda of the global democratic movement.

GLOBALIZATION OF DEMOCRACY

Since the mid-1970s, we have experienced a process of globalization of democracy. It began in Southern Europe in the 1970s, extended to Latin America in the 1980s, and culminated in the 1990s with the first democratic elections for national representative institutions taking place in 44 countries in Africa (22), Eastern Europe (19) and Asia (3). While the new democracies were spared authoritarian involutions in the 1970s and 1980s, military episodes against the democratic process were registered in 13 countries during the 1990s. As a result of independence and democratization the proportion of democratic countries compared to non-democratic countries rose from 27 percent in 1974 to 62 percent in 2000 (Linz, 2000; Freedom House, 2000).

This increase is important for the interpretation of political participation in the old and new democracies. First, as a result of the globalization of democracy, the heterogeneity of countries and regions that belong to the overall category of democratic countries has increased. Second, while the group of old democracies has remained almost entirely identical with the Western industrialized world (except for Costa Rica, India, Mauritius and Venezuela), the group of new democracies includes Southern European nations, Latin American countries, East European nations, and some African and Asian countries. In other words, the composition of the group of new democracies has undergone substantial change. Third, the categorization as "old" or "new" democracy itself is subject to change. Since it is assumed that after 20 years of practice democratic institutions can be considered consolidated - and consolidated is synonymous with old - countries can switch from one category to the other. In the literature, cases of new democracies in Europe in the 1970s - Greece, Portugal, and Spain - are now considered consolidated and are therefore included in the category of old democracies.

International IDEA has always understood voter turnout to be just one dimension of political participation. It has emphasized that no linear relationship exists between voter turnout and democratic development. It is true that turnout is simply one indicator of political participation - which is indeed a very complex term - and not always the most suitable one. Election specialists have long considered turnout percentages to be a reliable measurement not only for electoral participation but also for comparisons across countries and regions. Other dimensions of political participation are less amenable to quantification, therefore presenting substantial difficulties for cross-national or regional comparisons. Whether voter turnout in countries or regions is high or low, whether there are changes in one direction or another, whether these differ by country or by region or by old and new democracies is interesting data per se, but it does not reveal much about the state of democracy in the countries that are being compared. In other words, one can hardly extrapolate from higher or lower electoral participation to other characteristics of these democracies. In synchronic comparisons of countries, the limitations are immediately evident when consolidated democracies with relatively low voter turnout are compared to new democracies with relatively high voter turnout. Historical data of voter turnout for one country or region over time is a more meaningful basis for drawing conclusions or comparisons.

DIFFERENCES BETWEEN DATA AND ITS INTERPRETATION

Aggregate data analysis of electoral participation elucidates differences among countries and regions over a period of time. The correlation of specific characteristics of democracies with their participation rates can yield further comparisons depending on whether the selected phenomena correlate positively or negatively. Using this method, various factors that have an impact on voter participation figures can be identified. However, a number of questions remain which for various reasons, particularly the difficulty of translating the concepts operationally as well as their measurability, cannot be evaluated statistically.

Because the survey data approach is not very helpful in explaining voter turnout, current research strategy uses qualitative analysis to identify other factors, particularly contingent factors, which might explain variation in voter turnout. In the following analysis, the central theme will not be the differences between ratios of voter turnout, but rather between data and context. This approach rests on the premise that the voter turnout in a particular country or region is almost identical with any other country or region compared. The question is no longer what the difference in data explains, but what hides behind the data regardless of whether it differs by country or region. The basic premise is that voter turnout figures across nations conceal extremely diverse historical contexts, even if their numbers are equal. The difference dealt with is not voter turnout itself, but the conditions under which it was attained. For this differentiation among voter contexts, which can be applied to every single case, the classification of old and new democracies is critical.

DIFFERENCES OF CONTEXT

The distinction between old and new democracies represents fundamentally different social conditions which have a profound impact not only on the development of a democracy, but also on the meaning of elections and electoral participation. Generally speaking, four variables make a difference in voter participation and can explain the various meanings of voter turnout.

- Levels of social equality. High levels of social inequality in a society usually result in a greater bias against the political participation of socially deprived groups, regardless of voter turnout. Furthermore, when the level of poverty and social injustice is high, elections are not seen as an act of political empowerment by the majority of voters, but rather as an opportunity to trade votes for material profit or favour. Thus, depending on the degree of social inequality, high electoral participation can be coupled with entirely different expectations of politics.

- Governmental or societal focus of the political culture. While this variable primarily applies to the rate of voter turnout - recall the societal focus on political culture in the United States (so poignantly described by Alexis de Tocqueville) and the extremely low voter turnout there - it at the same time relieves a democracy of the necessity of high voter turnout. Societal participation can compensate for low political participation during elections to a great extent. When voter turnout figures are equal the question of coinciding governmental or societal focus of the political culture is an essential factor in interpretation.
- The centrality of a representative system of government in relation to other decision-making arenas, whether judiciary (formal), administrational or societal (informal). Whether a society has other means of enforcing its interests against veto powers than through traditional (violent) political conflict or via representational systems which lack democratically represented political power is a significant factor in interpreting voter turnout.
- Confidence in the political institutions. It makes a big difference whether constitutionally guaranteed political participation is based on trust and on a high level of political accountability, or whether distrust and low levels of vertical and horizontal accountability exist. Not only is the meaning of voter turnout strongly influenced by this factor, but so is the quality and legitimacy of democracy as a whole.

Certainly, these criteria alone do not allow for a distinctive classification of democracies as old or new. Nevertheless, a detailed look at the new democracies alone shows, despite some exceptions, the following common patterns:

- a comparatively high degree of social inequality;
- a distinct focus of the political culture on the government, although with considerable inconsistencies (resulting from an uneven modernization process) and social disparities (as in the post-socialist countries);
- lack of democratic governability and rule of law; and
- a comparatively strong distrust of political institutions and low accountability.

The validity and importance of each characteristic for the meaning of political participation (aside from voter turnout only) vary. Having discussed contextual differences between old and new democracies and similarities within the group of new democracies, let us now turn to the similarities across categories and to institutional factors.

Institutions and Voter Turnout

Regardless of whether a democracy is old or new, intervening factors tend to strengthen or weaken the importance of each pattern, partly by compensation. Such intervening factors are often results of the country-specific political culture or of the institutional design. An important factor is the presence of other forms of participation such as direct democracy, that is, referenda or political participation on various levels of political representation (local, regional, supra-national) that allow for multiple arenas for political participation, or intra-party elections (e.g., primaries). The more channels of political participation are available to voters the less important the central avenue of participation might be. In countries with elements of grass-roots democracy, voter participation in national elections is often valued far less. It is important to note that in new democracies forms of participation based on common cultural traditions, such as institutionalized political discussions in bars and cafés, are present, which deviate from the Western understanding of political participation.

Additionally, the following institutional factors previously identified as criteria for the evaluation of electoral systems are important:

- Parliamentary representation that mirrors the party preferences of the voters can very well increase turnout.
- The concentration process in the sense of reducing the number of parties in parliament as well as a majority-building system can have the opposite effect; this is often indicated by low electoral participation in the strongholds of parties where electoral campaigns are not fought with the same intensity as in marginal constituencies.
- The chance to select not only among preferred political parties but also among preferred candidates in an election can draw voters to the ballot box.

However, if all of the previously mentioned functions are built into the institutional engineering of an electoral system, the simplicity of the election system can suffer substantially and voters may be discouraged from voting by the complexity of the electoral process. No one wants to admit that they have difficulty understanding the ballot sheet.

- The legitimacy of the electoral system as a whole: doubts that the electoral system is "fair" and fear that one's political preference cannot be channelled in a subjectively satisfying way can decrease voter turnout.

Old and new democracies cannot avoid choosing an election system. Their similarities reflect similar institutional rules and regulations. Since electoral systems affect political parties in various ways depending on their context, they also affect the competition between parties, by means of fragmentation, polarization and patterns of interaction among parties, which in turn affects voter turnout. Differences and similarities are closely related.

FREE AND FAIR ELECTIONS

Now we turn to the difference that draws the most attention. Old democracies experience fewer problems with the electoral system, fewer irregularities in election procedures and fewer doubts regarding the election results. I would like to emphasize that this difference is relative. It is not true that old democracies have no problems with irregularities or electoral results. The United States presidential election of 7 November 2000, especially the dubious events in the state of Florida, have recently highlighted this assessment. Although there is surely a higher degree of acceptance of the democratic system and its rules and regulations in old democracies, nevertheless, the relative difference reflects varying degrees of trust in the political institutions and players. Mistrust of one's fellow citizens is more deeply ingrained in Latin America than in Europe, so that the deeply ingrained distrust of political institutions in Latin America is not surprising. Greater distrust leads to more elaborate institutional requirements to guarantee political participation through elections. To mention just one example, in most old democracies electoral administration is performed by a branch of the executive power, while in new democracies public distrust in the incumbent state authority has led to the establishment of independent electoral commissions. It is unimaginable what problems might arise in most of the young democracies if elections were organized by institutions similar to those responsible for elections in the old democracies. But even if elaborate election systems try to secure free and fair elections in the new democracies, it is not certain that they achieve their goals, even if international advisers and experts supervise the election process; it is also not certain that the voters would be convinced that their elections were free and fair. In Latin America, in spite of the fact that the organization of election procedures in the new democracies has been essentially improved, quite independent of voter turnout, more than half of the voters still claim that their elections are manipulated and election results are forged. This certainly does not mean that all election results are not trustworthy, but rather that voters misunderstand the meaning of elections and communicate to their parties that the candidates have fulfilled election promises, that voters did not receive anything in return for their votes, or that "fraud" is taking place.

OLD DEMOCRACIES AS MODELS FOR NEW DEMOCRACIES?

The preceding reflections indicate that simply imposing models of government adopted from old democracies cannot solve the problems of political empowerment in new democracies. Many attempts at political advising have failed because the suggested measures were based on the experiences of the old democracies and because the recommendations were too general. The institutional design must take into account that:

- there is no best system;
- there is no general institutional solution; and
- there is no way to impose a design-solution.

Furthermore, in order to improve political participation, constitutional design in new democracies must be fundamentally concerned with the specifics. It begins with the problems and issues of the specific social, cultural and political conditions of these countries that form the group of new democracies.

DEMOCRACY IN THE NEW MILLENNIUM

At the beginning of the twenty-first century the future of democracy must be seen in the context of a twofold process: first, a process of expansion of democracy in terms of an increase in the number of democracies in the world; and, second, a process of consolidation of democracy in the new democracies. The great wave of democratization in the first sense is almost complete. The expansion of democracy will continue, though not as explosively as in the recent past. New democracies will arise, while others will break down. In regions of the world that would profit from democratic forms of government, such as Africa and Asia, almost equally frequent relapses into dictatorial regimes will affect the trend. Thus it seems likely that deepening of democracy in the new democracies will be at the top of the agenda in the decades to come. Although this process may be less spectacular, it is actually more important for the future of democracy in the world. Strengthening of democracy, i.e., qualitatively higher degrees of participation combined with institutional reforms to improve its political efficiency, is the essential precondition to consolidate the new democracies. Age alone will not turn new democracies into old democracies. The new democracies must prove themselves able to solve the economic and social problems in their countries, particularly that of extreme poverty and extreme social inequality. To the extent that they achieve this, they will be able to overcome the other fundamental discrepancies that separate new democracies from old democracies, such as political participation as social participation, a system of representation and a justice system, and greater trust in political institutions. The understanding of the meaning of elections and of voter turnout will improve.

Both dimensions of the development of democracy require the commitment of all members of a society, particularly the intellectuals who would rather deal with the democracy of the future than with the future of democracy. The international community must continue its unflagging support for democracy worldwide: development and peace depend on it. Democracies maintain peace internally and abroad, and they uphold individual rights of freedom as well as human rights. Despite traditional development theories that claim modernization can best be achieved by authoritarian regimes, democracies too are efficient in achieving these goals. Indeed, citizen participation in the development process has proven indispensable for long-lasting sustainability. Democracy, peace and development - these goals all contribute to a vision of a better world.

REFERENCES

Corporacion Latinobarometro. 1998. *Latinobarómetro: Opinion Publica Latinoamericana*. Corporacion Latinobarometro: Santiago, Chile.

Freedom House. *Democracy's Century*. New York: Freedom House, 2000, www.freedomhouse.org/reports/century.html.

Linz, J. J. 2000. *Totalitäre und autoritäre regime*. Berlin: Berliner Debatte Wissenschaftsverlag.

Nohlen, D. 1998. *Sistemas Electorates y Partidos Políticos*. Mexico: Fondo de Cultura Económica.

Nohlen, D. et al. 1999. *Elections in Africa*. Oxford: Oxford University Press.

Nohlen, D. et al. 2001. *Elections in Asia and the Pacific*. Oxford: Oxford University Press.

VOTER REGISTRATION

Voter Registration and Inclusive Democracy: Analysing Registration Practices Worldwide

Rafael López Pintor and Maria Gratschew

This chapter discusses why voter registration is important for democracy, and in particular for the exercise of voting rights in producing genuine democratic elections. It outlines why the need to have all eligible voters registered poses a significant challenge to electoral authorities, particularly with regard to the use of different registration methods and citizen mobilization campaigns. It discusses why issues such as continuous versus periodic registers, compulsory versus voluntary registration, and citizen versus state- initiated registration are key questions for electoral administration and why the cost implications of such decisions are vital. The chapter concludes with a summary of findings on the types of voter registration systems used around the world.

WHY REGISTER PEOPLE TO VOTE?

Voter registration is crucial for political participation in a democratic context. There must be a guarantee that the right to vote in elections is universal, equal, direct and secret. The franchise is the means through which the governed agree to delegate their authority to those who govern. It is the link between the legitimacy of political governance and the liberty of human beings. In a democracy - "government (*cratos*) by the people (*demos*)" - voter registers constitute a concrete description of the "*demos*" (i.e., the citizens who constitute the sovereign). Citizenship is usually defined by nationality or by residence, or both. The sovereign politically active is the electorate, which may be required to register in order to exercise the franchise.

Voter registers, which work to safeguard the franchise, should be:

Universal. They should include every adult person belonging to the citizenry. The crucial question of who is a citizen (i.e., nationals or residents? nationality by *ius soli* or by *ius sanguinis* and issues of nationality and territoriality (i.e., non-resident, displaced and refugee populations) should be addressed before elections are held; indeed these issues should be decided when democracy is first being established. Voter registration is directly related to political participation in terms of both citizen mobilization and voter turnout. The operation of registering voters is in itself a mobilizing exercise in transitional democracies, as well as in established democracies where significant segments of the population may fail to register and vote.

Equal. The vote of every citizen should have the same value without discrimination. This does not mean that every vote has the same weight in producing institutionalized representation of the people. This is why issues of electoral formulae (i.e., majority/proportional/mixed), of voting districts (i.e., district boundaries and size) and of representation of minorities often are so highly debatable. The definition is relevant in connection to voter registration as a mechanism to ensure equality for the exercise of the right to vote. As a safeguard, voter registers that are clean and comprehensive contribute significantly to district delimitation as well as to the proper functioning of electoral formulae. They are also instrumental in organizing voting operations (e.g., allocating voters to polling stations or preparing polling places and voting materials). Another major benefit of undertaking voter registration before or at the beginning of the election period is that it allows disputes about the right of a person to vote to be dealt with in a measured way well before the polling takes place, and thereby minimizes disputes on Election Day (Maley, 2000, 9). Last but not least, properly compiled registers can also make difficult, and may discourage, attempts at double voting.

Direct. The right to vote should be personally exercised by every individual citizen at the polling station. This standard should be seen against the historical practice of double-step elections of assemblies, the "curia and estate systems" in nineteenth-century Central Europe. (Some in the United States may argue that the "electoral college" type of presidential election fails to meet the direct vote standard.) This standard also implies that the vote should not be delegated. This sometimes leads to controversy regarding issues of family vote, proxy vote, assisted vote, mail vote and external vote, including related problems with voter registers.

Secret. Secrecy of the vote must be guaranteed both legally and in practice. Factors that may impact negatively on secrecy of the ballot include intimidation and fraud practices, or inadequate design of polling station interiors. There may be other concerns in societies where secrecy of the ballot has not been culturally valued. Also, people with sustained experience of freedom and political pluralism may not take care to protect the content of their ballot papers; the opposite may occur among those without democratic experience for whom the idea of individual secret ballot is not so important.

In conclusion, the structuring of voter registers constitutes a main instrument for the political expression of the sovereign, i.e., the electorate. All-inclusive, clean voter registers should be considered a safeguard to the integrity of the suffrage, and therefore an essential condition for the legitimacy of democracy as well as for the political stability of the country (Rial, 1999, 15).

HOW TO STRUCTURE VOTER REGISTERS

In structuring a voter register the principal guiding principles are simplicity of procedures and convenience for the citizen. As we are dealing with the exercise of a right (i.e., the suffrage), political authorities and public officials must not hinder the exercise of that right by imposing obstacles. Simple administrative procedures must be put in place, and the process for citizens to register must be made as convenient as possible (e.g., avoiding long distances, payment of heavy fees on stamps and photos, or having to show up several times at registration centres). The main issues to consider in structuring voter registers are outlined below.

Which registration system?

Voter registration systems may be classified based on four main criteria: a) compulsory versus voluntary registration; b) continuously updated registers (e.g., much of Western, Central and Eastern Europe, Australia, Peru, Guatemala) versus ad hoc voter registers or a new register put together for each election (e.g., many emerging democracies, Canada before 1997); c) registration through state initiative versus responsibility placed upon the individual citizen; and d) voter-specific registers (standard practice) versus not a separate register of voters (e.g., Sweden, Denmark).

Which authority is responsible for voter registration?

The responsibility for voter registration may rest with different state apparatuses depending on political and administrative traditions and experiences. In emerging democracies voters are often registered by an administrative unit within Electoral Management Bodies. In older democracies, voter registers may be produced by civil registers with or without the involvement of Electoral Management Bodies. Voter registers may also be produced by the national office of statistics. Finally, there are cases where voter registers are directly compiled by international community organizations such as the United Nations or the Organization for Security and Co-operation in Europe (e.g., the Balkans, East Timor). In any case, the formation of voter registers often receives some input from civil registers and local governments.

How long does it take to produce an acceptable new voter register?

This may take from weeks to months depending on political and material conditions (i.e., political will, war and peace, logistics, administrative and financial conditions). Some examples of voter registration in emergency situations include: Nicaragua 1990, Albania 1992, Cambodia 1993, Kosovo 2000. On the other hand, most Western democracies' experience is with continuous registration, in which information is updated at the same time each year and within a given deadline.

Is enfranchisement genuinely universal, both legally and in practice?

The most often excluded or non-included populations, by law or *de facto,* are peasants, ethnic minorities, women, the illiterate and the poor. With the exception of a few countries, disenfranchisement around the world today tends to be more a matter of degree and of practice than of a legal phenomenon. Hence the relevance of presenting the problem as one of frontiers or of a territory which can be progressively settled by new waves of voters. It remains an empirical question in a given country to determine how much of the eligible population is actually being disenfranchised, and under whose responsibility.

Making registration procedures simple or complicated?

Making registration procedures simple involves: automatic registration based on civil registers where these exist, or requiring eligible voters to appear only once at registration posts; free-of-charge registration, and minimal costs for transport, certificates, and photos. A very sensitive question is why registration is sometimes difficult for eligible voters. International experience indicates that complicated and costly registration procedures are usually put in place for two main reasons: a) an intent by governments to prevent or discourage certain groups from voting (e.g., peasants, urban slum dwellers, ethnic groups, women); and b) the complexities of identifying eligible populations after civil conflicts (e.g., displaced persons, refugees, exiles), including situations where the mere spelling of names may be a problem (e.g., Cambodia, Western Sahara, Kosovo).

How to identify and quantify eligible voters

In principle, this may be expected to be a problem of varying dimensions in most new democracies. Determining the size of the electorate very much depends on the availability of reliable population census information, population estimates, and civil registers. When these are not available, making a reasonably comprehensive voter register may turn out to be the best possible basis for estimating the population of the country, including the size of internally displaced populations, refugees, and migrants. It may also allow for an estimate of regional and age distribution of the population and the scope of the urban rural divide.

Documents for identifying individual eligible voters

A variety of documents may be used for personal identification wherever a civil register is not automatically producing a voter register (i.e., national ID cards, driver's licenses, passports, civil register certificates). In cases where none of these are available, a voter's eligibility can be certified by witnesses. This may be arranged for culturally marginalized populations or for people in post-conflict situations where identification records have been destroyed or have disappeared. It is also typical in post-conflict scenarios to conduct registration by interviewing people (e.g., Western Sahara, Kosovo).

In registering eligible voters, is it necessary to produce a specially designed voter card?

This is not necessary as a matter of principle, as a properly registered voter may be identified by any other personal identification document; in some case identification may not even be required. Identification requirements depend on the specific environment and circumstances (i.e., whether such documents exist and cover all eligible voters, and whether an atmosphere of political mistrust may necessitate the issuance of a special voting card).

What should be the content of voter registers?

It is customary to include the personal details of voters such as name, gender, age and residence; photos may also be included, as is the case in Mexico, Peru and Kosovo. Voters in a national register are typically listed by family name in alphabetical order with breakdowns by polling centre; less frequently, they are listed by family clusters in each town/district (e.g., Albania 1992); the least frequently used method is to list voters chronologically by date of inscription (e.g., Pakistan). Necessary administrative information is also included in the voter registers, such as name and/or number of constituency, polling station and polling booth.

Breaking down of voter registers

National voter registers often, though not always, exist and can usually be extracted from a central aggregate register down to constituency and polling station levels. There are important benefits to having a centralized voter register: it allows for the clearing of duplications and double voting, facilitates redistricting when necessary, and processes external voting. In today's computer age, it can be particularly cost-effective to use a centralized register of voters.

Scrutiny of Voter Registers

Making provisional voter registers publicly available for corrections, deletions or additions is standard democratic practice. By not complying or not doing this in a timely manner, the transparency and fairness of the elections can be compromised. The main issues in this regard have to do with places and methods for publication, deadlines for changes and timely adjudication of complaints.

Publishing Final Voter Registers

How long before an election should final voter registers be known and made available to political parties and candidates as well as to other relevant groups, such as electoral observers and civil society organizations? A straightforward approach would recommend timely availability to allow political contenders a chance to make use of the registers for the organization of campaign activities and their Election Day operation. Moreover, election monitors and other civil society organizations can make use of the voter registers for civic education purposes and for distributing information to voters on where and how to vote.

Updating the Voter Registers

At least on technical and financial grounds, working to have permanently updated voter registers is the ideal situation. This would imply systematic inclusion of newly eligible voters; moving those who have changed residence; and removing the deceased, the convicted and the expatriates. As for the question of who shall be held responsible for initiating the update, a variety of legal alternatives have been offered in different countries. Quite often responsibility is placed upon individual voters, but it could also involve municipal authorities (i.e., matters of residence), judiciaries (i.e., criminal offences) and civil registers (i.e., births and deaths). The more regularly a voter register is updated the more likely it is that an update takes place under the exclusive responsibility of public authorities rather than the citizen.

Last Minute Voters

Are citizens who attain voting age shortly before or on Election Day eligible to vote? Will they appear on the standard voter register or on a separate register? Will they cast a regular or a tendered ballot? These are some of the questions that electoral authorities may face under certain circumstances, especially when emergency situations would recommend that a flexible approach be followed to allow as many people as possible to vote even if they were not previously registered. Tendered or conditional ballots can be collected and a separate register of voters compiled at the polling station in order to facilitate last minute voters showing up under critical circumstances (i.e., refugees, exiles, or ethnic minorities joining the electoral process at a very late stage). The question can be asked of how many tendered ballots are acceptable in an election. Political sensitivity and a problem solving approach would recommend that tendered ballots might be collected to the extent to which a new problem is not created, which would be larger or more serious than the problem which was intended to be solved.

How costly is it to produce adequate voter registers, and how can this be made cost-effective?

The most current research on this topic concludes that permanent registers promote both transparency and cost-effectiveness, particularly when they are periodically updated with corrections, additions, and deletions without obliging voters to re-register. Recent reforms in this direction are being implemented in a number of new as well as older democracies such as Botswana, Canada, Colombia, Chile, Namibia, Nicaragua and Venezuela. Among other recent developments, the computerization of voter registers has proved to be a reliable and effective mechanism for updating and cross-checking the registers at the national level. In addition, the single most important cost-cutting measure is probably continuous registration. Although there may be few countries in the world where continuous voter registration has been completely and successfully instituted, many countries are moving in that direction, among them Canada since 1997. Given the huge costs involved in undertaking voter registration operations for the first time, permanent registers that can be updated regularly will prove cost-effective in the long run.

Should voter registers be audited and how?

Registration practices (register formation and maintenance) can be assessed using different methods including visual inspection of voter registers and statistical samples that are verified through personal interviews of registered voters. In both transitional and established democracies observing and auditing voter registration can be part of an election observation programme. As Horatio Boneo points out, the traditional approach has been for observer teams to visit registration sites, as is done on Election Day. However, a preferred approach would be to conduct expert analysis of registration procedures and regional allocation of resources; to evaluate political party participation in identification of registration stations; to perform statistical analysis, including sample analysis of consistency of electoral registers; to follow up specific complaints concerning registration; and to visit registration stations randomly (Boneo, 2000, 187). In Peru, for example, the civil society organization Transparencia conducted a systematic audit of voter registers before the general elections in 2000 and 2001 with the support of electoral authorities. By so doing contributed significantly to the improvement of the quality of voter registers.

VOTER REGISTRATION SYSTEMS AROUND THE WORLD

Data has been compiled from 124 countries from all eight regions in the world. The two questions posed to electoral management bodies were:

- Is it compulsory or voluntary for the citizen to be registered for elections?
- Is a continuous or a periodic voter register used?

As can be seen from Figure 1, compulsory registration is quite common in Western Europe and Central and Eastern Europe but not widely practised in Africa or North America. Data collected for South America shows an even distribution between the two practices.

Some countries impose sanctions on those who fail to register, while in others it is considered a civic duty and high registration rates can be expected.

As discussed above, voter registers can be updated either on a continuous basis or at specified time periods (including at election time). Continuous registers are used more than periodic registers, despite the complex machinery required and high cost incurred in maintaining continuous registers. (See Figure 2)

Compulsory Registration

Based on the principle that voting is a right and duty of citizenship and that voters are obliged to register for an election.

Voluntary Registration

Predicated on the principle that voting is a right of citizenship and that voters may choose to register or not to register for an election.

Periodic Register

The result of election administration authorities developing a new register of eligible voters prior to each election. This process often occurs (although not always) in the period immediately preceding an election. Voter registration through a periodic voters' register is a more expensive operation than maintaining a continuous register or a civil register. Although more money is spent as a one-time cost for that electoral event, the ongoing maintenance costs of a continuous register tend to be higher while the cost of the periodic register is prorated over the period between elections.

Continuous Register

One in which the electoral register is maintained and continually updated, either by the election administration or as a civil register. This system requires an appropriate infrastructure to maintain the register, adding the names and other relevant information for those who satisfy eligibility requirements (attaining citizenship, satisfying residency requirements, attaining voting age) and deleting the names of those who no longer meet the eligibility requirements (through deaths, changes of residency etc.)

The full data set on registration systems can be found at www.idea.int/turnout

Figure 1: Is it compulsory to register?

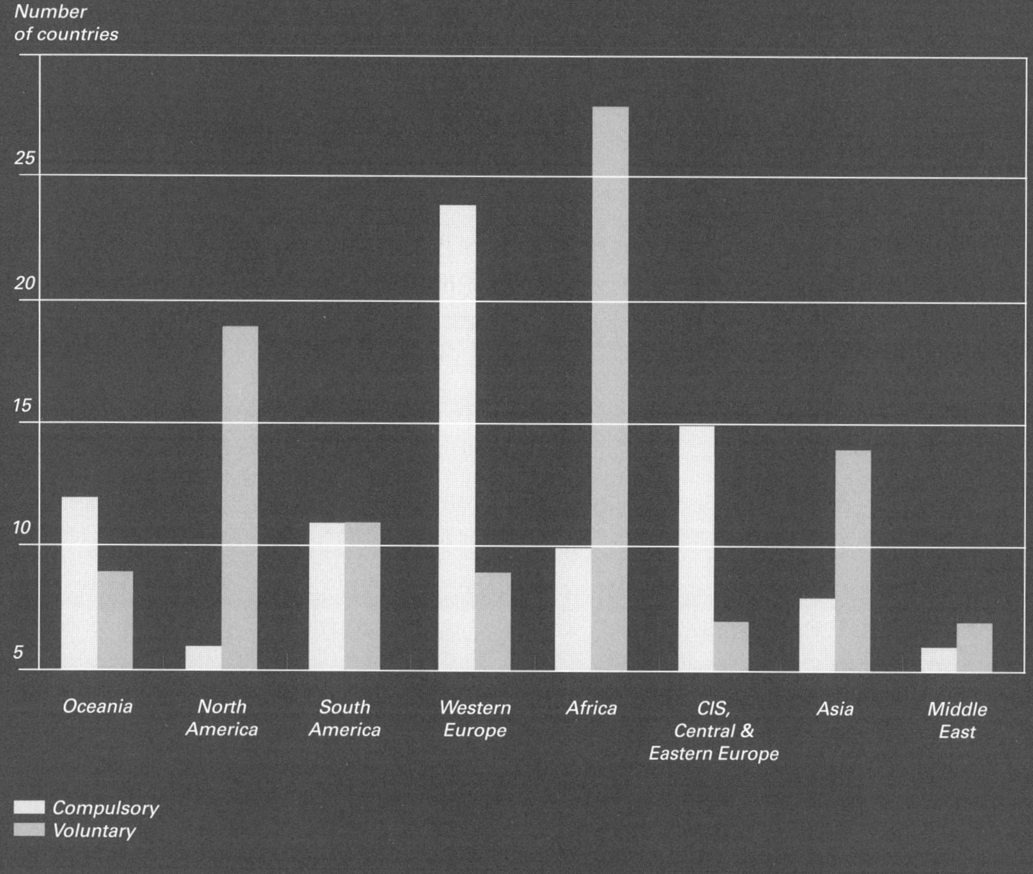

Figure 2: How often is the register updated?

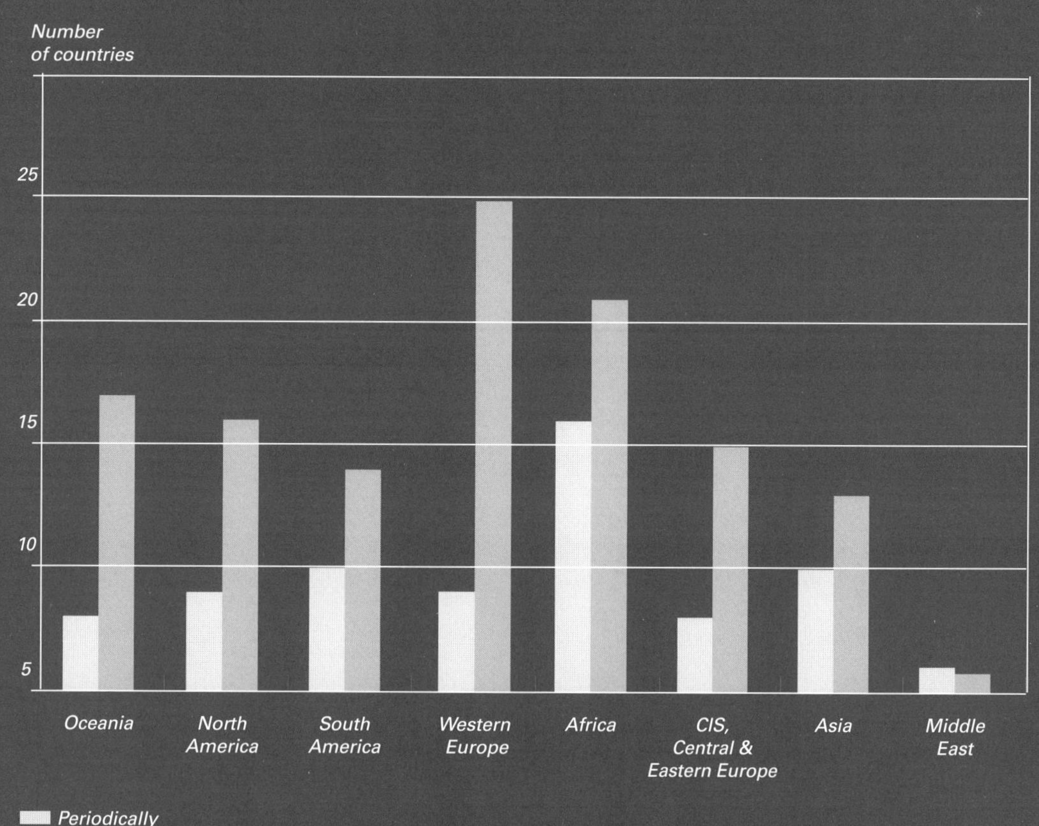

REFERENCES

Please refer to the Administration and Cost of Elections project (ACE) for more information about registration methods, types of registers and country case studies.

Administration and Cost of Elections Project (ACE). 1999. International IDEA, International Foundation for Election Systems (IFES), United Nations Department for Economic and Social Affairs (UN-DESA), www.ace-project.org.

Boneo, H. 2000. Observation of Elections. In *International Encyclopedia of Elections,* edited by R. Rose. London: Macmillan.

López Pintor, R. 2000. *Electoral Management Bodies as Institutions of Governance.* New York: United Nations Development Programme.

Maley, M. 2000. Administration of Elections. In *International Encyclopedia of Elections,* edited by R. Rose. London: Macmillan.

Rial, J. 1999. El Registro Electoral como Herramienta para la Consolidacion Democratica. In *Seminario Internacional sobre Legislacion y Organizacion Electoral: Una Vision Comparada.* Lima: Organizacion de Estados Americanos/ Transparencia.

Tremblay, M. January 2001. The right to vote: the heart of democracy. *Electoral Insight 3.*

Voter Registration Today: A Gateway to Enfranchisement

Rafael López Pintor and Maria Gratschew

Electoral registers are not just one additional element of the electoral process; they are in fact a crucial factor in the establishment and consolidation of a democratic system of government (Rial, 1999, 37). Having comprehensive, accurate voter registers should be considered a prerequisite for free and fair elections, although there have been exceptions to the rule such as the independence elections in Zimbabwe in 1980 and the election in South Africa in 1994 (Maley, 2000, 9). The main function of a good voter register is not only to promote high voter turnout, but also to enable any turnout at all. In general, it can be expected that comprehensive, continuously updated voter registers will produce higher voter turnout rates, although as an indirect effect. In fact, voter turnout rates are over 70 percent in most well-established democracies where comprehensive and continuously updated voter registers exist; the main exceptions are the United States and Switzerland. In both countries, fairly comprehensive voter registers have failed to produce turnout rates significantly over 50 percent of registered voters and both countries continue to rank among the lowest amongst established democracies in this respect. On the other hand, the experience of emerging democracies shows that whenever comprehensive voter registers are created, or existing registers of a limited scope are substantially improved, voter turnout rates tend to be, on average, as high as in most established democracies.

The delicate balance implicit in preparing election registers was succinctly characterized by the Electoral and Administrative Review Commission of Queensland, Australia: "Electoral rolls are a fundamental component of any voting system. Rolls constitute the official list of electors and are prima facie evidence of electors' right to vote. Enrolment procedures therefore need to strike the right balance between the need to be rigorous to ensure integrity of the rolls, and the need for flexibility to ensure that peoples' rights to enrol and vote are protected" (ACE, 1999).

More than a century after universal franchise was introduced in the western world, voter enfranchisement is becoming more and more universal in practice. If nation states are taken as a frontier reference for enfranchisement, there are only a few countries in the world where direct parliamentary elections are not held today, or where voter enfranchisement and registration are not required (e.g., some Arab countries and China). From a historical perspective, though, other more relevant frontiers for enfranchisement can be identified among and within states where the citizen's right to register and vote has been limited or impeded on grounds of gender, age, property, education or ethnicity. As it has been pointed out elsewhere "The history of the franchise is also the history of the abuses and harassment that prevented citizens legally entitled to vote from doing so. These included tricky rules and tests for voter registration, manipulation of residential requirements, choice of voting days, violations of the secrecy of the vote, district malapportionment and gerrymandering... *De facto,* however, these measures disenfranchised certain social groups" (Bartolini, 2000, 118). Registers which are all-inclusive constitute a guarantee that no significant segment of the population is impeded from registering and voting because of geographic, economic, ethnic-cultural, gender, or education reasons.

Several stages in the struggle towards universal suffrage have been identified; these phases were different in the United States and in Europe. In the United States, the franchise expanded slowly and by compromising steps and, despite the earlier start of franchise expansion, it took much longer to complete than in Europe. Administrative and legal obstacles were fully removed only in the 1960s (Bartolini, 2000, 118). The conquest of suffrage by women took longer and came later. Just as an example of how slow the road to suffrage has historically been for women, in Canada it was forty years after the first suffragette organizations emerged that one group of women - those employed by the army or who had a close male relative in the Canadian Forces - obtained the right to vote in 1917. The following year the right was extended to most Canadian women in recognition of their contribution to the war effort (Tremblay, 2001, 5). The situation was not the same in all Western countries, including the older Latin American democracies where women's right to vote was also established in the first half of the twentieth century (e.g., Uruguay in 1924). The United States and a number of European countries enfranchised women in the 1920s; but Italy, France and Belgium did so after World War II. The last country to grant women the right to vote was Switzerland in 1971, 123 years after the same right was granted to men (Bartolini, 2000, 125). Fortunately, after the Cold War the achievement of universal suffrage has progressed faster than ever before in history. As far as women's enfranchisement is concerned, at the beginning of the twentieth century, only 10 percent of the world's countries had enfranchised women; by the end of the century the figure was 95 percent (Rule, 2000, 384).

Limitations by law to the right to register and vote based on gender, age, property or education can hardly be found anywhere in the world today. What is more likely are situations where legislation is not enforced by competent authorities as a matter of ill will, negligence, lack of resources, or lack of capacity to face opposing reactionary elements in the society and culture. De facto if not legal disenfranchisement is frequently the case among certain sectors of society, most likely peasants, the illiterate, women and ethnic minorities. Any significant research on enfranchisement and voting should look at these particular segments in order to assess the actual state of affairs, no matter what the legal provisions may be.

The next section offers a mosaic of country case studies and interviews that are illustrative of progress and setbacks in voter registration around the world. Six countries were chosen to illustrate different challenges regarding voter registration that are being faced in established democracies like the United States, in countries with a long but uneven experience with democratization, like South Africa, Guatemala and Russia, and in some emerging democracies like Yemen and Indonesia. The case studies show a variety of situations where full enfranchisement of voters is facilitated or hindered by gender, socio-economic conditions or ethnicity. The studies provide examples of how voter enfranchisement is still an evolving process today.

REFERENCES

Administration and Cost of Elections Project (ACE). 1999. International IDEA, IFES, UN-DESA, www.ace-project.org.

Bartolini, S. 2000. Franchise Expansion. *In International Encyclopedia of Elections,* edited by R. Rose. London: Macmillan.

Maley, M. 2000. Administration of Elections. *In International Encyclopedia of Elections,* edited by R. Rose. London: Macmillan.

Rial, J. 1999. El Registro Electoral como Herramienta para la Consolidacion Democratica. *In Seminario Internacional sobre Legislacion y Organizacion Electoral: Una Vision Comparada.* Lima: Organizacion de Estados Americanos/ Transparencia.

Rule, W. 2000. Women Enfranchisement. *In International Encyclopedia of Elections,* edited by R. Rose. London: Macmillan.

Tremblay, M. January 2001. Women and political participation in Canada. *Electoral Insight* 3.

Guatemala

Rafael López Pintor and Edmundo Urrutia

Voter registration in Guatemala has been historically deficient because it has not included, de facto if not by law, large segments of the population. This applies in particular to women and peasants from different ethnic communities, who comprise almost half of the country's total population. Voter turnout has been limited to those sectors of the population who registered more actively. But even among these groups, the boundaries of the politically mobilized segments have shifted dramatically with the vicissitudes of various political crises. Voter turnout in Guatemala is one of the lowest in the world, ranking 155 in International IDEA's list of 170 countries.

After decades of protracted civil conflict in Guatemala, peace accords were signed in 1996 by the national government and the guerrilla organization Unidad Revolucionaria Nacional Guatemalteca (URNG), today a political party by the same name. Peace negotiations included legal and institutional reforms to increase voter participation. Since the 1995 general elections, slow but steady increases in voter registration and turnout can be measured.

THE PATH TO ENFRANCHISEMENT

Widespread suffrage for adult males was introduced in Guatemala in 1865, but it would not become truly universal, even from a legal point of view, until much later. In 1945, women were allowed to vote for the first time, but illiterate women were excluded. Voting was optional and secret for literate women but optional and public for illiterate men. It was not until 1965 that universal and secret suffrage was introduced with compulsory voting for all citizens 18 years and older; voting was still optional for all illiterates, and the illiterate vote was public.

Low voter turnout, as a percentage both of registered voters and of the eligible voting age population, ranks Guatemala low on International IDEA's list of 170 countries. The highest post-compulsory turnout at an election to the Constituent Assembly took place in 1985, when 69 percent of registered voters voted. It has been declining ever since, although the database indicates that there was an increase from 21 percent to 40 percent between 1994 and 1999.

A number of factors have been identified to explain the low turnout in Guatemala:

- lack of registration by significant sectors of eligible voters;
- location of polling stations only at the administrative centre of the municipalities, which creates transport problems for the poor and more distant citizens (this legal provision was introduced in response to complaints that electoral fraud was practised mostly at polling stations located in villages and country estates before 1985); and
- lack of confidence in government and the political elite (López Pintor, 1997; MINUGUA, 1999a and b; Boneo, 2000).

In Guatemala, both registration and voting were compulsory until 1985; since then they have been voluntary. Nevertheless, according to the law a citizen must initiate, but not necessarily complete, the voter registration process in order to obtain a passport or a driver's licence although many who initiate the process to get a passport no longer live in the country. Registration is not automatic, but once a citizen is registered he or she will remain on the register for a given municipality until a modification is made at the initiative of the citizen or municipality. Citizens must take the initiative to register by submitting application forms to registration offices of the Supreme Electoral Tribunal (one office is located in each administrative centre of 330 municipalities, under the supervision of 21 regional or departmental offices). Personal identification, an ID card (a valid *cédula de vecindad*), is required. An inscription is made, but the applicant must return at a later date to pick up the voter card. As the United Nations Mission in Guatemala (MINUGUA) has pointed out in several reports, the requirement that citizens visit registration offices several times partly explains why large sectors of the population do not register. Costs, such as those of transport and photographs, are also incurred as part of the registration process. Economic, geographic and cultural factors as well as lack of an ID card make the process even harder. Under-registration was estimated at over 30 percent of voting age population by 1999 (MINUGUA, 1999b), although the magnitude of the problem is probably much higher.

In 1982 the current voter register was introduced to prepare for elections to the Constituent Assembly in 1985 and the transition toward a more democratic system (Boneo and Torres-Rivas 2000, 8). Increases in the number of registered voters can be attributed to massive registration campaigns by the Supreme Electoral Tribunal, such as those undertaken after the discouraging results of the constitutional reforms referendum in May 1999. The electoral authorities established registration sites in several centres in the capital and in 180 sites in the provinces, and carried out a massive publicity campaign. The Rigoberta Menchú Tum Foundation has also carried out registration campaigns in 1995 and 1998 with significant media advertising and workshops in villages and municipalities throughout the country.

This development notwithstanding, increasing the number of registered voters has not improved the quality of the voter rolls. As time passed, voter rolls deteriorated by becoming inflated with non-existent or not fully eligible electors. At least 10 percent of already registered voters (an estimate of over 600,000 people) were never able to vote since they had not completed the registration procedures to receive their voter cards. Furthermore, significant numbers of deceased and permanent migrants abroad have not been removed from the rolls, and many who have changed residence within the country have not updated their voter information. Current estimates show that about 25 percent of all inscriptions are incomplete or out of date, or relate to deceased persons and migrants (Boneo and Torres-Rivas, 2000, 55).

REGISTRATION AS A BARRIER TO ENFRANCHISEMENT

Before 1999 it was considered that electoral registers in Guatemala were generally in line with international standards, with about 80 percent of the eligible population enrolled. As mentioned earlier, non-registration was more frequent among women and peasants in the indigenous parts of the country. It was thought that problems of political participation had more to do with low turnout among registered voters than with mobilization of non-registered voters. Contrary to conventional wisdom, however, recent in-depth research indicates that the main barrier to voter participation arises from sheer lack of registration. The eligible voting age population in 1999 was estimated at 5,785,000 persons (i.e., those aged 18 and over who were not legally impeded from voting; military and police personnel as well as condemned prisoners were excluded). The rolls included 4,459,000 people, about 77 percent of eligible voters - a reasonable figure according to international standards (Boneo and Torres-Rivas, 57).

At the November 1999 general election, 1,800,676 people turned out to vote, about 40.4 percent of those registered. Nevertheless, a more sophisticated analysis shows that once the registers are "cleaned", they actually include only 63.7 percent of the eligible population rather than 77 percent. Consequently, voter turnout as a percentage of registered voters is a much higher 71.7 percent rather than 40.4 percent. Turnout as a percentage of the total eligible population is 31.1 percent, which is much lower than the previous estimates. The fact is that 56

Figure 3: Voter Turnout in Guatemala, 1950-1999

Year	% of registered voters	% of voting age population
1950	71.5	30.4
1961	44.5	19.0
1970	53.3	25.9
1982	45.6	30.6
1985	69.2	49.8
1990	56.4	41.0
1995	46.8	33.4
1999	40.4	31.1

percent of the eligible population does not actually vote, and as many as 36 percent are not even registered (Boneo and Torres-Rivas 2000, 58). These findings reveal that the problem of non-voting in Guatemala is not one of motivating registered voters, but rather one of barriers to registration, either motivational and administrative or socio-economic and ethnic cultural.

NON-INCLUSION OF WOMEN AND INDIGENOUS PEASANTS

It was recently pointed out that the majority of those excluded from the registers in Guatemala are indigenous people of Mayan origin living outside the structures of the modern state (Rial, 1999, 31). Available evidence illustrates that under-registration is more frequent among women and indigenous peasants. While the gap between male and female registration has decreased, there are still significant gender imbalances, particularly in regions with large indigenous populations and high illiteracy rates. One reason is that these sectors have not been politically active historically, and often they do not possess personal identification papers: 15 percent of the adult population falls into this category according to estimates by the Supreme Electoral Tribunal. Another reason is that the recent civil war has uprooted and politically intimidated many people. Thus, low registration seems to be attributable more to historical and structural reasons than to the current situation and government. The main political powers and the international community recognize the need for important legal reforms and programmes to strengthen institutions and make the representational system more inclusive and the right to vote easier to exercise (López Pintor, 1999, 96).

Significant disparities in registration rates between men and women were found in both 1995 and 1999 among the 22 departments of the country, showing that the registration of women was much lower in departments with larger indigenous populations. Again, analysis indicates that this seems be based more on historical and structural grounds than on episodic and administrative difficulties (López Pintor, 1997; MINUGUA, 1999a). Recent analyses of the 1999 elections has shown that, although women as a whole turn out to vote less often than men, such gender imbalance tends to disappear if only registered women are taken into consideration. Once registered, women tend to turn out to vote in similar proportions to men (Boneo and Torres-Rivas, 2000, 77). Thus problems in the registration process appear to be the main barrier to suffrage.

Opinion poll data also supports the above conclusion that under-registration is more likely among women and indigenous people than among men and Ladino populations (In Guatemala, the term Ladino refers to the Spanish-speaking people not belonging to any indigenous community; they comprise about half of the total population). Three recent national surveys (conducted by the University of San Carlos, the University Rafael Landívar, and the ASIES Institute) reveal that non-registered people are more likely to be women (around 60 percent) than men (around 40 percent). Similarly, Ladinos tend to register more often (54 percent) than indigenous people (44 percent) (Boneo and Torres-Rivas, 2000, 83, 206). Among indigenous populations, the likelihood of getting registered is significantly higher among literate males (62 percent) than among illiterate females (27 percent). Correspondingly, literate indigenous males would more likely turn out to vote (81 percent) than illiterate females (51 percent) (UNDP, 1999).

Notwithstanding the above, under-registration of indigenous people has been diminishing, especially since the 1995 elections. Lower registration rates of the indigenous vis-à-vis the Ladino still persist, but relative improvement has taken place. While the national average for registration increased by 20 percent between 1995 and 1999, the proportion of increase was higher in those departments with larger indigenous populations. It is interesting to note that mobilization of indigenous people also increased at the time of the referendum for constitutional reforms in May 1999, even when the national average voter turnout was particularly low. Prior to the referendum, between October 1998 and February 1999, registration was higher in departments with larger indigenous populations. The rate of increase was 1.5 percent at the national level, but it was between 2.5 percent and 3 percent in Sololá, Totonicapán, Quiché, Alta Verapaz and Quiché. In fact, these were among the few departments where the constitutional reforms referendum was won, although it was defeated at the national level (MINUGUA, 1999b).

FUTURE CHALLENGES AND OPPORTUNITIES

The main barrier to the exercise of the right to vote has historically been and continues to be, in certain countries, non-inclusion of significant segments of the population in electoral registers. In Guatemala, historical deficiencies in voter registration were at least partly removed at the time of the 1999 general elections, with increasing rates of both voter registration and turnout, in particular among women and indigenous people. In fact, political mobilization started becoming more intense during the time of the 1995 general elections. A significant increase in voter registration took place after 1995 during two main polling events: the referendum for constitutional reform of May 1999, and the general elections the following November. On both occasions the number of new inscriptions mounted to over 300,000, and this was largely an effect of mobilization and campaigning efforts by the electoral authorities, political parties, civil society organizations and the international community (MINUGUA, 1999a and b).

A number of challenges and opportunities have been identified. First, the current state of affairs can be improved by disseminating current and reliable research and information concerning the problems of registration. This should facilitate public discussion of these issues as well as the search for viable solutions. Comprehensive in-depth research on voter participation was undertaken under the auspices of the Supreme Electoral Tribunal, International IDEA and the UNDP. Second, the cost of registration could be lowered by facilitating citizen access and alleviating the administrative procedures to register. The reasons and the logic for these administrative complexities are difficult to explain. On the other hand, the costs for non-registration could be raised, for example, by making it mandatory to obtain a personal ID card (the forthcoming *cedula de identidad personal* as a substitute for the current *cedula de vencidad*), and then to automatically register properly identified citizens. The Supreme Electoral Tribunal could take this responsibility. Third, civic education could be recommended on a long-term basis rather than only before a given election (Boneo and Torres-Rivas 2000, 143-171).

The Electoral Reform Commission, created under the peace accord, formally proposed the above-mentioned reforms in its 1998 report Guatemala, Peace and Democracy. The aim of the proposals was to attain a fully inclusive and participatory electoral system with special attention to the integration of indigenous Maya populations as citizens and voters. The Supreme Electoral Tribunal created by the Constitution of 1985 has been recognized to this day as a prestigious institution, which should be instrumental in implementing the above-mentioned reforms (International IDEA, 1998, 60, 61).

REFERENCES

Boneo, H. and E. Torres-Rivas. 2000. *¿Por qué no votan los guatemaltecos?* Estudio de participación y abstención electoral. Ciudad de Guatemala: IDEA, Tribunal Supremo Electoral, PNUD.

International IDEA. 1998. *Democracia en Guatemala: La Misión de un Pueblo Entero.* Stockholm: International IDEA.

López Pintor, R. 1997. Cultura Política y Elecciones en Guatemala. *In América Latina: Realidades y Perspectivas. I Congreso Europeo de Latinoamericanistas,* edited by M. Alcántara. Salamanca: Universidad de Salamanca (electronic book).

López Pintor, R. 1999. *Votos contra Balas.* Barcelona: Planeta.

MINUGUA. 1999a. Informe sobre resultados de las elecciones presidenciales, parlamentarias y municipales de 7 de noviembre y 26 de diciembre de 1999. Ciudad de Guatemala (photocopied report released to the press).

MINUGUA. 1999b. Informe preliminar sobre la consulta popular del 16 de mayo. Ciudad de Guatemala (photocopied report released to the press).

Nohlen, D. et al. 1998. *Tratado de Derecho Electoral Comparado de América Latina.* Mexico : Fondo de Cultura Económica.

Rial, J. 1999. El Registro Electoral como Herramienta para la Consolidacion Democratica. In *Seminario Internacional sobre Legislacion y Organizacion Electoral: Una Vision Comparada.* Lima: Organizacion de Estados Americanos/ Transparencia.

UN Development Programme. 1999. *Informe de Desarrollo Humano.* Guatemala: La Fuerza Incluyente del Desarrollo Humano, UNDP, New York.

INTERVIEW

with Mrs Nineth Montenegro Cottón, member of the Congress for Alianza Nueva Nación (ANN) and member of the Commission for Electoral Issues.

7 November 2000, Congress

What is the current state of voter registration and enfranchisement in Guatemala?

It still needs to be expanded. Several sectors, among them women, the indigenous population and the rural population are not registered due to the lack of opportunities, financial resources and infrastructure. Illiteracy as well as little information about the importance of registration and voting further limit the participation and development of true citizenship.

Have there been any major developments on voter registration recently?

There are registration campaigns but only when elections are approaching. In 1999 the electoral roll was expanded by 100,000 names, but this is very low considering the voting age population [VAP is 5,784,820; number of registered voters is 4,458,744]. Mapping of the electorate has been initiated, even if the previous mappings have been insufficient. There is hope that the reforms of the Electoral Law of Political Parties (that are based on the peace agreements) and the implementation of the Agreements on Constitutional Reform and Reform of the Electoral Regime that are being carried out will bring about new ways of improving enrolment opportunities.

What could be done to ensure enfranchisement of all eligible people and improve voter turnout?

More permanent information campaigns are necessary, preferably bilingual or multilingual in order to include the various languages of the Mayan culture. It is also imperative that we address the high illiteracy rate that exists amongst a large segment of the population. The enrolment and polling stations need to be closer and made more accessible to the rural population, since they now only exist in the administrative centres of each region.

Do you see registration as a barrier to voter turnout or as an incentive? Please explain why.

There is still a barrier that makes people abstain from voting due mainly to the malfunction of the electoral system. This is why it is indispensable to introduce, for example, a uniform system of identification. This would give each and every person a unique identification number in the citizen register, which would mean that he or she could be automatically included in the electoral roll once they reached voting age. The requirements to get an ID today are so complicated that it does not appear important enough for most inhabitants.

Rosa Tock
Faculty of Sociology and Political Science
Rafael Landívar University, Guatemala

Indonesia

Smita Notosusanto

HISTORY OF ENFRANCHISEMENT

Political circumstances have largely shaped the history of enfranchisement in Indonesia, as electoral laws have been affected by the ebb and flow of Indonesian politics.

The first law on elections was passed in 1953 in preparation for the long-anticipated 1955 general election, the first general election after the nation gained independence in 1945 (Feith, 1957).

In 1966, General Soeharto seized power from President Soekarno and created the authoritarian New Order regime, which lasted 32 years. Soeharto justified the *coup d'état* to prevent a communist takeover of the government indicated by the assassination of six army generals in 1965 by army officers in the communist September 30 Movement. One of the first actions taken by the New Order was to ban the Communist Party of Indonesia (Partai Komunis Indonesia, PKI) (Schwarz, 1994).

In 1969, a new electoral law was passed as a basis for the 1971 general elections. This law underwent several amendments in 1975, 1980 and 1985, in anticipation of the elections of 1977, 1982 and 1987, respectively. The general elections of 1992 and 1997 were held based on the last amendment made to the electoral law in 1985. The 1969 law and its amendments were more conservative than the 1953 law, as they restricted enfranchisement by prohibiting ex-members of the Communist Party of Indonesia from participating in the general elections during the New Order period (Umum, 1997, 36-37).

The 1999 general election, the first election held after the fall of General Soeharto, was based on a new electoral law (Law No.3/1999). Some of the important aspects and changes in this electoral law concerning enfranchisement are discussed below.

VOTING AGE

The 1953 law stipulated that the voting age was 18 years and older, or that the prospective voter had to be legally married at the time of registration. (Marital status was and is still seen as a sign of political maturity in Indonesia.) The voting age was reduced to 17 in the 1969 electoral law passed by the newly established New Order government, presumably to expand the participation of first-time voters. The government and the ruling GOLKAR Party may have assumed that politically naïve first-time voters would tend to vote for GOLKAR. In 1982, the law was amended to allow divorcees or widows, even those under 17, to register to vote in the general elections. This law allowed under-age voters an opportunity to vote in areas where child marriage was common.

NON-ELIGIBLE VOTERS

Individuals who were serving jail time as sanctioned by a court were not eligible to vote according to the 1953 law. This article was made more strict in the 1969 law, which stipulated that crimes must be punishable for a minimum of five years jail term. This stricter version was sustained until the 1999 election.

Individuals whose voting rights were removed by a court of law were also ineligible to vote according to the 1953 law. This law implies that a court can pass a decision that can remove an individual's voting right, but it does not explicitly state what cases would involve the removal of such rights. This article remained until the 1999 election. The electoral laws also prohibited individuals suffering from serious mental illness from participating in elections.

The most controversial part of the law regarding non-eligible voters was the exclusion or prohibition imposed on ex-members of the banned PKI or those who participated directly in the September 30 Movement 1965. This clause was later extended to ex-members of other banned organizations. In 1975, the government sought to soften this law by adding the possibility that the voting rights of ex-PKI members or other banned organizations could be re-evaluated, which implied that their voting rights could be restored. This could have been the result of international pressure on the Soeharto government to release ex-PKI members or those who were alleged to be ex-PKI members and had been imprisoned since 1965. After the fall of the Soeharto government in 1998, the law prohibiting the participation of ex-PKI members in the general elections was abolished, reflecting a more liberal and progressive view towards the Communist Party.

THE MILITARY

Members of the military or the armed forces were eligible to vote according to the 1953 elections law. But beginning in 1969 the election law stipulated that active members of the Indonesian armed forces would not be able to exercise the right to vote. The rationale given by the government was that, in order to perform their role as defender of the nation, the armed forces have to remain neutral and cannot be involved in partisan politics. It was thought that the 1955 general election caused political chaos because members of the military were involved in partisan politics. In reality, this law was used to justify the appointment of active military officers as voting members of the DPR (parliament) and the MPR (People's Consultative Assembly). The law did not prevent the military from becoming neutral political actors because the institution adhered to the "dual function" concept that justifies the military's role in politics. In practice, the military also tended to support the position of the government and the ruling GOLKAR Party.

VOTER REGISTRATION

Indonesia uses a periodic list voter registration system based on the most recent national census data. An automatically composed list is used in combination with a list demanding citizen initiative, allowing citizens to petition for changes in the list after the first automatic list is published prior to Election Day. Until the 1997 elections, voter registration was compulsory. Voter registration officials were largely responsible for registering voters through door-to-door canvassing. The first obvious problem with this method was the exclusion of those would-be voters with no residence. This problem was compounded by the practice of some election officials imposing stricter residential requirements, such as local residential registration forms that were not always available to those with no residential base. In this case, the registration process tended to exclude the poor who usually lacked documentation to show residence.

Compulsory registration also presented the possibility of fraud during voter registration. One of the most frequently reported types of fraud was the deliberate exclusion of would-be voters who were assumed to be supporters of the opposition parties. Voters in the island of Bali, for example, often had to suffer this particular abuse because Bali is known for its strong support of the Democratic Party of Indonesia (PDIP). There were also reports that local town or village officials often intimidated would-be voters by running "sweeping operations" to identify non-GOLKAR voters (Harjanto, 1997; Cahyono, 1998).

Another common practice was for government institutions or agencies to register their employees en masse using their place of employment or office as their residence address. Group registration was a common practice exercised by governmental institutions mainly to control how their employees voted in the elections. The civil service was GOLKAR's most important stronghold and therefore each civil servant was considered to be a GOLKAR member. During the New Order period, Election Day was not declared a holiday; thus, civil servants were often ordered to vote in their place of work instead of at the closest polling centre near their homes. This convinced many civil servants that their votes were monitored by their superiors.

Critics have frequently argued that the compulsory aspect of voter registration in Indonesia has actually turned voters into mere political objects of the government's mobilization programme rather than into active and autonomous citizens. The New Order regime thus treated the general elections as an exercise of mass political mobilization to legitimize the New Order's policies (Legowo, 1996).

In the 1999 electoral law, the compulsory registration process was abolished and a voluntary voter registration method was adopted. The requirement for registration has also been modified to allow only one form of legal identification as a requirement to register. Registration centres were established independently of local town or village bureaucracies. In practice, however, there were enormous problems surrounding the implementation of the new method of registration because of the lack of training and logistical preparation. The 1999 general election was hastily organized to serve the immediate need for new political leadership after the end of the New Order regime. Some of the problems reported were delays in the opening of registration centres, lack of information on registration procedures, and often inexperienced registration officials. In some remote areas, registration forms were delivered only a few days before the registration deadline. In the end, in order to accommodate the voters the government extended the voters' registration period. There was no serious fraud reported during the 1999 voters' registration process except some scattered and unsubstantiated reports of abuses by local party officials (KIPP, 1999).

VOTER TURNOUT

The key characteristic of elections in Indonesia has been high voter turnout. This can be attributed to high voter expectation of elections as a solution to existing or past political turmoil, as was the case with the general elections of 1955 and 1999. However, this conclusion can hardly be applied to the elections during the New Order period. High voter turnout during the New Order period can be attributed to "political mobilization" combined with intimidation by the government to move voters to the polling stations. In some cases, government officials or party officials often transported voters to polling centres to ensure that they cast their votes. This method is suspect because there was a tendency to only provide transportation to voters for the GOLKAR Party.

Unfortunately the government does not publish data on voter turnout, let alone turnout based on gender, residence, or other social and political groupings. The only data available on voter turnout is the data on voter registration and on valid votes cast during the elections.

In the 1997 election, out of almost 125 million registered voters, 113 million (90.5 percent) of registered voters cast their votes. In the 1999 election, out of 118 million registered voters, 105.5 million (89 percent) cast their votes. Indonesia experienced a slight decline in the total number of registered voters by 5 percent. The biggest slump occurred in the province of Aceh, which suffered a downturn in the number of registered voters from 2.2 to 1.4 million, a decline of 35 percent. However, the Aceh region experienced a bigger decline in the number of valid votes, from 2.1 million voters (95.2 percent) to only one million (69.3 percent). East Timor, which at the time of the 1999 general election was preparing to hold its own referendum to determine its independence from Indonesia, only experienced a slight downturn in the total number of registered voters (7 percent).

PROSPECTS

Voter turnout at the next election will depend partly on the successful conclusion of an amendment to the existing election law which could radically change the electoral system from the standard proportional representation system to a "first past the post" system, as proposed by the government. This plan can affect voter turnout in different ways. On the one hand, a new electoral system could have the potential of deterring would-be voters who do not understand the new system. On the other hand, the adoption of a new system could instil enthusiasm among voters to participate in greater numbers than at the last election.

Regardless of what the political development will be, the Indonesian government should strive to attain the principle of universal suffrage by gradually eliminating discriminatory barriers to voter registration and voter eligibility. One of the issues that needs to be reconsidered is the exercise of the right to vote for members of the armed forces. Also, the banning of prisoners from participating in elections should be re-evaluated to prevent court decisions from being manipulated or used to incriminate or bar individuals from exercising their voting right. Lastly, the government should allow ample time for the training of registration officials to allow for a successful voluntary registration process.

REFERENCES

Cahyono, H. 1998. Pemilu dan Pendidikan Politik. In Menggugat Pemilihan Umum Order Baru, edited by S. Harris. Jakarta: YOI.

Feith, H. 1957. The Indonesian Elections of 1955. Cornell Modern Indonesia Project, Interim Report Series. Ithaca, N.Y.: Southeast Asia Project, Cornell University.

Komite Independen Pemantau Pemilu (KIPP) Jakarta. 1999. Laporan Pemantauan Pemilihan Umum 1999 Jakarta, Depok, Tangerang dan Bekasi. Jakarta: KIPP.

Kristiadi, J., T. Legowo and Budi Harjanto (eds). 1997. Pemilihan Umum. Perkiraan, Harapan dan Evaluasi. Jakarta : CSIS.

Legowo, T. A. 1996. Revitalisasi Sistim Politik Indonesia. Jakarta: CSIS.

Lembaga Pemilihan Umum. 1997. Susunan dalam satu naskah dari UU No.15 tahun 1969 sebagaimana telah diubah pertama dengan UU No.4/1975, kedua dengan UU No 2/1980, dan ketiga dengan UU No.1/1985. Jakarta: LPU.

Schwarz, A. 1994. A Nation in Waiting. Boulder, Colo.: Westview.

Russia

Sergei Lounev

HISTORY OF ENFRANCHISEMENT

The first parliamentary elections in Russia were held as recently as 1906, but even then the franchise did not include women, persons under 25 years old, students, servicemen, foreigners, convicts and some other groups. The system of separate electorates provided advantages to socially and economically privileged groups, particularly landlords. After the February 1917 Revolution, Russian suffrage became the most democratic (universal) in history: the franchise was given to women (only some states in the United States allowed this at the time) and servicemen (for the first time in the world), and the age limit was the lowest anywhere (20 years). The October 1917 Revolution led to changes: the "exploiter" classes were disenfranchised. By 1937, the majority of restrictions were lifted and direct elections with secret voting were introduced. However, the very term "elections" was clearly a misnomer in the Soviet Union. There was no electoral competition whatsoever. A constituency could have only one candidate nominated by the powers that be.

By the early 1990s, Russia witnessed fundamental shifts. Competitive elections (with a multiplicity of parties and candidates) were one of the most significant achievements in the process of democratization. Elections are free, although doubts remain about whether they are fair. There are expert reports on numerous cases of intervention by authorities at various levels of the electoral process and other malpractice, especially in the so-called "national republics".

The changes did not affect the electoral procedure (the suffrage remains universal, equal and direct, and the voting is secret). The only significant amendment was a ban on voting by proxy. The 1993 constitution has no special section concerning the suffrage (there are only very general provisions), which remains regulated by different federal laws and federal constitutional laws. Active suffrage is granted to all citizens aged 18 and over (the age limit is not a constitutional norm and some politicians and experts, especially those from the southern regions, suggest bringing the age limit down to 16). There are only two restrictions on suffrage: serving convicts and citizens admitted incapable by a court have no right to vote (persons under criminal investigation have this right).

Voter registration in Russia is conducted periodically by the public authorities in an automatic manner. All Russian citizens are on the lists of voters compiled by constituency election commissions on the basis of information from the heads of local municipalities. Registration occurs twice a year (by 1 January and 1 July). The information is passed to a constituency election commission immediately after the announcement of an election date. The basis for registration is permanent or preferential residence in the constituency. The list of voters is supposed to be made public no later than 20 days before the election. Any citizen has the right to verify it and point out errors, if any, and a constituency election commission is supposed to either correct errors or provide a written reply within 24 hours.

Citizens who were omitted from the list or became residents in the constituency after the list had been compiled are included in an additional list on the basis of documents that identify the person and his or her residence.

There were no attempts to deprive particular groups of the franchise, with one exception: in the 1990s the people of Chechnya were not able to vote in the elections for federal bodies. However, such elections were held in 2000. There were also unsuccessful

Figure 4: Turnout in Russia, 1989 - 2000 (%)

1989	*1990*	*1991*	*1993*	*1995*	*1996*	*1996*	*1999*	*2000*
87.0%	*76.4%*	*74.7%*	*54.8%*	*64.7%*	*69.6%*	*67.8%*	*61.8%*	*68.7%*

Notes: *1989. the first free election to the USSR Congress of People's Deputies (the data is only for the Russian Federation)*

1990. the first free election to the Congress of People's Deputies of the Russian Federation

1991. the first election of the President of the Russian Federation

1993, 1995, 1999. parliamentary elections

1996, 2000. presidential elections (two rounds in 1996)

Figure 5: Parliamentary statistics for Bashkortostan
The difference in turnout compared with all-Russian indices (%)

Election district	*1993*	*1995*	*1999*
Oktiabr'skii (part of the Republic's capital city)	*- 5*	*0*	*0*
Kirovskii (part of the republic's capital city)	*0*	*+3*	*+4*
Sterlitamak (an industrial region)	*+ 7*	*+ 9*	*+ 10*
Sibaiskii (rural)	*+ 18*	*+ 13*	*+ 15*
Birskii (rural)	*+ 15*	*+ 15*	*+ 18*
Tuimazy (rural, on the boundary with Tatarstan)	*+ 14*	*+ 16*	*+ 20*

attempts in the Arkhangelsk and Tyumen' regions to disenfranchise individuals with dual citizenship.

TURNOUT TRENDS

Voting is voluntary in Russia. The problem of absenteeism has made it necessary, in order to ensure legitimacy, to make a legal provision regarding the turnout rate (a presidential election requires over 50 percent of voters; the turnout figure required for a parliamentary election is 25 percent). After a number of cases when the election for a particular district failed due to poor turnout, some experts discussed alternative measures including the idea of compulsory voting and punishing non-voting or rewarding voting.

It is well known that the Soviet authorities considered it a major task to ensure a full turnout and vote for the official slate. Abstention was treated as an open challenge to the authorities, and very few persons abstained. From World War II until the Gorbachev period, turnout varied from 99.74 percent to 99.99 percent, and the vote for candidates from 99.18 percent to 99.95 percent. The beginning of the democratization process has inevitably brought a marked decrease in turnout.

It is necessary to take into account that there are many "active" non-voters. The number of persons voting against all candidates or spoiling ballots can be very high; in 1993 they constituted 7.5 percent of voters.

There are not many general studies regarding turnout trends in Russia. It is common for researchers to state that many non-voters live in cities of over one million. Yet, both in 1993 and in 1999, the figures for the turnout in Moscow and St. Petersburg were higher than the average figure for Russia (by contrast, in 1995 they were lower). In general, in rural areas the turnout rate is higher than in urban areas (in the 1995 election 70 percent and 61 percent respectively). But, as a rule, turnout in cities like St. Petersburg and Ekaterinburg is higher than in the surrounding rural areas. The local authorities' control over the population is much stronger in rural areas and in the called national republics (see the parliamentary statistics for Bashkortostan as one example, in Figure 5). But, for reasons that depend on local situations, relations with the centre, and so on, the authorities may prefer either high or low results.

From the late 1980s to the early 1990s, the growth of popular political activity and the emergence of a feeling that an average person might affect the political process were the main reasons for the relatively high turnout. In the late 1990s, a sharp aggravation of the social and economic situation, government failures, and the growth of corruption and crime brought turnout rates down.

Public opinion surveys reveal that, in comparison with the Soviet period, Russians today perceive government to be less able to control ordinary life. They also believe that they can influence the government less. During the 1990s, trust in such institutions of civil society as parties and political movements, trade unions, the presidency, government and parliament was shockingly low. The primary reason for not voting in Russia is alienation or political apathy. Some surveys point to physical or legal impediments as the main obstacle to voting, but the majority of studies conclude that these factors are secondary (as a rule, only 25 to 30 percent of non-voters give this reason). On the other hand, presidential elections attract more voters than parliamentary ones: the 1993 Russian Constitution is "presidentialist", and Russians consider the presidency to be crucial for the general development of the country.

Different surveys detect certain, often hardly traceable, tendencies: a lower turnout of women and unemployed; a slightly higher percentage of votes from state employees than from those working for private companies; and retired people frequent election commissions more than the employed.

The most visible trend is the impact of age: the percentage of voters under 30 is significantly less than among older persons. The turnout is also lower among the supporters of democratization and reforms, young people and women (there are more women that men voting for democracy-oriented parties and candidates). In some cases the authorities tried to stimulate turnout among young people (this was one of Yeltsin's main strategies during the 1996 campaign).

In the future, the role of young people is likely to become a major challenge. In the mid-1980s, Russia had the highest birth rate that by 2000 led to an increasing percentage of 12- to 17-year-olds in the population. The number of jobs available for this age-group in areas such as industry, small and medium business, science, education, consumer services, and public service, however, is very small. This is spurring the growth of radicalism among young people, on the one hand, and is feeding apathy, on the other. As a result, teenagers and young people are often politically indifferent: only 8 percent of students show any interest in politics. They also display absenteeism: about 70 percent of young people said they would not interfere if democracy in Russia appeared to be in jeopardy. The level of social engagement is minimal. It is probable that, together with the decrease in the population of the older generation, this factor will lessen the turnout in the near future.

REFERENCES

Baglai, M. V. 1998. Konstitutsionnoe Pravo Rossiiskoi Federatsii [Constitutional Law of Russian federation]. Moscow: Norma-Infra.

Vestnik (to 1995 Byulleten') Tsentral'noi izbiratel'noi komissii Rossiiskoi Federatsii [Herald (Bulletin) of the Central Election Commission of the Russian Federation] (Moscow). 1991–2000.

White, S., R. Rose and I. McAllister. 1997. How Russia Votes. Chatham, N.J.: Chatham House Publishers, Inc.

South Africa

Julie Ballington

HISTORY OF ENFRANCHISEMENT

Universal suffrage and electoral registration are relatively new to South Africa's political history. South Africa's exclusionary apartheid regime formally came to an end with the country's first democratic national and provincial elections in 1994. These elections heralded a new political order in which the vast majority of previously disenfranchised people, most notably Africans, were finally able to cast their ballots and participate in electing a new democratic government. No voters' register was compiled for this election. The first common national voters' register was completed in 1999 in time for the second elections, with more than 19 million names. Since then, continuous registration has been available for South African citizens.

For most of the twentieth century, the franchise was racially restricted in South Africa. From the time of the Union in 1910, white males were enfranchised, but with certain property and education requirements in certain territories. In 1930 white women were enfranchised without qualification, and in 1931 the vote was extended to all white men. Few

Black, Asian and Indian voters were enfranchised before the Union, and until 1994 they were subject to severely restricted and inconsistent voting rights. For Black voters, the only elected bodies were those that functioned within the boundaries of the homeland system, which was a system of 10 homeland governments representing the African population (Lodge, 1999).

Indian and Coloured voters were removed from the common municipal registers in Natal and the Cape in 1964 and 1968, but were re-enfranchised in 1984 with the establishment of the Tricameral Parliament which established a House of Representatives for Coloured affairs and a House of Delegates for Indian affairs (Lodge, 1999). The House of Assembly represented the white population. The Tricameral Parliament ceased to exist in April 1994, being replaced by the Parliament and Senate (now the National Council of Provinces). All elections prior to 1994 were contested on a constituency basis. Racially segregated elections for African, Indian and Coloured voters generally did not attract high voter participation. However, white electors generally displayed higher levels of voter commitment during this time (Lodge, 1999).

South Africa's first democratic elections were conducted using a list proportional representation system. This system was considered the best option for a number of reasons, including the fact that it would not require the mammoth task of registering voters in time for the election in April 1994. Therefore, voter registration was not required and all citizens and permanent residents were able to vote with a wide range of prescribed identity documents, or with a temporary voting card. Voter turnout in this election was high, with over 19.7 million of the 22.7 million voters (86.9 percent) turning out to vote.

In 1995 and 1996, local government elections were held to elect councillors to transitional local authorities to include African, Indian, Coloured and white communities. Citizens 18 years of age or older were required to register for these elections in order to vote. Voters' registers were compiled on a provincial basis. Overall, registration was relatively high as over 17.7 million of the estimated 22.3 million voters registered (79.8 percent). However, voter turnout was low with 48.8 percent of registered voters turning out on polling day (Elections Task Group, 1996). Explanations for the low turnout included the fact that a drop in turnout rates between a national and a local election is not unusual. There was also speculation that insufficient voter education had been provided about the complicated electoral system and balloting procedures. The registers compiled for the 1995/1996 local election were discarded after the election, and a new voters' register compiled for the 1999 national elections.

South Africa's first all-inclusive voters' register was compiled over the course of 1998 and 1999, to be used for South Africa's second democratic election on 2 June 1999. The Electoral Act No. 73 of 1998 requires the Chief Electoral Officer to compile and maintain a common national voters' register. The franchise is confined to South African citizens in possession of an identity document or temporary certificate, who must apply for registration in the prescribed manner and in the voting district in which the person is ordinarily resident in order to vote. The Independent Electoral Commission (IEC) certified South Africa's first democratically compiled national voters' register on 30 April 1999.

REGISTRATION OF VOTERS

The registration of voters, in particular the stipulation that only those with the requisite identity document could register, proved to be a point of contention in the run-up to the election. The requirement for bar-coded identity documents arose from a concern to prevent people in possession of fraudulently obtained identity documents from taking part in the election, and to provide the framework for an orderly, free and fair election. However, this statute appeared to disenfranchise at least part of the eligible voting population, as not all citizens were in possession of the requisite bar-coded identity document.

The task of informing citizens of the requirements for registration, as well as places of registration, proved to be a critical task in the administration of the 1999 elections. The IEC embarked upon a number of public awareness campaigns and voter educators worked to inform the electorate about the requirement for the bar-coded identity document in order to register, and to encourage those without bar-coded documents to obtain them. However, the fact that a notable proportion of the voting population was unable to register was indeed a cause for concern. Opposition parties vehemently opposed the requirement for registration, arguing that it was discriminatory and affected certain sections of the population, such as young people, as well as many rural voters. Some parties called for an amendment to the Electoral Act to recognize all forms of identification so that citizens were not disenfranchised as a result.

The IEC used sophisticated technology including 25,000 "zip-zip" machines that were used to scan bar codes, linking their central communication system to over 14,000 voting stations. The majority of citizens registered during three "registration weekends" when voters registered at the polling station at which they would vote during the election. Disabled and elderly people and weekend workers were also encouraged to register at municipal offices daily in the run-up to the election. Based on research from other Southern African countries, the IEC considered a registration figure of about 70 percent to be acceptable (EISA, February 1999, 2).

Voter registration levels exceeded this expectation. Of the 22.8 million estimated voters, over 18.3 million (80.4 percent) registered. Registration was highest among those living in urban areas, where 85 percent of urban voters registered compared with 75 percent of rural citizens (EISA, April 1999, 1). National trends point to a higher registration of women than men. A significant 1.5 million more women than men registered meaning that the voters' register comprised of 53 of percent women. This perplexed observers anticipating a gender gap in terms of turnout, as historically men have often displayed higher levels of interest in politics than women. In the June 1999 election nearly 16 million voters turned out on polling day, representing a turnout of 86 percent of registered voters, or roughly 60 percent of the voting age population.

TURNOUT RATES AND TRENDS

Registration and voting across the different age cohorts increased with age. Those in the 50-to-60-year old age group had a registration rate of over 97 percent. Registration was lowest among first-time voters, where only 42 percent of the potential voters registered. Therefore, one group in particular that displayed lower levels of registration, and consequently voting, was first time voters. Nearly 3.3 million of the eight million people (41 percent) who did not vote (which includes the six million who did not register) would have been first time voters. Reasons cited for the low youth turnout included the fact that the election date was not declared early in the registration process, meaning that many students did not know where they would be at the time of the election and consequently did not know where to register. Opinion polls also suggested that a number of first-time voters did not possess the requisite identity document, or fully understand the voting process and identity requirement.

Other problems raised included lack of information disseminated about voter registration by the IEC: as a consequence some voters did not know where to register or did not possess the relevant documentation. Some people had registered but their names did not appear on the register, and they were unable to vote on polling day. Rural areas proved to present their own problems in terms of registration. People in rural areas were less likely than urban dwellers to possess the requisite identification and often had long distances to walk to registration posts. Rural areas often had high illiteracy rates and limited access to adequate information, which often caused confusion about the processes and identity documents required to register in order to vote.

Subsequent to the 1999 elections, continuous registration was made available by the IEC in order to maintain the voters' register. This allowed citizens to register or to amend their details on the voters' register (such as a change in residential address) at municipal electoral offices. Ahead of the local government elections in November 2000, targeted registration was undertaken to increase registration in areas that had recorded less than 60 percent turnout. It also allowed electors to correct details on the voters' register in instances where the boundary demarcation process undertaken for the local elections had affected voter details by splitting voting districts. Electors were also able to check their registration details using the Internet by entering their identity number into the database. The campaign also included door-to-door registration and information campaigns, as well as a registration weekend where all voting stations were opened to ensure accessibility for voters ahead of the local elections.

The IEC certified the voters' register for the local government elections in October 2000. The register contained the names of 18,476,519 verified voters. Of these, there were 1.6 million more women than men. Younger and first-time voters again displayed disappointing levels of interest in the registration process by registering in low numbers. The issue of statutorily defined identity documents did not surface as such a contentious issue ahead of the 2000 local government elections. However, there was confusion among some voters as to whether re-registration was required to participate in the local elections, and whether or not they could still vote in the voting district in which they registered for the national election. The splitting of some voting districts during the demarcation process also caused confusion and frustration for some voters as they were moved to other districts. Only 48 percent of those registered turned out to vote on polling day. Less than 50 percent turnout in local elections appears to be an emerging trend as voter turnout in South Africa's first local elections in 1995/1996 was 48.8 percent.

While a complex array of factors can explain turnout or non-participation in elections, clearly voter registration procedures have an important role to play. Compared with the 1994 national and provincial elections, the 1999 elections required far more stringent qualifications in order to register. Most notably, South African citizens required a green bar-coded identity document issued after 1986 to be eligible to register, which appeared to disenfranchise a small proportion of the eligible population. Other technical and procedural difficulties also confused voters. The other area of concern is the low level of participation displayed by young and first-time voters. As voter registration is a requirement for voting, it appears that voter education requires further attention in South Africa.

REFERENCES

Elections Task Group. 1996. CEEG Report on Local Government Elections in South Africa. Johannesburg: Community.

Electoral Institute of Southern Africa. Election Update 99(6) 12 February 1999.

Electoral Institute of Southern Africa. Election Update 99(11) 30 April 1999.

Electoral Institute of Southern Africa. Election Update 99(15) 25 June 1999.

Independent Elections Commission. 12 October 2000. State of the Voters' Register. Fact Sheet.

Lodge, T. 1999. Electoral Information Digest: South Africa. Johannesburg: EISA (unpublished paper).

United States of America

Craig Brians

In the United States, voter turnout has historically been closely linked to voter registration levels. This relationship has weakened in recent years as voter registration has become increasingly universal, while voter turnout continues to decline. National legislation making voter registration easier in most states was enacted in the 1990s. Easier registration has resulted in large increases in voter registration levels, but has had little effect on turnout. Research following the enactment of this new law finds that lower-income classes are now more likely to be registered, but are still under-represented among the voting electorate.

HISTORY OF ENFRANCHISEMENT

Historically, voter turnout for those with less education and lower income has been disproportionately low in the United States. From the earliest days of the country, few people who were not land-holding, white males were permitted to vote. By 1896, politics had permeated through much of the population to include many poorer white men and the country experienced high levels of turnout among those eligible to vote. In the face of rampant voter fraud in many jurisdictions, voter registration methods were developed. As voter registration became commonplace, turnout at national elections declined, particularly among the poor and less educated.

Women, minorities and younger citizens have slowly gained recognition of their right to vote following national government action in this traditionally state-dominant area of the law. Although permitted to vote in some localities earlier, women were constitutionally guaranteed the right to vote in 1920. But it took several generations before womens' turnout approached their proportion of the population. A growing population of Latinos and Asian-Americans are becoming increasingly politically active; these groups are largely concentrated in certain states and often face citizenship barriers in addition to registration hurdles. Although the 26th Amendment to the Constitution lowered the voting age to 18 years throughout the US, younger citizens still register and vote at disproportionately lower rates than do their elders.

In response to the egregious disenfranchisement of African-Americans in the South, the national government undertook several remedial steps. In the 1960s, federal registrars were sent to many of the states of the former Confederacy to register citi-

Figure 6: Voter registration statistics in the USA over time

Type	*Year*	*VAP*	*% of VAP*	*% Women*	*%Men*	*% White*	*% Black*	*% Hisp.*
Pres.	*1974*	*146336000*	*65.7%[1]*	*61.7%*	*62.8%*	*63.5%*	*54.9%*	*34.9%*
Pres.	*1978*	*158373000*	*65.2%*	*62.5%*	*62.6%*	*63.8%*	*57.1%*	*32.9%*
Pres.	*1982*	*169938000*	*65.1%*	*64.4%*	*63.7%*	*65.6%*	*39.1%*	*33.3%*
Pres.	*1984*	*174466000*	*71.2%*	*69.3%*	*67.3%*	*69.6%*	*66.3%*	*40.1%*
Pres.	*1988*	*182778000*	*69.1%*	*67.8%*	*65.2%*	*67.9%*	*64.5%*	*35.5%*
Pres.	*1992*	*189529000*	*70.6%*	*69.3%*	*66.9%*	*70.1%*	*63.9%*	*35.0%*
Pres.	*1996*	*196511000*	*74.4%*	*67.3%*	*64.4%*	*67.7%*	*63.5%*	*35.7%*
Parl.	*1976*	*152309190*	*69.0%*	*66.4%*	*67.1%*	*68.3%*	*58.5%*	*37.8%*
Parl.	*1980*	*164597000*	*68.7%*	*67.1%*	*66.6%*	*68.4%*	*60.0%*	*36.3%*
Parl.	*1986*	*178566000*	*66.3%*	*65.0%*	*63.4%*	*65.3%*	*64.0%*	*35.9%*
Parl.	*1990*	*185812000*	*65.2%*	*63.1%*	*61.2%*	*63.8%*	*58.8%*	*32.3%*
Parl.	*1994*	*193650000*	*67.3%*	*63.7%*	*61.2%*	*64.6%*	*58.5%*	*31.3%*
Parl.	*1998*	*183450000*	*67.1%*	*68.4%*	*65.7%*	*69.3%*	*63.7%*	*55.2%*

[1]Ex.Iowa

See www.fec.gov/pages/Raceto.htm for VAP clarification and linked pages for methodology

Hispanic may be of any race.

***Source:** All data in the table above taken from the website of the Federal Election Commission, United States of America under the section "Voter Registration and Turnout Statistics; www.fec.gov and www.fec.gov/elections.html.*

zens to vote. Less onerous registration and voting requirements were mandated and federal authorities must now approve changes in state election procedures. These changes have yielded large gains in registration and voting rates for both African-Americans and lower-income whites living in the South.

REGISTRATION LEGAL REFORMS

In the 1990s, the federal government enacted legislation to standardize voter registration procedures for all citizens. Previously, voter registration was offered idiosyncratically, with procedures and pre-election deadlines varying by state and even county. In 1993, the National Voter Registration Act became law. It requires states to register voters at motor vehicle offices and many other state and local government agencies. Implementation of the Act produced a marked increase in voter registration, particularly among under-represented groups. Younger Americans, minority citizens and lower socio-economic groups recorded large gains in registration.

Nonetheless, contrary to the expectations of those sponsoring this legislation, a turnout increase did not result from the registration increases associated with the new laws. In fact, national voter turnout has continued its downward trend that began in the 1960s. One scholarly explanation for the inability of the new procedure to stem the turnout slide hinges on the nature of the new voter registration procedures. Unlike when voter registration was primarily performed at the offices that ran the elections or by political party representatives, now registration is frequently accomplished by checking a box on a driver's license form, incidental to one's renewal. This transforms voter registration from a political act linked to voting into an administrative action.

Another factor underlying low turnout among new registrants is their lower level of partisan attachment. As has long been the case in American politics, those lacking allegiance to a political party are less likely to vote. In many states a large proportion of the new "motor voter" registrants identify themselves as independents.

The future of registration and voting administration in the US is likely to have a large federal component. Late in the twentieth century, federal legislation had already determined minimum voting age and registration availability, as well as mandated procedures to make the franchise fully available to minority group members. Additionally, the aftermath of the 2000 presidential election has been accompanied by calls for the national government to play a greater role in election administration.

It is doubtful, though, that procedural changes in election rules will profoundly affect turnout levels without mobilization efforts by political parties or candidates. Eased registration rules have increased the number eligible to vote in any given election, but a continued lack of political contact has kept these potential voters from the polls.

REFERENCES

Brians, C. L. March 1997. Residential mobility, voter registration, and electoral participation in Canada. Political Research Quarterly 50:215–227.

Brians, C. L. and B. Grofman. 2001. Election Day registration's effect on US voter turnout. Social Science Quarterly 82.

Brians, C. L. and B. Grofman. April 1999. When registration barriers fall, who votes? An empirical test of a rational choice model. Public Choice 161–176.

Grofman, B., L. Handley and R. G. Niemi. 1992. Minority Representation and the Quest for Voting Equality. New York: Cambridge University Press.

Powell, G. B., Jr. March 1986. American voter turnout in comparative perspective. American Political Science Review 80.

Rosenstone, S. J. and J. M. Hansen. 1993. Mobilization, Participation and Democracy in America. New York: Macmillan.

INTERVIEW

Stephenie Foster has served as Chief of Staff to two United States Senators, and as National Director of Women's Outreach for the Clinton/Gore 1996 campaign. Currently, she is an attorney in Washington, D.C.

At the beginning of the new millennium, many people are still disenfranchised either legally or de facto. How would you assess the current state of voter registration and enfranchisement in the United States?

In the United States, you must register in order to vote. It is easy to register to vote and the US Congress and state legislatures are making registration easier all the time. Every state has its own laws regarding registration; some even allow voters to register at the polling place on Election Day (e.g., Wisconsin). Some states are experimenting with online registration and voting (e.g., Arizona) and voting exclusively by mail (e.g., Oregon).

Having said that, of the over 196 million Americans eligible to vote in 1996, only 75 percent (about 146 million) actually registered to vote; 61 percent of those registered went to the polls (96 million people). Unfortunately, that means that only 49 percent of those Americans eligible to vote actually voted.

As these figures indicate, we have challenges. As Americans, we need to work harder to make registration easier and to make voting easier, but we also need to work harder to give people a reason to register and vote. Voters need to understand that voting matters; that it matters who wins an election and that the democratic process is important. These are challenges that candidates, activists, and political parties face every day.

Have there been any major developments on voter registration recently?

The most recent major development is the National Voter Registration Act of 1993 (the "motor voter" law), which is designed to increase voter registration and participation by making it easier to register to vote.

Specifically, this law requires states to provide people with the opportunity to register to vote, or to update their registration for change of address, when they get or renew drivers' licenses, or when they apply for services at public assistance, disability and other designated offices within a state. The "motor voter" law also requires that states offer voter registration through the use of a simple mail-in form.

The motor voter law went into effect for most states on 1 January 1995. The most recent result shows a marked increase in voter registration, with over 12 million new registrants at the time of the 1996 elections.

What could be done to ensure enfranchisement of all eligible people and to improve voter turnout?

On the technical side, voter registration and the actual voting process needs to be made even easier. Whether it is through Internet registration and voting or by expanding hours at polling places, we need to address the fact that many Americans cannot always get to an office to register to vote or to a polling place to vote during normal working hours.

On the political side, we need to make politics relevant to people. We need to give people a reason to vote. We need to make sure that candidates clarify how they are different from their opponents, what their priorities will be if elected to office, and how their election will make a difference. We need to seriously work for campaign finance reform, so that Americans don't believe that elective office in the United States can be bought.

Do you see registration as a barrier to voter turnout or as an incentive? Please explain why.

It is both. The voter registration system in the United States is an incentive to vote in that people believe that the system is transparent and relatively free of manipulation. Therefore, they believe that their vote counts and will be counted appropriately. It is a barrier in that almost all states require registration 30 days before Election Day.

Yemen

Jamal Adimi

RULES ON THE RIGHT TO VOTE

The Parliament

After Yemen's unification in 1990, the first parliament was constituted in 1993 and the second in 1997. New parliamentary elections were due in April 2001. However, a constitutional amendment presented to parliament by the president of the republic providing for the term of parliament to be extended from four years to six years was approved and submitted to a national referendum at the time of local elections in February 2001.

The constitution stipulates that the republic be divided into equal electoral districts on the basis of population, give or take 5 percent (Article 62). The parliament comprises 301 members of parliament (MPs) representing 301 electoral districts, each district electing one MP. The parliament is elected every four years and the president of the republic calls the election 60 days before the election is to take place.

The President

The president of the republic is elected by direct popular vote. The candidate who receives an absolute majority of votes in the elections is considered the winner. If none of the candidates obtains such a majority the elections are held once again between the two candidates who received the greatest number of votes. The president's term of office is five years and the post may not be held for more than two terms. In 1999 the first president of the republic was elected by direct popular vote. Prior to this, the president was elected by parliamentary vote. A constitutional amendment extending the term of office of the president to seven years was submitted and approved in 2001.

Voting Rights

The right to vote is guaranteed by the constitution to every Yemeni citizen 18 years of age or older. The 1996 Electoral Law does not permit naturalized persons to exercise the right to vote or to be nominated in elections until 15 years after they have acquired Yemeni nationality. This is inconsistent with the text and provisions of the constitution, which state that all citizens are equal in rights and duties and that each citizen has the right to contribute to the political life of the country. These provisions also provide that every citizen has the right to vote, be nominated and express an opinion in a referendum. Furthermore, the Penal and Criminal Law of 1994 grants the courts the right to prevent persons convicted of a crime from being nominated to political office or from exercising the right to vote as a complementary penalty alongside the original penalty. This is a perpetual deprivation that does not end except through rehabilitation. It may be a temporary deprivation for a period of no less than one year and no more than three years starting from the date of completion of the original penalty.

As a general matter, each citizen may cast one vote in an election, which must be done in person at the electoral district that is the electoral domicile and in the election centre where his or her name is registered. Shortly before the 1999 presidential elections the Electoral Law was amended. The amendment granted voters in presidential elections the freedom to cast their vote in any election centre, regardless of where the voter's name is registered. It is thought that this severely limits the benefit of having electors' rolls and significantly increases the possibility of election fraud. Each voter receives a permanent election card which has his or her photograph and includes the date of birth, election domicile, number and date of registration in the electors' rolls of the election district and centre and the election centre where he or she is entitled to vote, as well as the signature of the district primary committee representative.

REGISTRATION OF ELIGIBLE VOTERS

Legal Framework

The law provides that each electoral district have a permanent electors' roll that contains the name of every citizen in the district who meets the constitutional and legal conditions required for exercising electoral rights, as well as the title, occupation, date of birth and election domicile of each citizen. Registration in more than one electoral district is prohibited.

The age of a person who wants to register

Figure 7: Registration divides, Yemen
Registered voters and the voters who cast their votes in 1993, 1997 and 1999

	Parliamentary election 1993	Parliamentary election 1997	Presidential election 1999
Total eligible [1]	6,282,939	5,921,542	6,500,000
Eligible male	3,075,056	3,464,570	3,250,000
Eligible female	3,206,833	2,456,992	3,250,000
Total registered	2,688,323	4,737,701	5,621,829
Registered male	2,209,944	3,364,627	3,897,346
Registered female	478,379	1,273,073	1,702,773
Cast their vote	2,271,185	2,843,216	3,772,941
Void ballots	38,612	100,609	47,713

[1]Figures for 1999 are estimates from the population census breakdown of the number of persons 15 years or older.
Source: Produced by the author from official statistics.

his or her name in the electors' rolls is verified either through that person's personal identity card or any other official document, or, if these documents are not available, the evidence of two witnesses.

The roll is published in five copies signed by the chairman of the committee and its members (at the premises of the committee in the electoral district). The committee retains the first copy, the second is kept by the Supreme Elections Committee, the third by the parliament secretariat, the fourth by the Supreme Court, and the fifth at the premises of the Governorate Supervisory Committee.

The rolls are periodically revised and amended. No amendment to the rolls may be made after elections have been announced. The rolls are considered conclusive proof at the time of elections and no one may participate in the elections unless his or her name appears on the rolls.

Official copies of the electors' rolls are posted in public spaces and places for a period of 15 days following the end of the registration process. Every citizen resident in the electoral district has the right to have his or her name included in the rolls if it has been excluded or deleted without justification. Any person included in the rolls may request the inclusion of the name of any eligible person whose name has been excluded from the rolls. Applications are submitted during a period of 20 days starting from the first day the rolls are posted. Every citizen who has been registered in the electors' rolls is given a temporary certificate to that effect. An election card replaces this temporary certificate after the entry of his or her name in the electors' rolls becomes final.

GETTING REGISTERED TO VOTE

Since 1993 voter registration has been increasing, with an especially dramatic rise among women and the rural population. This is a very important trend in a country where there are 7 million illiterate people and 6 million of the 17 million population are poor. Despite these dramatic developments in voter registration, it is still women, the illiterate, and the poor that are the least likely to register. Figure 8 below reveals, the registration divide is first between men and women, second between the educated and the illiterate and third between urban and rural populations.

The overall registration rate more than doubled as a percentage of eligible voters between 1993 and 1999 (42.8 percent in 1993, 80.0 percent in 1997, and 86.5 percent in 1999). Changes in women's registration were still more dramatic as the registration rate more than tripled during the same period of time, moving from a meagre 15 percent of all eligible women in 1993 to over 55 percent in 1997. This latest figure implies that around one-third of all registered voters are currently women. Registration in 1993 was higher in the southern provinces, though the north made great efforts to increase women's registration in time for the

Figure 8: Some Relevant socio-demographics and voter registration figures by province, Yemen, 1999

PROVINCE	*Total population (thousand)*	*% Rural population*	*% Illiterate 10 years and over*	*Registered voters as % of population 15-64* [1]	*Women registered as % of all registered*
Sana'a city	*1373*	*0.0*	*23.9*	*76.5*	*22.7*
Sana'a	*1242*	*98.0*	*57.3*	*61.7*	*26.4*
Aden	*471*	*1.9*	*19.8*	*83.4*	*30.9*
Taiz	*2157*	*77.6*	*44.8*	*74.7*	*35.6*
Lahj	*616*	*95.6*	*39.9*	*66.2*	*32.8*
Ibb	*1893*	*85.5*	*50.0*	*69.9*	*32.3*
Abyan	*404*	*79.2*	*38.1*	*67.3*	*35.3*
Al-Baida'a	*558*	*82.8*	*49.9*	*58.4*	*31.3*
Shabwa	*520*	*88.4*	*48.7*	*49.2*	*35.1*
Hadramout	*862*	*63.9*	*38.6*	*61.2*	*34.1*
Al-Maharah	*64*	*65.6*	*50.8*	*96.8*	*32.2*
Hodeidah	*1994*	*61.7*	*60.9*	*56.5*	*27.4*
Dhamar	*1106*	*88.1*	*58.7*	*74.8*	*35.7*
Al-Mahwit	*428*	*92.5*	*62.2*	*65.9*	*31.2*
Hajjah	*1409*	*90.0*	*64.7*	*51.5*	*28.3*
Saadah	*574*	*87.4*	*63.9*	*52.6*	*15.2*
Al-Jawf	*499*	*87.3*	*64.5*	*28.0*	*25.7*
Mareb	*240*	*87.9*	*56.5*	*55.8*	*23.8*
TOTAL	*17676*	*73.9*	*49.5*	*66.0*	*30.3*

[1] This age bracket has been taken from the 1999 Census, as no better source is available.

Source: *Table produced by author with data from the Statistical Yearbook 1999.*

1997 parliamentary election. The increase in women's registration after 1993 was particularly high in the more rural provinces. The higher increase rates between 1993 and 1997 took place in those provinces with the largest rural population (i.e., Al-Mahwit with a 24 percent increase, Dhamar with 22 percent, Ibb with 18 percent, Hajjah and Al-Jawf with 16 percent each, Al-Baida'a with 15 percent, Sana'a rural with 14 percent, and Shabwah and Saadah with 10 percent each). Nevertheless, despite this dramatic trend of women's enfranchisement, almost half of the eligible women in Yemen are not included in the electoral rolls as yet.

Examining registration rates in general as well as among women does not entirely answer the question of who is more likely to register in Yemen, and whether there are other social segments still excluded from the voter lists, as a matter of fact if not legally. Comparative international experience shows that the history of enfranchisement is a history of enhancing the participation of larger and larger segments of the society in political life. Women, peasants and the illiterate are usually the last to be fully enfranchised. The case of Yemen is not unique.

It is also worth noting that voter registration has been lower in those areas of the country with the highest illiteracy rates. In seven out of eight provinces with illiteracy rates above the national average of 50 percent, voter registration ranks below the national average: Sana'a rural, Hodaida, Mahwit, Hajjah, Saadah, Al-Jawf and Mareb. On the other hand, a correlation exists between living in rural areas and not getting registered as a voter, although this is weaker than in the case of illiteracy. This can perhaps be explained by the registration efforts made in rural areas in the last few years. In fact, seven out of thirteen provinces with a rural population above the national average of 73 percent show voter registration rates below the national average, five of them also included as highly illiterate provinces: Sana'a, Al-Baida'a, Shabwa, Hajjah, Saadah, Al-Jawf and Mareb.

In conclusion, the least likely Yemeni national to be registered to vote is an illiterate female peasant; the most likely to get registered is an educated urban male.

CHALLENGES FOR GRANTING THE YEMENIS THE RIGHT TO VOTE

The most important and prominent difficulties that confront the exercise of voting rights in Yemen are the following: illiteracy, the fabrication of ballots, deprivation of naturalized persons of the right to vote, pressure of living conditions of most categories of the population, and most important the competence of those managing the electoral process and the continual amendment of the electoral law and the constitution.

If there is to be democratic voting in the country, a number of basic preconditions must be fulfilled. Among these are the following: the eradication of illiteracy; nullification of all provisions related to deprivation of naturalized persons from exercising their electoral rights; a candidate should not be declared the winner except if the counting of votes is true and correct; the judiciary should decide on the validity of membership of parliament (parliament should not by itself decide this matter); amendment of the elections system; the judiciary should supervise the election process; and a precise mechanism should be put in place for registration of voters to ensure clarity and correctness of the electors' rolls.

Through our consideration of the election process, we have found that there exist some prospective challenges that have to be met by the operation itself and those responsible for it. These must be resolved in a sound and clear manner. Among the most significant challenges are the following:

Registration

The level of awareness of the importance of parliamentary and other forms of elections among unregistered citizens is very low. However, this does not mean that those that are registered are aware of the importance of participating in elections. There are many citizens who do not go to polling centres to cast their votes. Despite the awareness of a huge proportion of unregistered citizens and those eligible to register of the immense significance of registration, and of the elections themselves, participation in the electoral process is low. This may be attributed largely to indifference and lack of planned and considered awareness of the significance of elections, particularly among illiterates, the rural population and recently eligible young people. These citizens usually lose the opportunity to cast their votes due to not having been made properly aware of the significance of registration and elections.

Family bonds still assume a vital role in social participation, both among men and women.

There is still an immense need for awareness in some basic information pertaining to elections, such as informing citizens of registration, its purposes and timing, which entails undertaking the following steps:

- an urgent awareness campaign for those categories in the rural areas, such as the Bedouins;
- an election awareness campaign for women, provided that an initiative is undertaken to inform men of the importance of participation of women in the elections;
- illiteracy may not form an obstacle with regard to registration for elections, but may form a tremendous barrier with regard to exercising the election process. Therefore, a campaign to raise awareness among the illiterate, especially women; and
- activating the role of non-partisan local leaderships in order to enable those responsible for elections to benefit from them when undertaking awareness campaigns.

Women's Participation

Customs and traditions play an influential and strong role in the electoral choices of both Yemeni men and women. Some studies indicate that these customs and traditions are the major reasons for opposition to women's participation in elections. In fact, some of them reject the idea due to their belief that women have no knowledge of politics.

Although religious beliefs are for the choice of the voter in a conservative country like Yemen, religious reasons that hamper women from participating in elections cannot be rationalized.

Modifying inherited customs and traditions is, no doubt, very difficult and requires intensive and continuous efforts, particularly if quick results are desired. But long-term awareness campaigns will have an effective and vital impact, particularly in rural areas.

There is a common factor between non-registration of a large number of women and their failing to attend polling centres to cast their votes, represented by the feeling that nothing would benefit from the elections in the future as men also do not go themselves cast their votes or otherwise they lack political tendencies.

REFERENCES

The Constitution and elections law of Yemen.

Republic of Yemen. Ministry of Planning and Development. Central Statistical Organization. 2000. Statistical Yearbook 1999. Sana'a.

www.al-bab.com/yemen/pol/tab3.htm

Voter Turnout Rates from a Comparative Perspective

By Rafael López Pintor,
Maria Gratschew and Kate Sullivan

This section provides a brief overview of worldwide voter turnout statistics since 1945 for both parliamentary and presidential elections. It is based on the International IDEA database of elections, which covers 170 independent states and includes data for 1,256 parliamentary elections and 412 presidential elections. It examines trends over time since 1945, such as differences in turnout between geographical regions and between different types of electoral systems. Finally, the survey provides some comparison between voter turnout and selected political, institutional and socio-economic factors that are often cited as determinants of differing voter turnout rates. All figures refer to parliamentary elections unless otherwise indicated.

OPERATIONALIZING VOTER TURNOUT

Voter turnout is one measure of citizen participation in politics. It is usually expressed as the percentage of voters who cast a vote (i.e., "turnout") at an election. This total number of voters includes those who cast blank or invalid votes, as they still participate.

The pool of eligible voters can be defined in different ways. International IDEA uses two measures: the number of registered voters and estimated voting age population (VAP). Information on the number of registered voters has been compiled from electoral management bodies around the world and an estimate on voting age population has been made using population statistics from the United Nations. Further information on the methodology can be found on page 9.

There are advantages and disadvantages in using either of these calculations as the basis for turnout statistics. Registration is useful in that in many countries it is a prerequisite for voting, so the number of registered voters reflects those who may actually be able to cast a vote. However, in some countries registration may not be used or the register itself may be inaccurate.

The use of voting age population allows for an estimate of the potential number of voters, were all systemic and administrative barriers to be removed. However, as an estimate, it is not able to exclude those within a population who may not be eligible for registration or voting due to factors such as non-citizenship, mental competence or imprisonment.

The material presented here is a summary both of the tables later in this book and of the data collected for the International IDEA Voter Turnout Database. More information on the database can be found in this report's appendix and at International IDEA's website at www.idea.int/turnout.

Figure 9: Worldwide turnout, 1945-2001

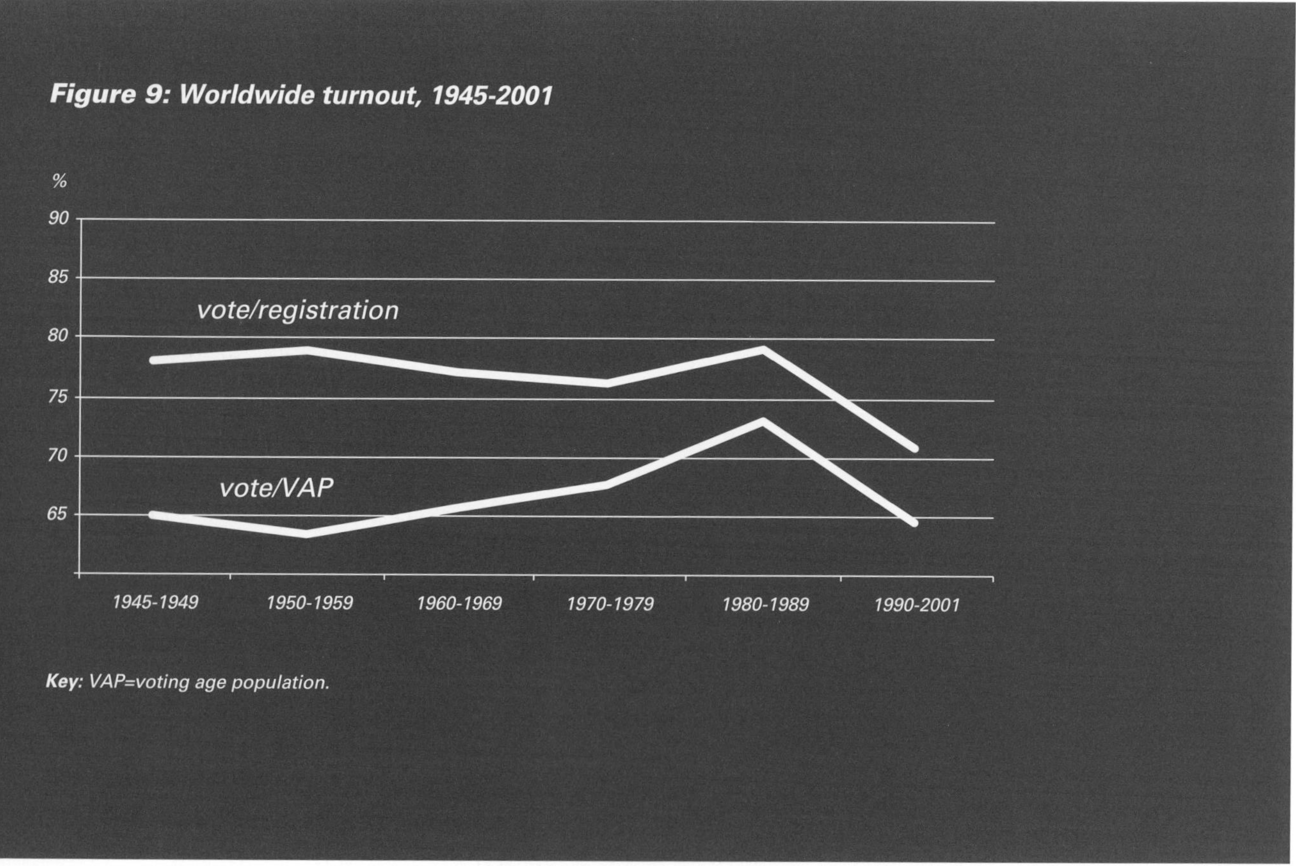

Key: *VAP=voting age population.*

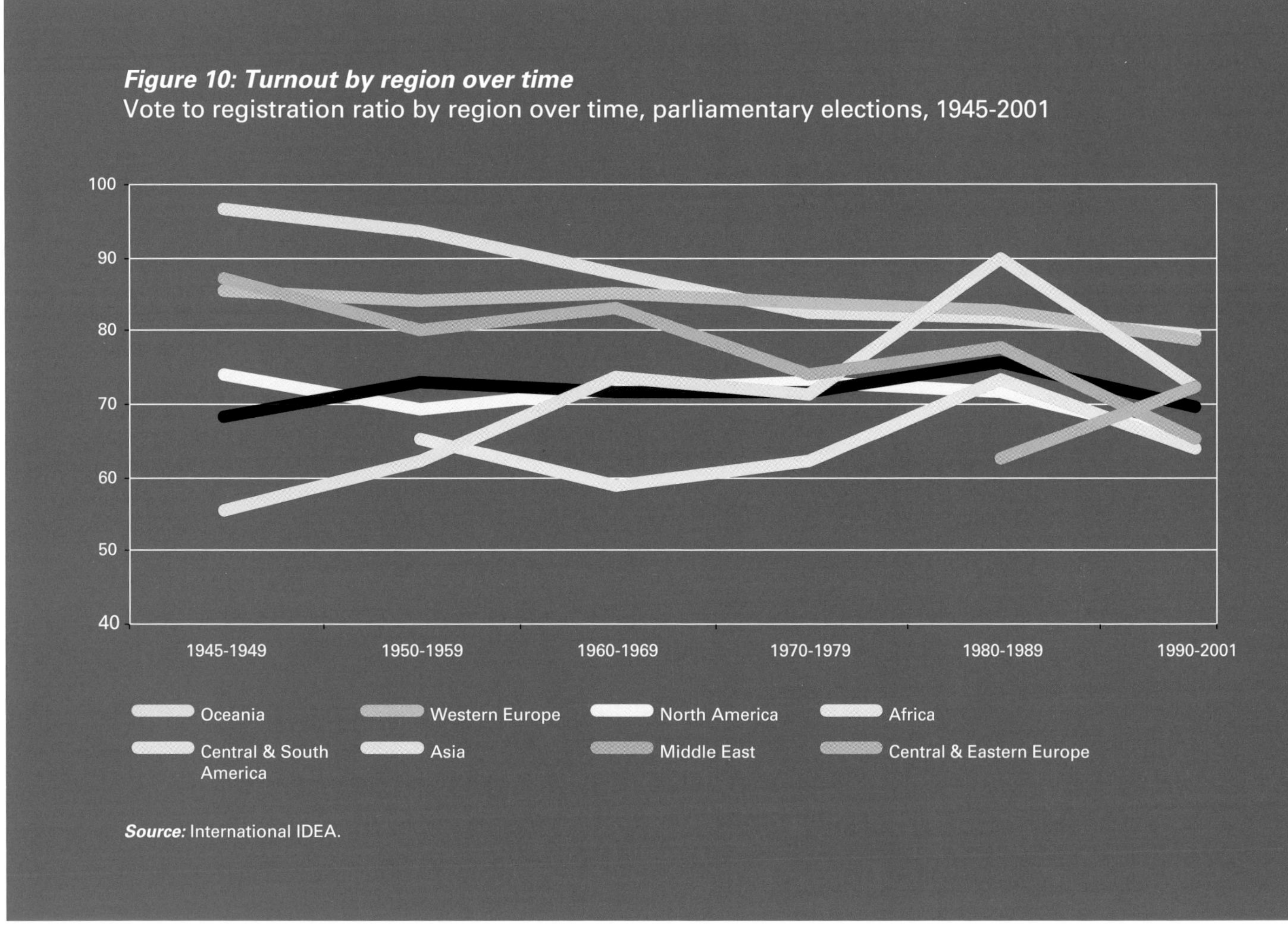

Figure 10: Turnout by region over time
Vote to registration ratio by region over time, parliamentary elections, 1945-2001

Source: International IDEA.

Figure 9: *Worldwide turnout, 1945-2001* shows a notable decline in voter turnout since the mid-1980s. This decline is similar whether turnout is measured as a percentage of registration or as a percentage of the voting age population. However, this global trend is not consistently reflected across regions.

Figure 10: Turnout by region over time
Africa experienced a pronounced increase in turnout, riding the wave of democratization to the mid-1980s. After ten years of elections, Central and East European countries are still increasing voter turnout. Turnout in North and South American countries has remained stable across the time period, as has that of Oceania and Western Europe. The Middle East has a varied turnout record, but Asia has seen the most pronounced variations.

Average turnout from 1990 to 2001 peaked at 79 percent in Oceania, just ahead of Western Europe with 78 percent. Both Asia and the Central and Eastern European region had average voter turnout of 72 percent. The average in Central and South America was 69 percent; the average in North America and the Caribbean was 65 percent, the same as in the Middle East. Africa's average turnout was the lowest at 64 percent.

Figure 11: League table by country vote to registration ratio, parliamentary elections, 1945-2001

Country (no. of elections)	vote/reg %
1 Australia(22)	94.5
2 Singapore(8)	93.5
3 Uzbekistan(3)	93.5
4 Liechtenstein(17)	92.8
5 Belgium(18)	92.5
6 Nauru(5)	92.4
7 Bahamas(6)	91.9
8 Indonesia(7)	91.5
9 Burundi(1)	91.4
10 Austria(17)	91.3
11 Angola(1)	91.2
12 Mongolia(4)	91.1
13 New Zealand(19)	90.8
14 Cambodia(2)	90.3
15 Italy(15)	89.8
16 Luxembourg(12)	89.7
17 Cyprus(7)	89.7
18 Iceland(17)	89.5
19 South Africa(1)	89.3
20 Cook Islands(1)	89.0
21 Tajikistan(2)	88.7
22 Guyana(7)	88.5
23 Thailand(15)	88.3
24 Malta(14)	88.2
25 Albania(4)	88.0
26 Netherlands(16)	87.5
27 Sweden(17)	87.1
28 Seychelles(2)	86.6
39 Tunisia(5)	86.2
30 Malawi(2)	86.2
31 East Timor(1)	86.0
32 Denmark(22)	85.9
33 Germany(14)	85.4
34 Slovakia(4)	85.2
35 Mauritius(6)	84.4
36 Argentina(18)	84.2
37 Czech Republic(4)	82.8
38 Western Samoa(3)	82.3
39 Bolivia(11)	82.2
40 Tuvalu(2)	81.9
41 Palau(6)	81.7
42 Bulgaria(4)	81.4
43 Andorra(3)	81.4
44 Turkey(10)	81.3
45 Fiji(3)	81.0
46 Philippines(7)	80.9
47 Belize(5)	80.4
48 Norway(15)	80.4
49 Peru(9)	80.3
50 Israel(15)	80.3
51 Venezuela(10)	80.0
52 Uruguay(11)	80.0
53 Greece(16)	79.9
54 Kuwait(5)	79.6
55 Chile(11)	78.9
56 Latvia(4)	78.7
57 Namibia(3)	78.6
58 Aruba(3)	78.5
59 Bahrain(1)	78.4
60 San Marino(7)	78.4
61 Paraguay(9)	78.3
62 Mozambique(2)	78.0
63 Kiribati(4)	77.9
64 Brazil(14)	77.8
65 Costa Rica(12)	77.7
66 Iran(1)	77.3
67 Azerbaijan(2)	77.0
68 Portugal(10)	77.0
69 Slovenia(3)	76.6
70 Kazakhstan(1)	76.2
71 Finland(16)	76.0
72 Nicaragua(6)	75.9
73 Panama(4)	75.5
74 Armenia(2)	75.4
75 Palestinian Authority(1)	75.4
76 United Kingdom(16)	75.2
77 Tanzania(2)	74.6
78 Dominica(12)	74.4
79 Sri Lanka(11)	74.3
80 St. Kitts & Nevis(11)	74.2
81 Suriname(6)	74.2
82 Cameroon(4)	74.0
83 Canada(18)	73.9
84 France(15)	73.8
85 Spain(8)	73.6
86 Gambia(5)	73.4
87 Ireland(16)	73.3
88 Ukraine(2)	73.2

89 Republic of Korea(10)	72.9
90 Honduras(11)	72.8
91 Moldova(3)	72.8
92 Romania(3)	72.5
93 Madagascar(5)	72.5
94 St. Vincent & the Grenadines(14)	72.2
95 Lesotho(4)	72.1
96 Maldives(2)	72.0
97 Togo(2)	71.9
98 Malaysia(6)	71.5
99 Morocco(5)	71.2
100 Croatia(3)	71.2
101 Democratic Rep. of Congo(1)	70.9
102 Monaco(7)	70.9
103 Uganda(3)	70.8
104 Yemen(2)	70.7
105 Taiwan (Republic of China)(5)	70.5
106 Comoros Islands(2)	70.3
107 Grenada(6)	70.3
108 Anguilla(8)	69.5
109 Japan(22)	69.5
110 Nepal(7)	69.1
111 Ecuador(12)	68.9
112 Georgia(3)	68.9
113 Barbados(11)	68.8
114 Cap Verde(3)	68.6
115 Vanuatu(5)	68.3
116 Estonia(4)	68.1
117 Jamaica(12)	68.1
118 Hungary(3)	67.0
119 Dominican Republic(6)	66.6
120 United States of America(17)	66.5
121 Benin(3)	65.9
122 Mexico(19)	65.2
123 Sao Tome e Principe(3)	64.5
124 Papua New Guinea(8)	64.1
125 St. Lucia(12)	64.1
126 Solomon Islands(4)	63.8
127 Trinidad & Tobago(12)	63.3
128 Central African Republic(2)	63.2
129 Burma(2)	62.7
130 Kyrgyzstan(3)	62.5
131 Guinea Bissau(2)	62.5
132 Algeria(2)	62.3
133 Antigua & Barbuda(11)	62.2
134 Kenya(2)	62.1
135 Guinea(1)	61.9
136 Syria(1)	61.2
137 Botswana(6)	60.7
138 Belarus(2)	60.6
139 Sierra Leone(1)	60.3
140 Bosnia & Herzegovina(3)	60.2
141 India(13)	59.4
142 Russia(3)	58.4
143 Bangladesh(6)	58.2
144 Sudan(2)	57.6
145 Switzerland(14)	56.5
146 Tonga(4)	56.3
147 Niger(3)	56.2
148 Macedonia(2)	54.1
149 Senegal(6)	53.8
150 Lithuania(3)	52.7
151 Djibouti(2)	52.6
152 Jordan(3)	51.8
153 Zambia(3)	51.7
154 Guatemala(16)	51.6
155 Ghana(6)	50.5
156 Poland(5)	50.3
157 Nigeria(3)	50.3
158 Chad(1)	50.1
159 El Salvador(11)	49.6
160 Zimbabwe(3)	48.7
161 Colombia(18)	47.6
162 Haiti(3)	47.1
163 Mauritania(2)	45.5
164 Pakistan(6)	45.3
165 Egypt(5)	45.1
166 Burkina Faso(4)	41.7
167 Lebanon(3)	39.5
168 Ivory Coast(2)	37.0
169 Mali(2)	21.3

Key: no.=number of elections.

* Argentina included women in the franchise from 1947.
* Bahrain only includes men in the franchise.
* Belgium included women in the franchise from 1948.
* Czech Republic includes elections in Czechoslovakia 1990 and 1992.
* Greece included women in the franchise from 1986.
* Kuwait only includes men in the franchise.
* Liechtenstein included women in the franchise from 1986.
* Switzerland included women in the franchise from 1971.

COMPARING TURNOUT ACROSS NATIONS

Figure 11, p.78 shows the turnout ranking for all countries in the International IDEA database. The high ranking of certain countries may be a surprise; it certainly refutes the notion that only Western countries have high voter turnout.

This table is based on voter turnout as a percentage of registered voters, which may explain some apparent anomalies. Turnout may be high if a voters' register is not of high quality or is outdated. Five of the top seven countries - Australia, Nauru, Singapore, Belgium, and Liechtenstein - enforce compulsory voting laws, which may explain their high turnout.

Figure 12: League table by region, vote to registration ratio.

Ranking of average turnout since 1945 Country (no. of elections)	*vote/reg %*
Oceania	
Australia(22)	*94.5*
Nauru(5)	*92.4*
New Zealand(19)	*90.8*
Cook Islands(1)	*89.0*
Western Samoa(3)	*82.3*
Tuvalu(2)	*81.9*
Palau(6)	*81.7*
Fiji(3)	*81.0*
Kiribati(4)	*77.9*
Vanuatu(5)	*68.3*
Papua New Guinea(8)	*64.1*
Solomon Islands(4)	*63.8*
Tonga(4)	*56.3*
Average(86)	*83.1*
Western Europe	
Liechtenstein(17)	*92.8*
Belgium(18)	*92.5*
Austria(17)	*91.3*
Italy(15)	*89.8*
Luxembourg(12)	*89.7*
Cyprus(7)	*89.7*
Iceland(17)	*89.5*
Malta(14)	*88.2*
Netherlands(16)	*87.5*
Sweden(17)	*87.1*
Denmark(22)	*85.9*
Germany(14)	*85.4*
Andorra(3)	*81.4*
Turkey(10)	*81.3*
Norway(15)	*80.4*
Greece(16)	*79.9*
San Marino(7)	*78.4*
Portugal(10)	*77.0*
Finland(16)	*76.0*
United Kingdom(16)	*75.2*
France(15)	*73.8*
Spain(8)	*73.6*
Ireland(16)	*73.3*
Monaco(7)	*70.9*
Switzerland(14)	*56.5*
Average(339)	*82.6*
North America	
Bahamas(6)	*91.9*
Aruba(3)	*78.5*
Dominica(12)	*74.4*
St. Kitts & Nevis(11)	*74.2*
Canada(18)	*73.9*
St. Vincent & the Grenadines(14)	*72.2*
Grenada(6)	*70.3*
Anguilla(8)	*69.5*
Barbados(11)	*68.8*
Jamaica(12)	*68.1*
Dominican Republic(6)	*66.6*
United States of America(17)	*66.5*
St. Lucia(12)	*64.1*
Trinidad & Tobago(12)	*63.3*
Antigua & Barbuda(11)	*62.2*
Haiti(3)	*47.1*
Average(162)	*69.6*

Africa	
Burundi(1)	91.4
Angola(1)	91.2
South Africa(1)	89.3
Seychelles(2)	86.6
Tunisia(5)	86.2
Malawi(2)	86.2
Mauritius(6)	84.4
Namibia(3)	78.6
Mozambique(2)	78.0
Tanzania(2)	74.6
Cameroon(4)	74.0
Gambia(5)	73.4
Madagascar(5)	72.5
Lesotho(4)	72.1
Togo(2)	71.9
Morocco(5)	71.2
Democratic Republic of Congo(1)	70.9
Uganda(3)	70.8
Comoros Islands(2)	70.3
Cap Verde(3)	68.6
Benin(3)	65.9
Sao Tome e Principe(3)	64.5
Central African Republic(2)	63.2
Guinea Bissau(2)	62.5
Algeria(2)	62.3
Kenya(2)	62.1
Guinea(1)	61.9
Botswana(6)	60.7
Sierra Leone(1)	60.3
Sudan(2)	57.6
Niger(3)	56.2
Senegal(6)	53.8
Djibouti(2)	52.6
Zambia(3)	51.7
Ghana(6)	50.5
Nigeria(3)	50.3
Chad(1)	50.1
Zimbabwe(3)	48.7
Mauritania(2)	45.5
Egypt(5)	45.1
Burkina Faso(4)	41.7
Ivory Coast(2)	37.0
Mali(2)	21.3
Average(126)	64.5

Central & South America	
Guyana(7)	88.5
Argentina(18)	84.2
Bolivia(11)	82.2
Belize(5)	80.4
Peru(9)	80.3
Venezuela(10)	80.0
Uruguay(11)	80.0
Chile(11)	78.9
Paraguay(9)	78.3
Brazil(14)	77.8
Costa Rica(12)	77.7
Nicaragua(6)	75.9
Panama(4)	75.5
Suriname(6)	74.2
Honduras(11)	72.8
Ecuador(12)	68.9
Mexico(19)	65.2
Guatemala(16)	51.6
El Salvador(11)	49.6
Colombia(18)	47.6
Average(220)	71.5

Asia	
Singapore(8)	93.5
Indonesia(7)	91.5
Mongolia(4)	91.1
Cambodia(2)	90.3
Thailand(15)	88.3
East Timor(1)	86.0
Philippines(7)	80.9
Sri Lanka(11)	74.3
Republic of Korea(10)	72.9
Maldives(2)	72.0
Malaysia(6)	71.5
Taiwan (Republic of China)(5)	70.5
Japan(22)	69.5
Nepal(7)	69.1
Burma(2)	62.7
India(13)	59.4
Bangladesh(6)	58.2
Pakistan(6)	45.3
Average(134)	74.0

(...Figure 12)

Middle East	
Israel(15)	*80.3*
Kuwait(5)	*79.6*
Bahrain(1)	*78.4*
Iran(1)	*77.3*
Palestinian Authority(1)	*75.4*
Yemen(2)	*70.7*
Syria(1)	*61.2*
Jordan(3)	*51.8*
Lebanon(3)	*39.5*
Average(32)	*72.2*

Central & Eastern Europe	
Uzbekistan(3)	*93.5*
Tajikistan(2)	*88.7*
Albania(4)	*88.0*
Slovakia(4)	*85.2*
Czech Republic(4)	*82.8*
Bulgaria(4)	*81.4*
Latvia(4)	*78.7*
Azerbaijan(2)	*77.0*
Slovenia(3)	*76.6*
Kazakhstan(1)	*76.2*
Armenia(2)	*75.4*
Ukraine(2)	*73.2*
Moldova(3)	*72.8*
Romania(3)	*72.5*
Croatia(3)	*71.2*
Georgia(3)	*68.9*
Estonia(4)	*68.1*
Hungary(3)	*67.0*
Kyrgyzstan(3)	*62.5*
Belarus(2)	*60.6*
Bosnia & Herzegovina(3)	*60.2*
Russia(3)	*58.4*
Macedonia(2)	*54.1*
Lithuania(3)	*52.7*
Poland(5)	*50.3*
Average(75)	*71.9*

Key: no.*=number of elections.*

If this data is presented regionally, the differences within each region can be seen more clearly. The difference between the highest and lowest average turnout in Western Europe - Liechtenstein's 93 percent and neighbouring Switzerland's 56 percent - may be explained by the use of compulsory voting in Liechtenstein. On the other hand the Bahamas enjoys a non-compulsory average of 92 percent, compared to the Haitian average of 47 percent. (Figure 12)

Turnout by population

If we rank countries according to turnout as a percentage of voting age population, the results are quite different. Our estimate of voting age population is based on an estimate of the adult population, and does not account for legal or systemic barriers to registration.

None of the top ten countries from Figure 11 are among the top ten when we express turnout as a percentage of voting age population; however five countries maintain their top twenty ranking (Uzbekistan, New Zealand, Belgium, Austria and Australia).

Countries from diverse regions are among the top ten: three from Africa, three from Western Europe, two from Asia, one from Central and Eastern Europe, and one from Latin America.

Figure 13: League table by country. vote to voting age population ratio. Parliamentary elections. 1945-2001

	Country (no. of elections)	vote/vap %
1	Suriname(8)	93.8
2	Comoros Islands(2)	93.6
3	Seychelles(2)	93.1
4	Albania(5)	92.4
5	Italy(15)	92.0
6	Cambodia(2)	90.5
7	Iceland(17)	89.3
8	Angola(1)	88.3
9	Portugal(10)	88.2
10	Indonesia(7)	87.9
11	Uzbekistan(3)	87.7
12	Cook Islands(1)	87.3
13	Somalia(1)	87.1
14	Malawi(2)	86.9
15	Western Samoa(3)	86.4
16	Guyana(8)	86.0
17	New Zealand(19)	86.0
18	Belgium(18)	84.8
19	Austria(17)	84.4
20	Australia(22)	84.2
21	Sweden(17)	84.1
22	Netherlands(16)	83.8
23	Denmark(22)	83.6
24	Slovakia(4)	82.9
25	Czech Republic(4)	82.8
26	Canada(18)	82.6
27	San Marino(7)	82.5
28	Mauritius(7)	82.4
29	Thailand(14)	82.1
30	Palau(1)	81.7
31	Greece(18)	80.8
32	Aruba(3)	80.4
33	Israel(15)	80.3
34	Germany(14)	80.2
35	Mongolia(4)	79.5
36	Norway(15)	79.2
37	Tajikistan(2)	79.0
38	Malta(14)	78.9
39	Finland(16)	78.1
40	Slovenia(3)	77.9
41	Croatia(3)	77.2
42	Spain(8)	76.4
43	Bulgaria(4)	76.1
44	Uruguay(11)	76.1
45	Maldives(2)	76.0
46	Namibia(3)	75.7
47	Burundi(1)	75.4
48	Palestinian Authority(1)	75.4
49	Ireland(16)	74.9
50	South Africa(2)	74.7
51	Turkey(10)	74.2
52	St. Vincent & the Grenadines(14)	74.1
53	United Kingdom(16)	73.8
54	Republic of Korea(10)	72.9
55	Dominica(12)	72.9
56	Cap Verde(3)	72.4
57	Papua New Guinea(8)	72.2
58	Romania(3)	72.2
59	Azerbaijan(2)	71.9
60	Cyprus(7)	71.4
61	Ukraine(2)	70.8
62	Taiwan (Republic of China)(4)	70.1
63	Togo(4)	69.3
64	Argentina(18)	69.3
65	Japan(22)	68.7
66	Costa Rica(13)	68.1
67	Hungary(3)	68.1
68	Dominican Republic(11)	67.8
69	Lebanon(3)	67.8
70	Iran(2)	67.6
71	France(15)	67.3
72	Belize(5)	67.2
73	Venezuela(11)	67.2
74	Algeria(2)	67.1
75	Nepal(7)	67.0
76	Trinidad & Tobago(12)	66.5
77	Madagascar(5)	66.1
78	Grenada(12)	66.1
79	Vanuatu(5)	65.7
80	Fiji(3)	64.9
81	Lesotho(4)	64.3
82	Barbados(11)	63.9
83	Georgia(3)	63.7
84	Liechtenstein(17)	63.6
85	Luxembourg(13)	63.5
86	Bahamas(6)	63.4
87	St. Lucia(13)	62.5
88	Sri Lanka(11)	62.4
89	Kiribati(5)	62.4
90	Mozambique(2)	62.3
91	Benin(3)	62.0

92 Nicaragua(10)	62.0
93 Moldova(3)	61.6
94 India(13)	61.5
95 Bolivia(13)	61.4
96 Philippines(7)	60.6
97 St. Kitts & Nevis(11)	60.6
98 Latvia(4)	60.3
99 Guinea(1)	59.9
100 Andorra(3)	59.5
101 Solomon Islands(5)	59.0
102 Belarus(2)	58.9
103 Jamaica(12)	58.6
104 Bosnia & Herzegovina(3)	58.3
105 Syria(1)	58.0
106 Panama(5)	58.0
107 Tunisia(5)	57.9
108 Malaysia(8)	57.8
109 Anguilla(2)	57.7
110 Morocco(5)	57.6
111 Lithuania(3)	56.9
112 Russia(3)	56.6
113 Sao Tome e Principe(3)	56.6
114 Paraguay(11)	56.0
115 Niger(3)	56.0
116 Bangladesh(6)	56.0
117 Gambia(6)	55.8
118 Zimbabwe(6)	55.7
119 Honduras(12)	55.3
120 Peru(9)	54.8
121 Kyrgyzstan(3)	54.3
122 Cameroon(4)	53.9
123 Estonia(4)	53.5
124 Guinea Bissau(2)	52.6
125 Tonga(3)	52.4
126 Central African Republic(2)	51.9
127 Switzerland(14)	51.9
128 Poland(5)	51.4
129 Singapore(8)	51.2
130 Uganda(3)	50.6
131 Burma(2)	50.0
132 Antigua & Barbuda(11)	49.6
133 Haiti(3)	48.8
134 Macedonia(2)	48.4
135 Brazil(14)	48.2
136 Mexico(19)	48.1
137 Armenia(2)	48.0
138 United States of America(28)	47.7
139 Nigeria(3)	47.6
140 Sierra Leone(3)	46.8
141 Tanzania(2)	46.8
142 Botswana(7)	46.2
143 Micronesia(2)	46.2
144 Ghana(6)	46.1
145 Chile(11)	45.9
146 Mauritania(2)	45.1
147 El Salvador(16)	43.9
148 Kenya(2)	43.8
149 Ecuador(15)	42.6
150 Senegal(7)	42.3
151 Zambia(3)	41.4
152 Pakistan(6)	40.7
153 Democratic Rep. of Congo(2)	39.0
154 Nauru(8)	38.8
155 Burkina Faso(4)	38.4
156 Yemen(2)	36.8
157 Colombia(20)	36.2
158 Bahrain(1)	32.6
159 Sudan(2)	32.0
160 Ivory Coast(2)	31.9
161 Jordan(3)	29.9
162 Guatemala(16)	29.8
163 Djibouti(2)	28.1
164 Chad(1)	25.6
165 Egypt(5)	24.6
166 Kazakhstan(1)	22.7
167 Mali(2)	21.7
168 Kuwait(5)	14.0
169 Monaco(7)	13.2

Key: VAP= voting age population; no.=number of elections.

* Argentina included women in the franchise from 1947.

* Bahrain only includes men in the franchise.

* Belgium included women in the franchise from 1948.

* Czech Republic includes elections in Czechoslovakia 1990 and 1992.

* Greece included women in the franchise from 1986.

* Kuwait only includes men in the franchise.

* Liechtenstein included women in the franchise from 1986.

* Switzerland included women in the franchise from 1971.

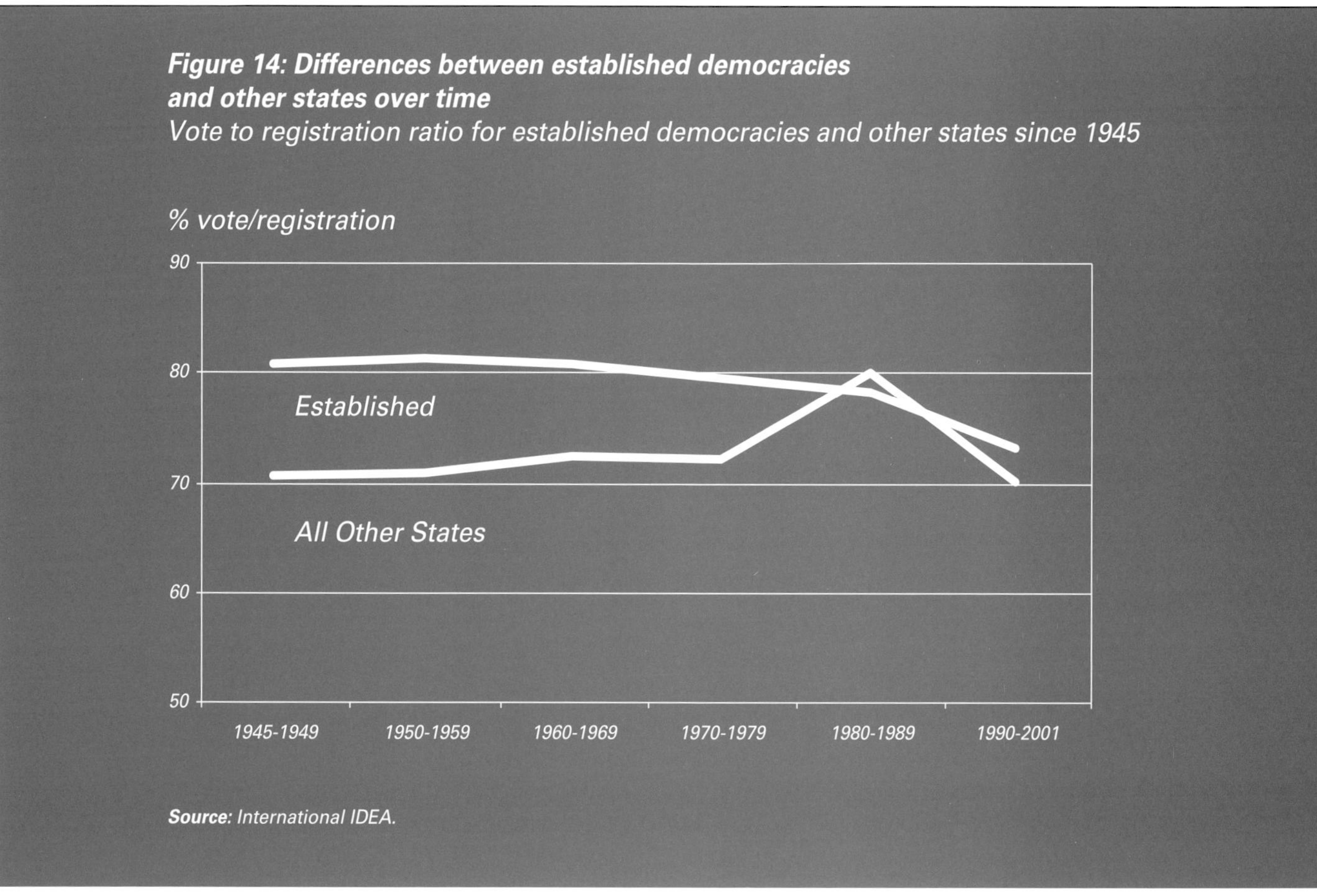

Figure 14: Differences between established democracies and other states over time
Vote to registration ratio for established democracies and other states since 1945

Source: *International IDEA.*

VOTER TURNOUT AND SOCIO-ECONOMIC FACTORS

Figure 14: *Differences between established democracies and other states over time*

Our data reveals that high-turnout countries are neither exclusively new nor established democracies. Arend Lijphart has defined thirty six countries* as "established democracies" if they are democratic now and have been for twenty years (democracy assessed using a Freedom House scale, as below). These established democracies have seen a slow but steady decline in turnout since the 1970s. During the 1970s, however, as a result of the democratization movement, "other states" experienced an increase in voter turnout, peaking at about 80 percent. The current turnout in "other states" is about 70 percent, lower than the 73 percent in established democracies.

Our data shows however that a high level of political freedoms and civil liberties may contribute to a high level of voter turnout.

The 457 elections conducted in a political system rated by Freedom House as being "free" yielded an average turnout of 76 percent. However, being in either a "partly free" or a "not free" environment seems less of an influence on turnout, as both ratings see an average turnout of 70 percent.

**Australia, Austria, Bahamas, Barbados, Belgium, Botswana, Canada, Colombia, Costa Rica, Denmark, Finland, France, Germany, Greece, Iceland, India, Ireland, Israel, Italy, Jamaica, Japan, Luxembourg, Malta, Mauritius, Netherlands, New Zealand, Norway, Papua New Guinea, Portugal, Spain, Sweden, Switzerland, Trinidad and Tobago, United Kingdom, United States of America, Venezuela.*

Source: *Lijphart, A. 1999. Patterns of Democracy, Government Forms and Performance in Thirty-Six Countries. New Haven: Yale University Press.*

Figure 15: Freedom House rating and voter turnout
Vote to registration ratio by Freedom House rating, 1945-2000

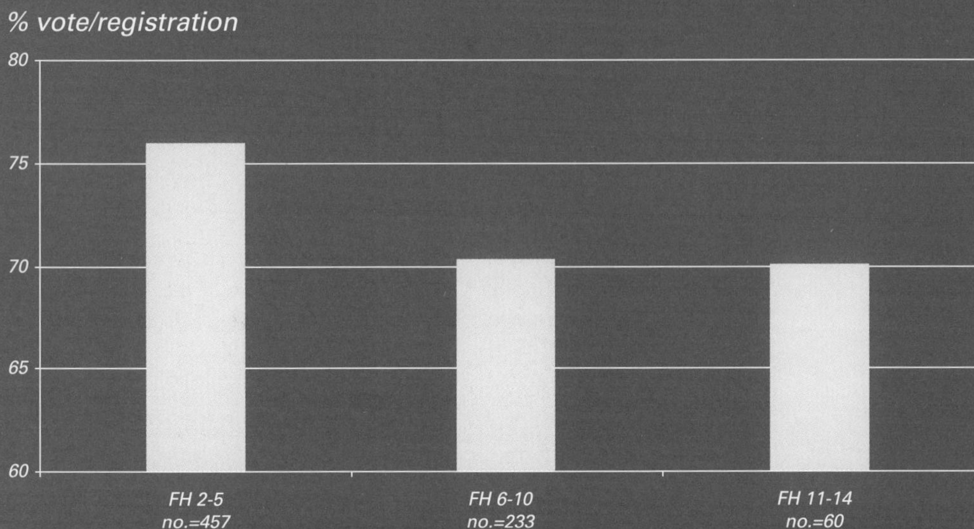

Source: *International IDEA.*
Key: no.*=number of elections, FH= Freedom House rating of political rights and civil liberties. "2" indicates the highest possible level of rights and freedoms and 14 the lowest.*

Figure 16: Literacy and Turnout
Vote to registration ratio by literacy rate (1997), most recent parliamentary elections

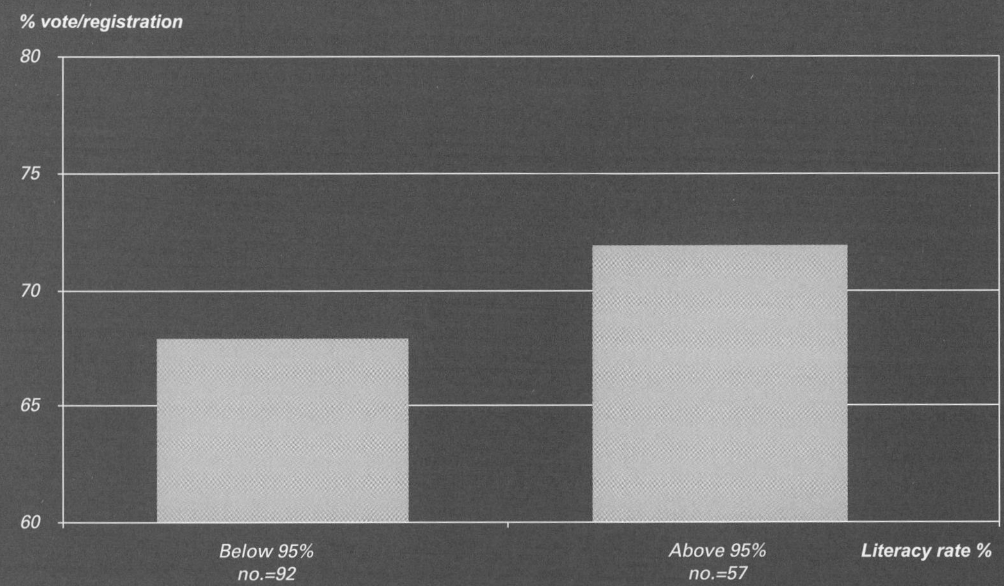

Source: *International IDEA and Human Development Report (1*
Key: no.*=number of elections.*

Figure 17: Vote to registration ratio by GDP per capita, most recent parliamentary elections

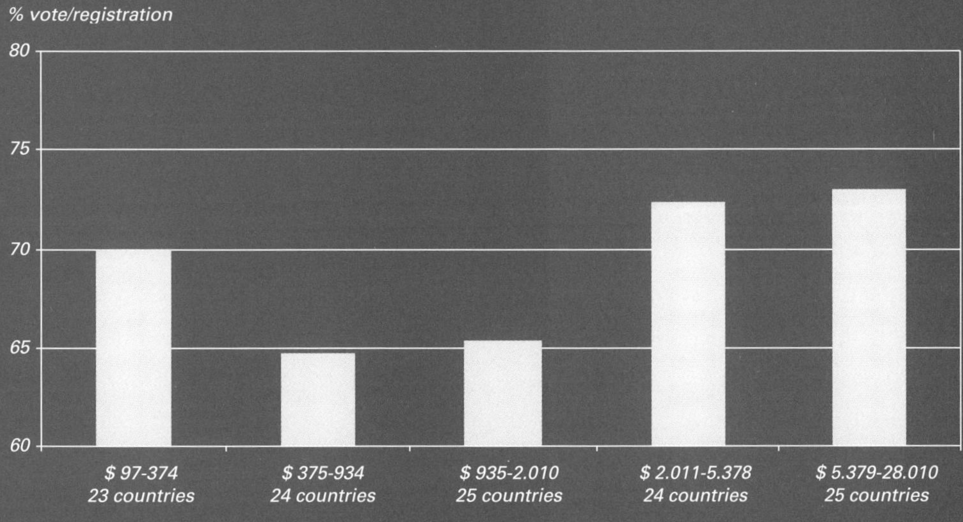

Source: International IDEA and Human Development Report (1999).

Figure 18: Vote to registration ratio by population size, parliamentary elections, 1945-2001

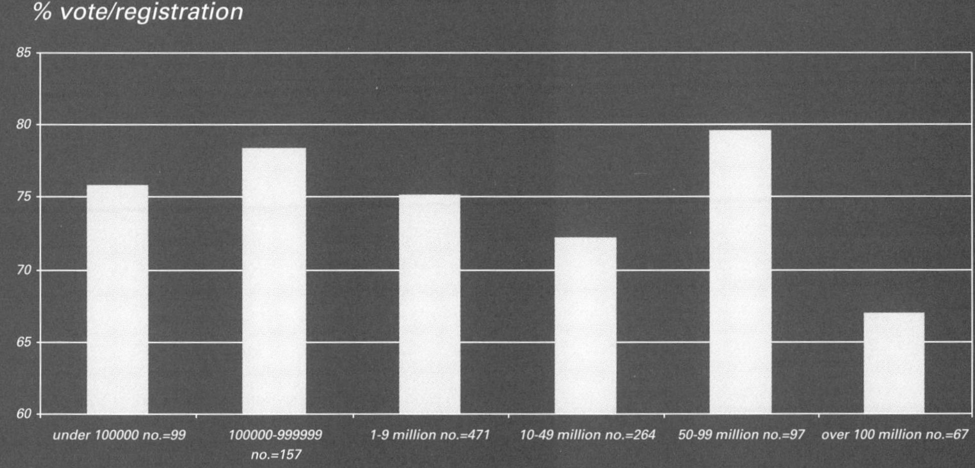

Key: no.=number of elections.

While the capacity to read and write does not necessarily equate to an ability to make coherent and informed political decisions, turnout does increase with literacy, before declining in societies where literacy exceeds 90 percent.(See Figure 16)

Similarly, if we measure the wealth of a country against its gross domestic product and examine voter turnout performance a similar effect is seen, although it stays relatively static at the highest levels. (See Figure 17)

If we examine population size and voter turnout a clear correlation with regional results can be seen. Many African countries, whose low turnout is discussed above, fall into the 10-49 million group. In the over 100 million group, twenty seven elections are US congressional elections, with consistently low levels of turnout. (See Figure 18)

ELECTORAL SYSTEMS AND TURNOUT

Within parliamentary elections, there are nine major electoral systems in use around the world, as categorized in the International IDEA Handbook of Electoral System Design

Alternative Vote (used in the three Oceania countries of Australia, Fiji and Nauru) leads with an average turnout of 91 percent, while the two countries with Single Non-Transferable Vote (Jordan and Vanuatu) have an average of only 43 percent. The other systems do not have such a large deviation, with Single Transferable Vote at 80 percent and Two-Round System at 63 percent. An interesting result is the relatively small difference between the two most widely used systems, List Proportional Representation at 73 percent and First Past the Post at 67 percent.

Figure 19: Electoral system & turnout
Vote to registration ratio by type of electoral systems, most recent parliamentary elections

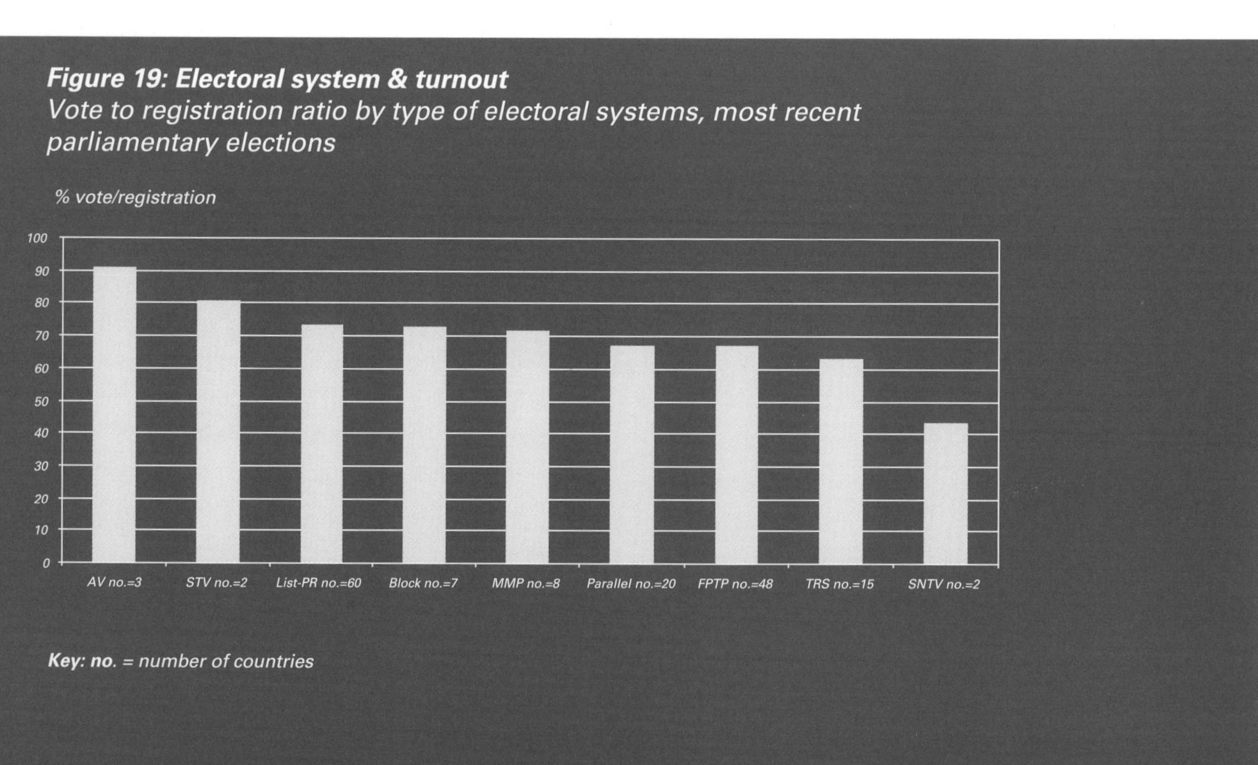

Key: no. = number of countries

Electoral Systems: The Nine Sub-families

ALTERNATIVE VOTE (AV)
A preferential, plurality majority system used in single-member districts in which voters use numbers to mark their preferences on the ballot paper. A candidate who receives over 50 percent of first preferences is declared elected. If no candidate achieves an absolute majority of first preferences, votes are reallocated until one candidate has an absolute majority of votes cast.

BLOCK VOTE (BLOCK)
A majority plurality system used in multi-member districts in which electors have as many votes as there are candidates to be elected. Voting can be either candidate-centred or party-centred. Counting is identical to a First Past the Post system, with the candidates with the highest vote totals winning the seat(s).

FIRST PAST THE POST (FPTP)
The simplest form of plurality majority electoral system, using single-member districts, a categorical ballot and candidate-centred voting. The winning candidate is the one who gains more votes than any other candidate, but not necessarily a majority of votes.

LIST PROPORTIONAL REPRESENTATION (LIST PR)
In its simplest form List PR involves each party presenting a list of candidates to the electorate. Voters vote for a party, and parties receive seats in proportion to their overall share of the national vote. Winning candidates are taken from the lists.

MIXED MEMBER PROPORTIONAL (MMP)
Systems in which a proportion of the parliament (usually half) is elected from plurality majority districts, while the remaining members are chosen from PR lists. Under MMP the PR seats compensate for any disproportionality produced by the district seat result.

PARALLEL SYSTEM (PARALLEL)
A Proportional Representation system used in conjunction with a plurality majority system but where, unlike MMP, the PR seats do not compensate for any disproportions arising from elections to the plurality majority seats.

SINGLE NON-TRANSFERABLE VOTE (SNTV)
A Semi-Proportional system which combines multi-member constituencies with a First Past the Post method of vote counting, and in which electors have only one vote.

SINGLE TRANSFERABLE VOTE (STV)
A preferential Proportional Representation system used in multi-member districts. To gain election, candidates must surpass a specified quota of first-preference votes. Voters' preferences are reallocated to other continuing candidates if a candidate is excluded or if an elected candidate has a surplus.

TWO-ROUND SYSTEM (TRS)
A pluralitymajority system in which a second election is held if no candidate achieves an absolute majority of votes in the first election.

Figure 20: Differences between parliamentary and presidential elections
Vote to registration ratio by parliamentary and presidential elections, 1945-2001

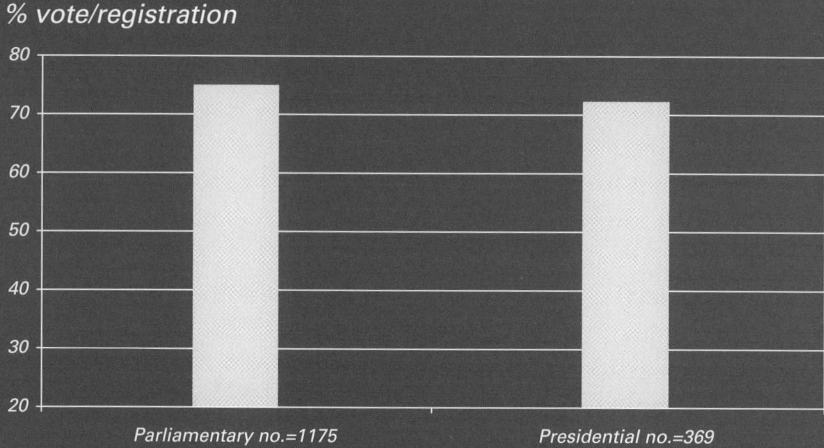

Key: no=number of elections.

Figure 21. Presidential elections by region
Vote to registration ratio by region, presidential elections 1945-2001

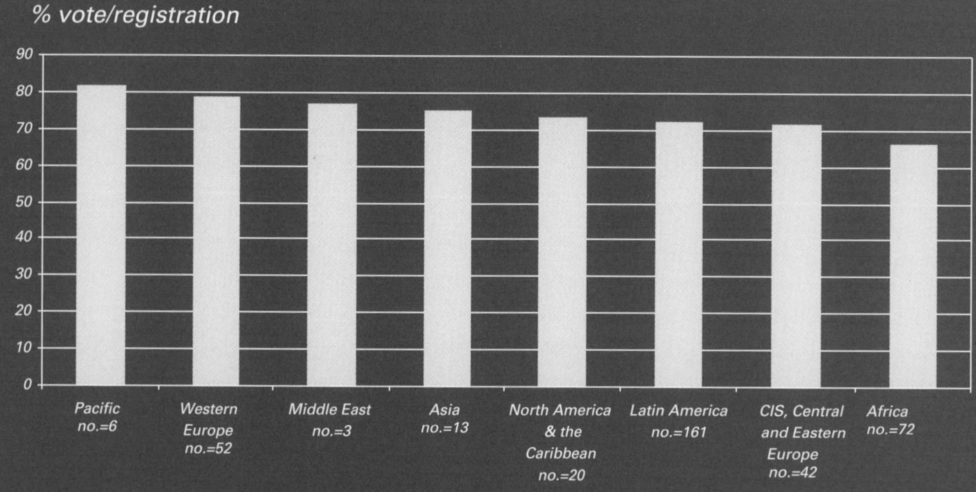

Key: no=number of elections.

DIFFERENCE BETWEEN PARLIAMENTARY AND PRESIDENTIAL ELECTIONS

Participation at parliamentary elections is only marginally higher than at presidential elections, although it should be noted that the database contains more than three times as many parliamentary elections as presidential elections. The 1,175 parliamentary elections saw an average turnout of 75 percent.(see Figure 20)

Across regions, Oceania still has the lead in turnout from Western Europe, while Africa has the lowest turnout in both parliamentary and presidential elections.(see Figure 21)

Choosing Politicians by Lottery: An Option for the Future?

For many people today, democracy ("rule of the people") has become equal to elections -to a system of representation and political parties where ordinary citizens are only engaged in politics at election day once every four or five years. Recently, however, voter participation has decreased, new technologies have challenged the old system, and the established democracies have experienced what has been called a crisis of political parties. Elections as the only means by which people can select who is going to govern are no longer taken for granted. In many corners of the world, new ways to achieve rule of the people are being discussed. Why not use direct, Internet-based discussions? Or lottery? The ideas are not as unusual as they may seem.

There is nothing new about selecting politicians and civil servants by lot. In Classical Athens, lot was used to select most secular officials, from members of the Executive Council to port authorities. Some key positions were rotated daily to prevent people from abusing power. The arguments for the use of the lot are highly valid today. The lot was used to prevent the cementation of political elites and thus allow larger segments of the population to take an active part in the governing of society; it guaranteed a balanced representation between the tribes and groups in society and it was believed to protect the equality of the citizens and allow them an opportunity to experience how to govern as well as be governed. The selection by lot also distributed the duty and responsibilities of running the state among all citizens.

The ideas from ancient Athens have, together with the development of new technologies, lead to a wave of experimentation with citizen juries and other forms of involving people in the governance of democratic countries. During the last two decades, programmes in Germany, Denmark, the United States and Britain, for example, have tried to find ways to gather more or less randomly chosen citizens to discuss political issues in an environment where they can get their questions answered and their opinions heard and respected.

The first of these projects is called "Policy Juries" at the Jefferson Center for New Democratic Processes. In this case a high-quality telephone survey is conducted to randomly selected individuals in a given community (a city, organization, county, state, nation, etc.). Survey respondents who show an interest in participating are entered into the jury pool, where they are coded for certain demographic information such as age, gender, geographic location, and so on. The final jury of about twenty-four citizens is then selected to reflect the general public. Over several days, the jurors are provided with information from expert witnesses regarding all sides of the issue (ranging from public health and the federal budget to US peacemaking in Central America), and the results of the jury are issued in a public forum.

In the German "planning cell" project, twenty-five people are selected at random through the official registration offices. Their task is to evaluate problems or solutions, preparing new laws or planning local projects. The jurors sit in small groups of five discussing the issues for a limited time before the membership in the groups is rotated at random. The idea is that the jurors should be faced with four new group members six times a day to be confronted with a variety of opinions and knowledge.

Another interesting project is the "citizen juries" of the Institute for Public Policy Research in the United Kingdom, a project built on the idea from the U.S. Policy Juries, but with one important distinction; the results of the citizen jury are binding for the government or administration that ordered the jury. If it does not want to implement the results of the jury, it has to give a press conference to present its reasons for not doing so.

Women's Power at the Ballot Box

Pippa Norris

The Convention on the Elimination of All Forms of Discrimination against Women, adopted by the United Nations General Assembly in 1979 and subsequently signed by 165 nation states, emphasizes the importance of equal participation of women with men in public life. Yet two decades later women remain far from parity worldwide at the apex of power, as heads of state at prime ministerial and presidential levels, in the executive branch as ministers and as senior public officials, and within parliamentary assemblies (International IDEA 1998; UN 2000). But what is the situation today at the most fundamental level of citizenship: in terms of women's voting participation? Laws restricting women's rights to vote and to stand for election persist in a handful of Middle Eastern countries, including Kuwait, Qatar, Saudi Arabia, Oman and the United Arab Emirates (UNDP, 2000). In newer democracies, such as Namibia and South Africa, most women have only recently acquired voting rights. In established democracies, however, women have had the legal franchise for many decades; since the 1920s in most western countries.

GENDER AND POLITICAL PARTICIPATION

The earliest studies of voting behaviour in Western Europe and North America established that gender, along with age, education and social class, was one of the standard demographic and social characteristics used to predict levels of civic engagement, political activism, and electoral turnout (Tingsten, 1937; Almond and Verba, 1963; Rokkan, 1970; Verba and Nie, 1972), although observers noted that these gender differences were narrowing even in the 1950s in advanced industrialized societies such as Sweden (Lipset, 1960). Based on a seven-nation comparative study of different dimensions of political participation, ranging from voter turnout to party membership, contact activity and community organizing, Verba, Nie and Kim (1978) concluded: "In all societies for which we have data, sex is related to political activity; men are more active than women." The study established that these gender differences persisted as significant, even after controlling for levels of education, institutional affiliations like trade union membership, and psychological involvement in politics. During the same era, women were also found to be less engaged in unconventional forms of participation, like strikes and protest movements (Barnes and Kaase, 1979).

In recent decades, however, the orthodox view that women are less active has been challenged. More recent studies have found that traditional gender differences in voting participation diminished in the 1980s and 1990s, or even reversed, in many advanced industrialized countries (Christy, 1987; DeVaus and McAllister, 1989; Verba, Schlozman and Brady, 1995; Conway et al. 1997). In the United States, for example, in every presidential election since 1980, the proportion of eligible female adults who voted has exceeded the proportion of eligible male adults who voted, and the same phenomenon is found in non-presidential mid-term elections since 1986 (CAWP, 2000). This pattern is clearly generational: in the 1998 election, for instance, among the youngest cohort, (the under-25's), 35 percent of women and 30 percent of men reported voting, while among the oldest generation (75 years and up) 59 percent of women but 68 percent of men reported voting. In addition, overall women outnumber men in the American electorate, so that the number of female voters has exceeded the number of men in every presidential election since 1964, a difference of some 7.2 million votes in 1996. Similar trends are evident in Britain, where the gender gap in turnout reversed in 1979 so that by the 1997 election an estimated 17.7 million women voted compared with around 15.8 million men. Long-term secular trends in social norms and in structural lifestyles seem to have contributed towards removing many factors that inhibited women's voting participation.

Nevertheless studies commonly suggest that women remain less involved in more demanding forms of civic engagement. For example, a national survey of political participation conducted in 1990 in the United States found that, compared with men, women are less likely to contribute to political campaigns, to work informally in the community, to serve on a local governing board, to contact a government official or to be affiliated with a political organization (Schlozman, Burns and Verba, 1994). Political knowledge and interest in public affairs are important preconditions to the more active forms of engagement. Studies have found that American women continue to express less knowledge and interest in conventional politics, so that they are less likely to discuss politics, to follow events in the news, or to care deeply about the outcome of elections (Bennett and Bennett, 1989).

What explains gender differences in political participation? Patterns of voting turnout can be affected by the legal structure of opportunities, by the mobilizing role of organizations like parties and NGOs in civic society, and by the resources and motivation that people bring to political activity. The most popular socio-psychological explanations of why women have commonly been less engaged in the past have been based on theories of sex role socialization and the persistence of traditional attitudes towards women's and men's roles in the private and public sphere. Alternative structural approaches have emphasized the social and economic barriers facing women, such as the social isolation of full-time homemakers who are excluded from political networks based on occupational, trade union and professional associations. The movement of women into the paid labour force is one of the prime candidates for explaining changing patterns of civic engagement. Educational attainment is also thought likely to play a role, since education provides cognitive and civic skills necessary for information processing in the civic world.

POST-WAR TRENDS IN OFFICIAL RATES OF VOTER TURNOUT

Therefore what does evidence about trends in voter turnout suggest about the pattern of gender differences in civic engagement and how this varies worldwide, and what explains any significant differences that are apparent? There are two main sources of cross-national evidence that can be analyzed here. First, official statistics breaking down voter turnout by gender can be examined in the eight democracies where trend data is available in the post-war period, namely in Barbados, Finland, Germany, Iceland, India, Malta, New Zealand, and Sweden. This limited range of countries is far from representative of the broader universe of established democracies but, nevertheless, it does contain both large and small nation states, as well as societies like Sweden and India at widely different levels of socio-economic development.

Figure 22 shows the gender gap in voting turnout, measured as the difference between the proportion of men and women officially recorded as voting in general elections in these societies. The size of the gender gap displays considerable variations among the nations under comparison although at the same time most countries show a secular rise in female participation rates during the post-war era. In two nations, Barbados and Sweden, the data suggests that more women than men have consistently turned out to cast their ballot. In most countries under comparison, however, in the 1950s and 1960s women participated less often than men, producing a modest gender gap in Germany, Finland and Iceland,

and a substantial gap evident in India. By the end of the time series, in the 1990s, the gender gap has closed or even reversed in all societies except India, where women continue to turnout at markedly lower rates than men, although even here the trend is towards a slight closure of the gap. While the official data cannot tell us the reasons for these trends, multiple explanations can be suggested for the closure of the gender gap in turnout, including generational shifts in lifestyles and social norms.

SURVEY DATA ON REPORTED TURNOUT

In addition to examining official voter turnout statistics, to examine the picture more systematically we need to turn to survey data estimating reported levels of electoral participation. This study draws on the Comparative Study of Electoral Systems, based on national election surveys conducted in 19 countries from 1996 to 1999. The nations under comparison vary significantly along multiple dimensions, including levels of democratic and socio-economic development, as well as cultural and geographic regions of the world. The comparison includes four Anglo-American democracies (Australia, the United States, Britain, New Zealand), five West European nations ranging from the Scandinavian north to the far southern Mediterranean (Spain, Germany, the Netherlands, Norway, Israel), six post-

Figure 22: The gender gap in voter turnout

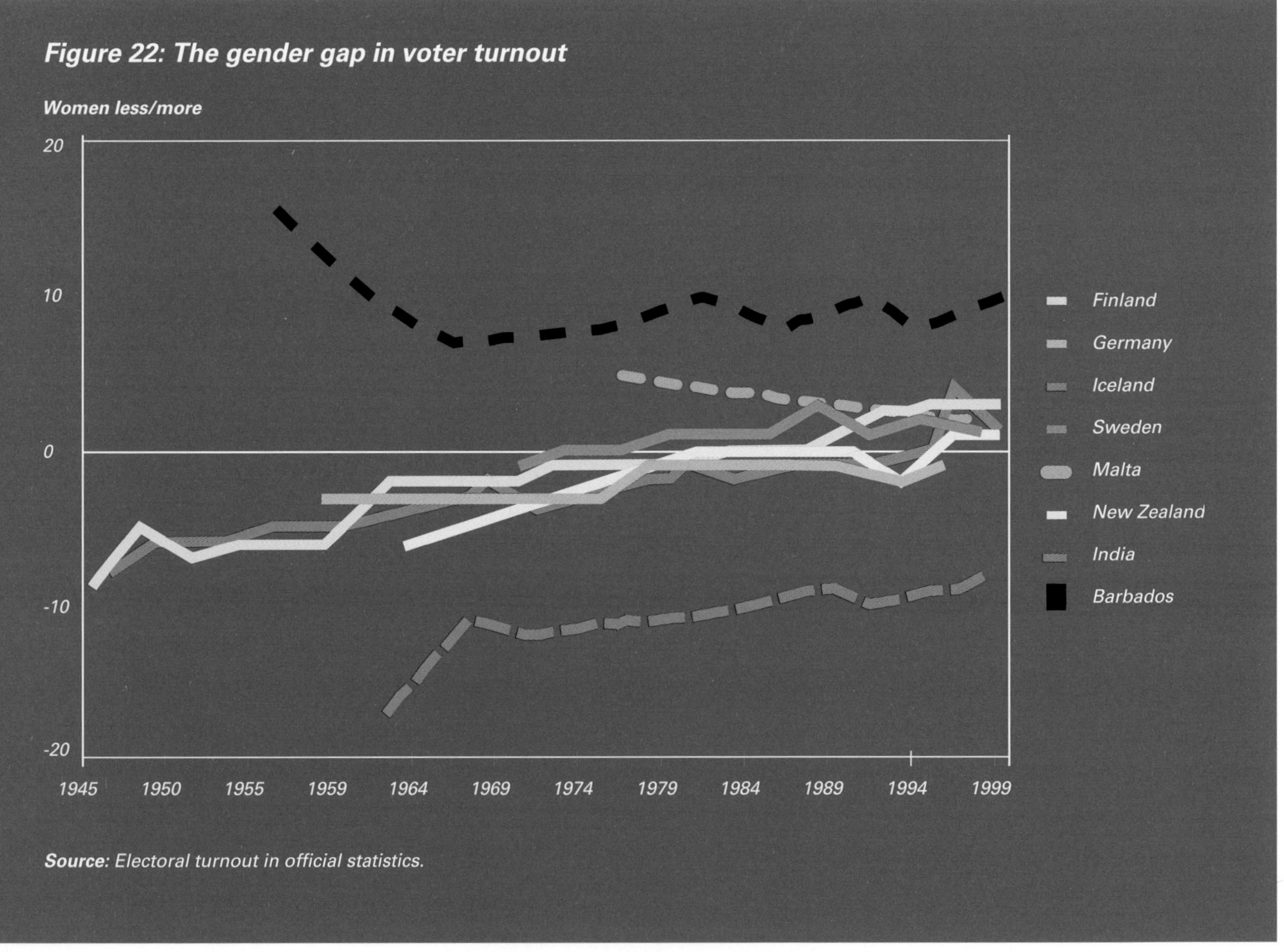

Source: *Electoral turnout in official statistics.*

Figure 23: The proportion of men and women who reported not voting

Nation	Men	Women	Difference women/ men	Sig.
Norway	15.7	12.2	-3.5	.021
Britain	17.5	17.1	-0.4	.779
Germany	7.3	7.2	-0.1	.919
Spain	10.3	10.5	+0.2	.909
Taiwan	8.3	8.6	+0.3	.860
Israel	16.9	16.5	+0.4	.868
New Zealand	5.0	5.5	+0.5	.438
Japan	15.8	16.8	+1.0	.611
Australia	3.6	5.5	+1.9	.048
Mexico	23.1	25.0	+1.9	.327
Czech Republic	9.3	11.6	+2.3	.192
Ukraine	21.9	24.2	+2.3	.354
USA	21.8	24.7	+2.9	.180
Netherlands	20.1	23.1	+3.0	.092
Poland	40.4	44.6	+4.2	.056
Hungary	23.9	28.7	+4.8	.035
Romania	7.6	15.6	+8.0	.000
ALL	13.7	15.5	+1.8	

Turnout: *The question measured whether the respondent cast a ballot in the general election. Functionally equivalent but not identical items were used in each national election survey. The significance of the difference is measured by gamma.*
Source: *Comparative Study of Electoral Systems, 1996-1999.*

communist nations in Central and Eastern Europe (Ukraine, Czech Republic, Lithuania, Poland, Romania, Hungary), two Latin American societies (Mexico, Argentina), and two Asian countries (Japan, Taiwan). In comparing levels of turnout among women and men in different nations we need to control for intervening factors that can be expected to influence this process, including levels of democratization, as well as standard social background factors at individual level including age, education, occupational status and income that previous studies have found to be commonly associated with levels of political participation.

Figure 23 shows the proportion of men and women who reported not voting in general elections in the mid-to late 1990s, the gender difference in turnout, and the significance of the gap. The evidence shows that women reported voting at significantly higher levels than men in only one nation (Norway), in thirteen nations there was no significant gender difference, and women

Figure 24 : The gender gap in turnout by social group

	Men	Women	Gap	Sig.
Age-group				
Younger	27.5	27.1	0.4	0.64
Middle	14.9	16.1	-1.2	0.08
Older	13.1	16.8	-3.7	0.00
Income				
Lowest	19.9	23.1	-3.2	0.01
Low	18.9	20.9	-2.0	0.07
Moderate	17.7	18.7	-1.0	0.33
High	16.1	19.3	-3.2	0.01
Highest	17.8	17.9	-0.1	0.96
Length of democracy				
Established	12.5	13.1	-0.6	0.26
Newer	32.4	34.0	-1.6	0.05
Urbanization				
Rural	20.1	23.4	-3.3	0.00
Small town	20.5	22.8	-2.3	0.02
Suburbs	13.5	13.7	-0.2	0.76
Large city	17.7	19.3	-1.6	0.07
Education				
Incomplete primary	22.9	29.1	-6.2	0.01
Primary	22.7	25.3	-2.6	0.04
Secondary	20.6	20.6	0.0	0.98
Post-secondary trade	24.4	26.1	-1.7	0.18
Undergraduate incomplete	20.2	18.7	1.5	0.47
Graduate	14.1	15.8	-1.7	0.12
Work Status				
Employed FT	18.6	21.9	-3.3	0.02
Employed PT	16.2	13.9	2.3	0.07
Unemployed	32.5	35.5	-3.0	0.11
Student	28.3	25.3	3.0	0.05
Retired	15.1	18.9	-3.8	0.06
Homeworker		20.4		
Disabled	20.4	27.9	-7.5	0.07

Note: *The gap represents the difference between men and women's reported turnout in general elections. The significance of the difference is measured by gamma.*

Source: *Comparative Study of Electoral Systems, 1996-1999*

reported significantly lower levels of turnout in the remaining three newer democracies in Central and Eastern Europe (Poland, Hungary, Romania), by a margin of four to seven percentage points. Therefore this picture provides further confirmation of the pattern already observed in the official data; any tendency for women to vote less frequently than men in the past seems to have disappeared in established democracies, and this pattern only remains significant in some (but not all) of the post-communist societies.

If we turn to the breakdown of the difference between men's and women's reported turnout by social group, it is apparent that the gap is evident across most demographic categories. The age gap reverses: older women (over 65 years) are significantly less likely to turn out to vote than older men, a gap which shrinks to become insignificant among younger cohorts. What this suggests is that the process of generational change is behind the secular trends that we have already observed in the official statistics, so that as younger cohorts gradually replace older ones the residual gender gap in participation will disappear. The pattern by household income (as a proxy measure of socio-economic status) varies, with the strongest gap among the lowest quintile but also among the high category. The gap is not therefore simply reducible to inequalities between rich and poor. The gap is significant among newer democracies but not established ones, as observed earlier. Level of urbanization proves a weak predictor, although the gap is least significant among those living in the suburbs while it is most marked in rural areas. The education gap is sharp, especially for those who failed to complete even primary education, and the gap shrinks with higher levels of education. Lastly, in terms of work status in the paid labour force, the pattern is somewhat mixed, with the gap sharpest among the disabled, the retired (reflecting the age profile already observed), and the unemployed, but also among those in full-time paid employment. Although it is difficult to compare against men, because of the small number of cases, the level of non-voting among female home-workers is not a particularly strong predictor of electoral participation compared with women in the paid labour force.

CONCLUSIONS

The comparison based on the limited official data on voter turnout presented here suggests that many countries have seen a gradual shrinking of the disparities in participation between women and men during the post-war era. Countries like Sweden, Iceland, Malta and Germany have seen women's turnout gradually rise to achieve parity with or even slightly exceed that of men's, although the survey data indicates that some of the post-communist countries are lagging behind this trend. The breakdown in the CSES survey data suggests many of the factors underlying this phenomenon, especially the role of generational replacement that has closed the gap in most of the post-industrial societies under comparison. As the younger generation gradually becomes the majority, this promises to have important implications for women's influence at the ballot box.

REFERENCES

Note: I am most grateful to the Comparative Study of Electoral Systems (CSES), based at the Center for Political Studies, University of Michigan, Ann Arbor, Mich., for release of this dataset, particularly Phil Shively, and all the national collaborators who made this possible. More details of the research design are available at www.umich.edu/~nes/cses.

Almond, G. A. and S. Verba. 1963. The Civic Culture: Political Attitudes and Democracy in Five Nations. Princeton, N.J.: Princeton University Press.

Barnes, S. and M. Kaase. 1979. Political Action: Mass Participation in Five Western Democracies. Beverly Hills, Calif.: Sage.

Bennett, L. and S. Bennett. 1989. Enduring gender differences in political interest. American Politics Quarterly 17:105–122.

Centre for American Women and Politics. 2000. Sex Differences in Voting Turnout, www.cawp.org.

Christy, C. 1987. Sex Differences in Political Participation: Processes of Change in Fourteen Nations. New York: Praeger.

Conway, M., G. A. Steuernagel, and D. Ahern. 1997. Women and Political Participation. Washington, D.C.: CQ Press.

DeVaus, D. and I. McAllister. 1989. The changing politics of women: gender and political alignments in 11 nations. European Journal of Political Research 17:241–262.

International IDEA. 1998. Women in Parliament: Beyond Numbers. Stockholm: International IDEA.

Lipset, S. M. 1960. Political Man: the Social Bases of Politics. Garden City, N.Y.: Doubleday.

Norris, P. 1999. A Gender–Generation Gap? In Critical Elections: British Parties and Voters in Long-term Perspective, edited by G. Evans and P. Norris. London: Sage.

Rokkan, S. 1970. Citizens, Elections, Parties: Approaches to the Comparative Study of the Processes of Development. Oslo: Universitetsforlaget.

Schlozman, K. L., N. Burns and S. Verba. 1994. Gender and pathways to participation: the role of resources. Journal of Politics 56:963–990.

Tingsten, H. L. G. 1937. Political Behavior: Studies in Election Statistics. London: P. S. King.

United Nations. 2000. The World's Women 2000: Trends and Statistics. New York: United Nations.

UN Development Programme. 2000. United Nations Development Report 2000. New York: Oxford University Press for UNDP.

Verba, S. and N. Nie. 1972. Participation in America: Political Democracy and Social Equality. New York: Harper and Row.

Verba, Sidney, N. Nie and Kim. 1978. Participation and Social Equality. Cambridge, Mass.: Harvard University Press.

Verba, S., K. Schlozman and H. E. Brady. 1995. Voice and Equality. Cambridge, Mass.: Harvard University Press.

Voting for the Disabled

Turnout rates can differ greatly both between countries and over time. One of the factors that can influence an individual voter's decision regarding whether or not to vote is access to the polling station. Long queues in bad weather can prevent large numbers of voters - especially the elderly, the sick, or single parents that cannot leave their small children - from voting. Increasing accessibility of the polling station and facilitating absentee voting can address some of these problems and at least slightly increase the level of direct participation in the elections.

The disabled often experience physical obstacles hindering their right to vote. Since voting typically takes place in schools or offices, or even outdoors, the polling station itself is often not suitable for those with impaired mobility, and resources are not always available to adjust to special needs. Ramps at stairs, increased space around the polling stands, low tables and voting tables located right at the entrance can often be sufficient to increase accessibility for voters in wheelchairs or other disabilities. Other measures can be taken to help other groups of disabled, such as having large symbols on ballot papers for those with bad eyesight or low literacy. All possible measures should be taken to enable voters to mark their ballot papers without assistance, thereby ensuring their right to secret voting.

Some countries have adopted special rules, extending the possibility of postal voting for disabled persons, and new technologies have now led to Internet voting as a possible option where resources are available. There are international and domestic NGOs advocating facilitation of the vote by the disabled.

Compulsory Voting

Maria Gratschew

CONCEPTUALISING COMPULSORY VOTING

All democratic governments consider participating in national elections a right of citizenship and a citizen's civic responsibility. Some consider that participation in elections is also a citizen's duty. In some countries, where voting is considered a duty, voting at elections has been made compulsory and has been regulated in the national constitutions or electoral laws. Some countries impose sanctions on non-voters.

Compulsory voting is not a new concept. Belgium (1892), Argentina (1914) and Australia (1924) were among the first countries to introduce compulsory voting laws. Countries such as Venezuela and the Netherlands practised compulsory voting at one time but have since abolished it.

Advocates of compulsory voting argue that decisions made by democratically elected governments are more legitimate when higher proportions of the population participate. They argue further that voting, voluntarily or otherwise, has an educative effect upon the citizens. Political parties can save money as a result of compulsory voting, since they do not have to spend resources convincing the electorate that it should turn out to vote. Lastly, if democracy is government by the people, presumably this includes all people, so that it is every citizen's responsibility to elect his or her representatives.

The leading argument against compulsory voting is that it is not consistent with the freedom associated with democracy. Voting is not an intrinsic obligation and the enforcement of such a law would be an infringement of the citizen's freedom associated with democratic elections. It may discourage the political education of the electorate because people forced to participate will react against the perceived source of oppression. Is a government really more legitimate if high voter turnout is achieved against the will of the voters? Many countries with limited financial resources may not be able to justify the expense of maintaining and enforcing compulsory voting laws. It has been proved that forcing the population to vote results in an increased number of invalid and blank votes compared to countries that have no compulsory voting laws.

Another consequence of compulsory voting is the possible high number of "random votes". Voters who are voting against their free will may check off a candidate at random, particularly the top candidate on the ballot paper. The voter does not care whom they vote for as long as the government is satisfied that they have fulfilled their civic duty. What effect does this immeasurable category of random votes have on the legitimacy of the democratically elected government?

A figure depicting the exact number of countries that practise compulsory voting is quite arbitrary. The simple presence or absence of compulsory voting laws is in itself too simplistic. It is more constructive to analyse compulsory voting as a spectrum ranging from a symbolic, but basically impotent, law to a government that systematically follows up each non-voting citizen and implements sanctions against them.

This spectrum implies that some countries formally have compulsory voting laws but do not, and have no intention to, enforce them. There are a variety of reasons for this.

Not all laws are created to be enforced. Some laws are created merely to state the government's position regarding what the citizen's responsibility should be. Compulsory voting laws that do not include sanctions may fall into this category. Although a government may not enforce compulsory voting laws or even have formal sanctions in law for failure to vote, the law may have some effect upon the citizens. For example, in Austria voting is compulsory in only two regions, with sanctions being weakly enforced. However, these regions have a higher turnout than the national average.

Other possible reasons for not enforcing the laws could be the complexity of the law or the resources required for enforcement. Countries with limited budgets may not place the enforcement of compulsory voting laws as a high priority; still they hope that the presence of the law will encourage citizens to participate. The cost of enforcement may lead some electoral administrations to lower their standards of enforcement.

Can a country be considered to practise compulsory voting if the compulsory voting laws are ignored and irrelevant to the voting habits of the electorate? Is a country practising compulsory voting if there are no penalties for not voting? What if there are penalties for failing to vote but they are never or scarcely ever enforced? Or if the penalty is negligible?

Many countries offer loopholes, intentionally and otherwise, which allow non-voters to go unpunished. For example, in many countries it is required to vote only if you are a registered voter, but it is not compulsory to register. People might then have incentives not to register. In many cases, like Australia, voters will face sanctions unless they can provide an excuse that is acceptable under the legal framework.

The diverse forms that compulsory voting has taken in different countries focus the attention not on whether compulsory voting is present or absent but rather on the degree and manner in which the government forces its citizens to participate.

LAWS, SANCTIONS, AND ENFORCEMENT

Figure 25 lists all the countries that have a law that provides for compulsory voting. The first column lists the name of the country, the second column lists the type of sanctions that the country imposes against non-voters, and the third column states to what extent the compulsory voting laws are enforced in practice. The numbers listed in the column for "type of sanction" stand for different types of sanctions, as follows:

Explanation. The non-voter has to provide a legitimate reason for his or her failure to vote to avoid further sanctions, if any exist.

Fine. The non-voter faces a fine. The amount varies by country: three Swiss francs in Switzerland, between 300 and 3,000 schillings in Austria, 200 pounds in Cyprus, 10 to 20 pesos in Argentina, 20 soles in Peru, and so on.

Possible imprisonment. The non-voter may face imprisonment as a sanction (we do not know of any such documented cases). This can also happen in countries such as Australia where a fine is common. In cases where the non-voter does not pay the fines after being reminded or after refusing several times, the courts may impose a prison sentence. This is, however, imprisonment for failure to pay the fine, not imprisonment for failure to vote.

Infringements of civil rights or disenfranchisement. In Belgium, for example, it is possible that the non-voter, after not voting in at least four elections within 15 years, will be disenfranchised. In Peru, the voter has to carry a stamped voting card for a number of months after the election as a proof of having voted. This stamp is required in order to obtain some services and goods from certain public offices. In Singapore the voter is removed from the voter register until he or she reapplies to be included and submits a legitimate reason for not having voted. In Bolivia, the voter is given a card when he or she has voted as proof of participation. The voter cannot receive a salary from the bank if he or she cannot show proof of voting during three months after the election.

Other. In Belgium, for example, it might be difficult to get a job within the public sector. In Greece if you are a non-voter it may be difficult to obtain a new passport or driver's licence in. There are no formal sanctions in Mexico or Italy but there may be possible social sanctions or sanctions based on random choice. This is called the "innocuous sanction" in Italy, where it might for example be difficult to get a place in childcare for your child, but this is not formalized in any way.

The figure shows that not all countries that have compulsory voting laws provide for sanctions against non-voters or enforce these in practice. The actual presence and enforcement of sanctions varies dramatically between countries and regions. All regions except for North America and Central and Eastern Europe have countries with compulsory voting laws. Latin America, Western Europe, Asia and Oceania all have countries where compulsory voting is strictly enforced in practice. The table shows that the most common sanction practised is the explanation sanction alone or together with a fine.

Less common is deprivation of civil rights or disenfranchisement, which is only possible in a small number of countries, as is imprisonment. Imprisonment has, as the sole sanction, never been imposed on a non-voter according to the sources.

According to Figure 26, there is clearly a strong correlation between the level of enforcement of compulsory voting laws and voter turnout. The obvious theory supporting the positive relationship between compulsory voting and higher participation at elections is simple; each citizen's desire to avoid being punished for not voting increases the likelihood of them making the effort to vote. As shown in Figure 26, enforced compulsory voting increases turnout by a little more than 15 percent, compared with countries where voting is voluntary. However, compulsory voting is not the only factor to increase turnout in a country. Socio-economic, political and institutional factors have all been proposed as having an impact on voter turnout.

Figure 25: *Compulsory voting and sanctions*

Country	*Sanctions*	*Level of Enforcement*
Argentina	*1, 2, 4*	*Weak*
Australia	*1, 2*	*Strict*
Austria (Tyrol)	*1, 2*	*Weak*
Austria (Vorarlberg)	*2, 3*	*Weak*
Belgium	*1, 2, 4, 5*	*Strict*
Bolivia	*4*	*Not available*
Brazil	*2*	*Weak*
Chile	*1, 2, 3*	*Weak*
Costa Rica	*None*	*Not enforced*
Cyprus	*1, 2*	*Strict*
Dominican Republic	*None*	*Not enforced*
Ecuador	*2*	*Weak*
Egypt	*1, 2, 3*	*Not available*
Fiji	*1, 2, 3*	*Strict*
Gabon	*N/A*	*Not available*
Greece	*1, 5*	*Weak*
Guatemala	*None*	*Not enforced*
Honduras	*None*	*Not enforced*
Italy	*5*	*Not enforced*
Liechtenstein	*1, 2*	*Weak*
Luxembourg	*1, 2*	*Strict*
Mexico	*None / 5*	*Weak*
Nauru	*1, 2*	*Strict*
Netherlands	*-*	*Enforced until 1970*
Paraguay	*2*	*Not available*
Peru	*2, 4*	*Weak*
Singapore	*4*	*Strict*
Switzerland (Schaffhausen)	*2*	*Strict*
Thailand	*None*	*Not enforced*
Turkey	*2*	*Weak*
Uruguay	*2,4*	*Strict*
Venezuela	*-*	*In practise 1961-1999*

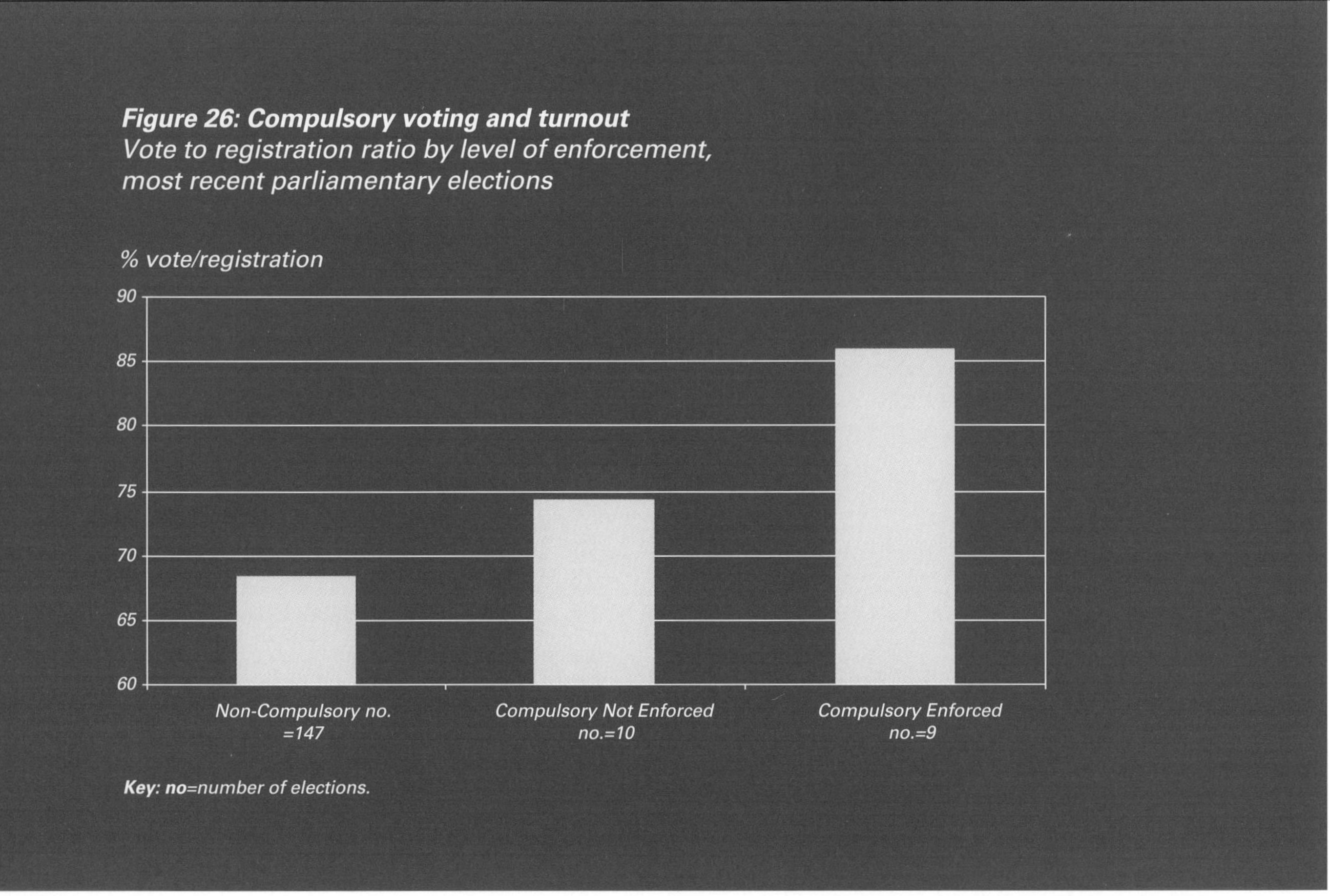

Figure 26: Compulsory voting and turnout
Vote to registration ratio by level of enforcement, most recent parliamentary elections

Key: no=number of elections.

REFERENCES

Electoral Management Bodies of the above-mentioned countries and extracts from electoral laws that these institutions have provided. Please refer to the list of Country-Specific Sources.

Administration and Cost of Elections Project (ACE) by International IDEA, IFES and the United Nations, www.aceproject.org.

Australian Electoral Commission, Electoral Backgrounder 8: Compulsory Voting, at www.aec.gov.au/pubs/backgrounders/vol_8/main.htm.

Australian Electoral Commission. Voting. Fact Sheet 22 at www.aec.gov.au/pubs/factfiles/factsheet22.htm.

Gratschew, Maria, July 2001, Compulsory Voting, ARENA, Association of Electoral Administrators, Oxonian Rewley Press Ltd, United Kingdom.

Hirczy de Mino, W. 1994. The impact of mandatory voting laws on turnout: a quasi-experimental approach. Electoral Studies 13:64–76.

International IDEA. 1997. Voter Turnout from 1945 to 1997: A Global Report on Political Participation. Stockholm: International IDEA. www.idea.int/turnout

LeDuc, L., R. Niemi and P. Norris (eds). 1996. Comparing Democracies: Elections and Voting in Global Perspectives. Thousand Oaks: Sage Publications.

Lijphart, A. March 1997. Unequal participation: democracy's unresolved dilemma. Presidential Address. American Political Science Review 91(1).

Major, S.. 1995. To Vote or Not to Vote? Compulsory Voting in Australia. Western Australian Electoral Commission.

The Parline Database of the Inter-Parliamentary Union in Geneva, Switzerland, www.ipu.org.

Puplick, C. and P. McGuiness. 1998. The pros and cons of compulsory voting. Elections Today 7(3).

Youth Voter Turnout

Julie Ballington

This is a summary of several reports of on youth electoral behaviour which were commissioned and published by International IDEA. The degree to which citizens, particularly young people, participate in democracy has become an area of increased interest in recent years. Moreover, recent research seems to point to growing dissatisfaction and apathy among young people in new and old democracies alike.

In an effort to analyse turnout among young people, International IDEA published a study, *Youth Voter Participation: Involving Today's Young in Tomorrow's Democracy* (1999). Mostly based on survey data, the study attempts to document the scope of the problem internationally, investigating its causes and identifying potential strategies to increase youth participation. Included in the study is a comparative analysis of the participation rates of young people in 15 Western European democracies.

One classical finding of election research appears well documented in the sense that voter turnout is indeed lowest among young voters (18-29 years). The average for voters aged 60-96 was 93 percent (Eva Anduiza Perea, in International IDEA 1999b, 24). The average turnout rate for all citizens across the 15 nations was 88.6 percent, and 80 percent for those aged 18-29. Further, in countries where overall voter participation is relatively low, the difference between youth turnout and the average turnout is greater than in countries with higher overall turnout rates. Unsurprisingly, where voting is compulsory, the turnout of young voters is substantially higher than in countries with voluntary voting. For example, in Switzerland (with voluntary voting in 25 out of 26 cantons), the average turnout is around 63 percent, while the 18-29 age cohort rate is over 13 percent lower. This is in contrast to Belgium (with compulsory voting) where the youth turnout rate was less than one percentage point lower than the average of 97 percent (*idem*).

Surveys from other countries confirm lower levels of electoral turnout among young people. In Britain, age has been found to be a key factor in explaining involvement in formal politics, with widespread non-participation and political withdrawal apparent among young people, especially in voter registration. Ahead of the election in Britain in 1997, young people were less likely to register to vote than other age-groups: 20 percent of 18 to 25-year-olds were not registered in 1995. Up to 40 percent of those aged 18-24 did not vote in the 1997 British elections (Fahmy, 1999). A similar trend was evident during the 2001 election, where the Market and Opinion Omnibus Survey (MORI surveys) found that 29 percent of 18 to 24 - year-old non-voters did not register to vote. The survey also estimates that turnout among 18-24 year olds fell to around 39 percent (Electoral Commission, 2001, 15).

Low levels of youth participation are apparent not only in developed democracies but also in emerging democracies, for example an analysis of South Africa's voters' roll revealed that registration for the 1999 election decreased noticeably with age. Those citizens 80 years or older demonstrated the highest rate of registration at 97 percent of potential voters, and the lowest was among first-time voters aged 18 to 20 where not even 50 percent of those eligible registered to vote. As with many other countries, participation rates in the June 1999 election were not disaggregated by age or gender. However, given the low rate of registration by eligible young people, it is likely that turnout among potential first-time voters was well below 50 percent.

However, it should not be concluded that age is the only variable that accounts for low voter turnout. Research has established that turnout is affected by a number of other factors, some relating to the individual micro-level (income, education, interest in politics) and others to the macro-level of the political system (the party system, the electoral system, election procedures). A multi-continental study commissioned by International IDEA (Lagos and Rose, 1999) attempted to assess the extent of young people's political involvement and how their outlook differed from that of older people. Their findings demonstrate that, while older people are more likely to vote than younger people, age is only one variable (albeit important) that affects participation in the political process. Prosperity and education also show a positive correlation with democratic involvement. These conclusions are substantiated by research in other countries, for example the MORI Omnibus survey in Britain found that respondents who were unemployed or living on low incomes were less likely to be politically active than respondents with average or above-average incomes (Fahmy, 1999). The cumulative effects of age, class and income seemingly influence patterns of political participation.

Macro-level explanations, focusing on institutions and the political environment, go even further in accounting for low turnout among young people. The International IDEA study, *Youth Voter Participation* highlights a number of factors that may affect participation:

- the nature of the electoral system and whether all votes are seen to have equal weighting in the final result;
- the registration system, if automatic or compulsory, facilitates higher voter turnout;
- the frequency of elections is another factor, as "voter fatigue" increases with the number of elections;
- the competitiveness of elections and the number of parties contesting them may also influence voting patterns. Highly competitive contests tend to increase interest and turnout; and
- Countries with compulsory voting, like Australia, have higher levels of turnout (International IDEA, 1999, 31 - 32).

In 1999, one hundred young people participated in the annual International IDEA Democracy Forum *"What's So Great about Democracy? The Youth Speak Up!"*. Key discussions centred on the future of democracy and the challenges and opportunities that confront young people. Participants noted several factors affecting youth participation in politics, from "not understanding how the system works, to a growing distrust of political institutions and leaders, to a lack of time in today's competitive environment". They also emphasized that they are not apathetic about politics but rather that they feel alienated from traditional political processes and are not convinced their participation can make a difference.

Some participants said that they lacked confidence in the system and its leaders and felt that politicians only appeal to them during elections. "This gap between those who govern and those being governed seems to be getting wider and appears to be a fundamental reason for low participation." Other reasons cited include lack of interest and disillusionment with the political and electoral system, doubts about the effectiveness of their votes, complaints about corruption in politics, and that they were not informed about where or how to vote (International IDEA 1999c, 8, 33). It is also possible that young people take time to develop an interest in politics, as they lack experience with political matters and are less socially and politically integrated.

While traditional party politics may be

unappealing to many, this is not to say that young people are not politically active. They are interested in specific issues, such as education, the environment and health care, and are consequently joining interest groups, non-governmental organizations or other associations that address their specific concerns. In turn, they are finding new ways to express themselves politically. However, in order to draw young people into the electoral process, different strategies may be considered:

- *Make it easier to register to vote:* In most countries, registration is a prerequisite for voting. It is therefore strategic to encourage young people to register, through public information campaigns, school visits, information displays, by placing registration facilities in places frequented by young people or by making registration available over the Internet.
- *Facilitate easy voting:* By making voting procedures simple and accessible and by disseminating information widely, young people may be more encouraged to participate.
- *Lower the voting age:* Although considered somewhat controversial, this is one way to encourage the early politicisation of young people as participants in democracy. Minimum voting ages vary from 15 to 21 years, but 18 years is the most common worldwide.
- *Support preparatory exercises like mock elections:* This allows first-time voters to explore the practical workings of electoral procedures (International IDEA, 1999, 42-56).

REFERENCES

Electoral Commission. 2001 run on
Election 2001: The official Results.London, Politicos

Fahmy, E. 1999. Young people's political participation: results from a 1996 MORI [Market and Opinion] Omnibus survey. Radical Statistics 70, www.radstats.org.uk/no070/article3.htm.

International IDEA. 1999. Youth Voter Participation: Involving Today's Young in Tomorrow's Democracy. Stockholm: International IDEA.

International IDEA. 1999. Democracy Forum Report. Youth and Democracy: Is There a Crisis? Stockholm: International IDEA.

Lagos, M. and R. Rose. 1999. Young People in Politics: A Multi-Continental Survey. International IDEA Democracy Forum, Stockholm, June 1999 (unpublished paper).

Internet Voting

There has been much discussion on the use of Internet voting as a method for boosting turnout at elections and governments have shown an increasing willingness to experiment with the Internet.

However, there is relatively little experience that suggests that Internet voting would increase turnout to any significant extent. Very few government level elections have featured Internet voting, so comparisons are not easily made.

The 2000 report of the California Internet Voting Task Force predicts that Internet voting would increase turnout, especially among the young and busy professionals, who have easy access to the Internet and whose turnout rates are low. On the other hand, Internet voting may only make voting easier for the already privileged and not increase access for marginalized groups. In the United States, for example, black and Latino households are much less likely to have access to the Internet than white households.

Much of the "hype" surrounding such elections comes from private companies and suppliers. Very few studies have examined the issue to determine if Internet voting can really increase access and therefore turnout.

Several-Day Polling

The most cost-effective and practical procedure is to hold elections in one day. By doing so, ballot papers and ballot boxes do not have to be stored overnight, alleviating security concerns, and the workload of election officials is reduced. Only about 10 percent of the democracies in the world practise several-day polling. One example is India, the largest electorate in the world with 600 million voters, where elections are held on a staggered timetable across the country. There are countries, like Sierra Leone or Lesotho, where elections were held on one day but for logistical reasons polling time was extended in certain regions.

Day of Election

There is an active debate, especially in older democracies on how to increase voter turnout. Some of the factors that may increase turnout would require complicated changes in electoral laws and even in constitutions, while others, like changing the day of election, would require little effort but could have a significant impact.

Of the 86 countries that Freedom House labelled as democratic in 1996, and that held election in one single day almost half of them had their latest election on Sunday. Saturday and Monday were the second most frequent election days. More recent figures also suggest that about half of the countries hold their elections on a non-business day.

A study in 2000 suggested that weekend voting increases turnout rates far above statistical relevance. One analysis found that turnout figures would on average increase between five and six percentage points if Election Day for national elections changed from a weekday to a rest day. When it comes to elections for the European Parliament (which feature extremely low turnout in most EU countries), the same change could account for a nine percentage point increase.

If election day were moved from a weekday to a Saturday or a Sunday, religious groups that worship on these days might be offended, but there is another possible solution to follow the example of a vast number of countries, including South Africa, Germany, India, Chile, Samoa, Vanuatu and the Philippines, where the election day automatically becomes a holiday.

THE INTERNATIONAL IDEA DATABASE:

VOTER TURNOUT FROM 1945 TO 2001

Definitions

DEFINITIONS FOR THE STATISTICAL TABLES

The International IDEA Database of Voter Turnout contains a global collection of election results and voter turnout statistics. Starting with elections in 1945 it is continuously updated with the most recent elections. The Database is available at *www.idea.int/turnout.*

Electoral System

For each country in the table we have listed the electoral system currently used, i.e. PR, Majority or Mixed. This information is taken from The International IDEA Handbook of Electoral System Design (1997) published by International IDEA. Please refer to the chapter on Voter Turnout Rates in a Comparative Perspective for a brief explanation of each electoral system.

Freedom House (FH)

Freedom House from which we use the ratings calculated as an indicator of the levels of freedom in a country's political system. We have added together the "political rights" and "civil liberties" ratings to yield a number from 2 to 14, where 2 indicates the highest possible level of rights and freedoms and 14 the lowest. Data was collected from the Freedom House website at *www.freedomhouse.org*, where more information about the survey methodology is available.

Gross Domestic Product (GDP)

Gross Domestic Product per capita measured in $US as listed in the Human Development Report 1999.

Human Development Index HDI

The Human Development Index tracks a nation's level of human development based on a combination of indicators and is more sophisticated than GDP per capita. For more details see the UNDP Human Development Report 1999.

Invalid

The number of invalid votes, as reported by each country.

Literacy

Literacy rates as a percentage of the adult population. These are estimates and projections from UNESCO's assessment as listed in the Human Development Report 1999.

Population

The total population as described under Voting Age Population.

Registration

The number of registered voters. The figure represents the number of names on the voters' register at the time that the registration process closes, as reported by the electoral management body.

Total vote

The total number of votes cast in the relevant election. Total vote includes valid and invalid votes, as well as blank votes in cases where these are separated from invalid votes. More information on valid, invalid and blank votes can be found at *www.aceproject.org*.

Vote/Registration

The number of votes divided by the number of names on the voters' register, expressed as a percentage.

Vote/VAP

The number of votes divided by the Voting Age Population figure, expressed as a percentage.

Voting Age

The lowest age at which the right to vote is obtained in the relevant country.

Voting Age Population (VAP)

The estimated voting age population is based on a country's population over the age of 18. It is not intended to be an exact measure of the VAP as it does not take into account legal or systemic barriers to the exercise of the franchise or account for non-eligible members of the population, such as resident non-citizens. It is intended as indicative only.

The VAPs shown here have been calculated from statistics produced by the Population Division of the UN Department of Economic and Social Affairs. Most estimates are based on the latest census data report in the

Demographic Yearbook 1998. Estimates for Barbados, the Central African Republic and Niger are based on census data reported in the *Demographic Yearbook 1996*. Estimates for Albania, Djibouti, Ghana, Guinea, Guyana, Côte d'Ivoire, Samoa, Tanzania, and Togo are based on the medium variant population estimate in *World Population Prospects: the 1998 Revision Volume II.* The following countries were not included in the statistics produced by the UN Department for Economic and Social Affairs: Anguilla, Fiji, Grenada, Nauru and Palau. For these countries the *CIA World Factbook* has been used.

In all cases the population data selected is either that for the election year or the latest reported before the election year. In the latter case, the growth rates presented in table A11 of *World Population Prospects: the 1998 Revision Volume 1* were applied to form an estimated population for the election year. The data was then adjusted to remove population under the age of 18; the result forms our estimated voting age population.

PARLIAMENTARY ELECTIONS

PRESIDENTIAL ELECTIONS

PARLIAMENTARY ELECTIONS

1945-2001

Parliamentary Elections

Year	Total vote	Registration	Vote/Reg	VAP	Vote/VAP	Invalid	FH	Population
Albania		**CIS, Central and Eastern Europe**			**Electoral system: Parallel**		**Voting age: 18**	
2001[1]	2 468 000	N/A	N/A	2 040 574	120.9%	N/A	N/A	3 132 301
1997	1 412 929	1 947 235	72.6%	2 228 430	63.4%	N/A	8	3 510 500
1996	1 963 344	2 204 002	89.1%	2 193 030	89.5%	N/A	8	3 481 000
1992[1]	1 830 000	2 000 000	91.5%	2 051 430	89.2%	N/A	7	3 363 000
1991	1 963 568	1 984 933	98.9%	1 985 550	98.9%	N/A	8	3 255 000
Algeria		**Africa**			**Electoral system: List-PR**		**Voting age: 18**	
1997	10 999 139	16 767 309	65.6%	14 838 069	74.1%	4.6%	12	29 245 552
1991	7 822 625	13 258 554	59.0%	13 021 830	60.1%	11.8%	8	25 553 000
Andorra		**Western Europe**			**Electoral system: Parallel**		**Voting age: 18**	
2001	10 892	13 342	81.6%	68 338	15.9%	5.7%	N/A	N/A
1997	8 842	10 837	81.6%	10 837	81.6%	N/A	2	70 000
1993	7 829	9 675	80.9%	9 675	80.9%	N/A	3	63 000
Angola		**Africa**			**Electoral system: List-PR**		**Voting age: 18**	
1992	4 402 575	4 828 486	91.2%	4 986 230	88.3%	10.4%	12	10 609 000
Anguilla		**North America & the Carribbean**			**Electoral system: FPTP**		**Voting age: 18**	
2000	4 825	7 520	64.2%	8 531	56.6%	1.0%	N/A	12 132
1999	4 847	6 578	73.7%	8 231	58.9%	0.9%	N/A	11 797
1994	4 495	5 980	75.2%	N/A	N/A	1.0%	N/A	N/A
1989	3 801	5 190	73.2%	N/A	N/A	1.1%	N/A	N/A
1984	2 694	3 733	72.2%	N/A	N/A	1.6%	N/A	N/A
1980	2 777	3 508	79.2%	N/A	N/A	1.4%	N/A	N/A
1976	2 725	3 802	71.7%	N/A	N/A	3.7%	N/A	N/A
1972	1 457	3 105	46.9%	N/A	N/A	2.4%	N/A	N/A
Antigua & Barbuda		**North America & the Caribbean**			**Electoral system: FPTP**		**Voting age: 18**	
1999	33 318	52 385	63.6%	46 053	72.3%	0.7%	7	69 750
1994[2]	27 263	43 749	62.3%	31 850	85.6%	0.5%	7	65 000
1989[2]	22 390	36 876	60.7%	30 870	72.5%	3.0%	5	63 000
1984[2]	19 223	31 453	61.1%	38 710	49.7%	0.6%	5	79 000
1980[2]	22 280	28 906	77.1%	36 750	60.6%	1.1%	N/A	75 000
1976[2]	24 879	26 197	95.0%	34 790	71.5%	1.5%	N/A	71 000
1971[2]	17 309	30 682	56.4%	34 300	50.5%	2.3%	N/A	70 000
1965[2]	9 223	21 525	42.8%	30 360	30.4%	N/A	N/A	60 000
1960[2]	2 559	6 738	38.0%	27 540	9.3%	2.2%	N/A	54 000
1956[2]	6 500	11 400	57.0%	27 454	23.7%	2.2%	N/A	53 000
1951[2]	4 843	6 886	70.3%	24 288	19.9%	1.2%	N/A	46 000
Argentina		**Latin America**			**Electoral system: List-PR**		**Voting age: 18**	
1999[3]	18 953 456	24 109 306	78.6%	23 877 270	79.4%	N/A	5	36 554 185
1998	18 135 267	23 184 491	78.2%	23 230 160	78.1%	6.2%	6	35 739 000
1995	17 939 156	22 158 612	81.0%	22 488 050	79.8%	3.7%	5	34 597 000
1993	17 090 830	21 443 951	79.7%	21 886 150	78.1%	6.9%	5	33 671 000
1991	18 609 221	20 742 631	89.7%	20 812 743	89.4%	7.7%	4	32 863 366
1989	16 867 095	20 022 072	84.2%	20 552 960	82.1%	2.1%	3	32 114 000
1987	16 263 572	19 452 790	83.6%	20 293 650	80.1%	5.3%	3	31 221 000
1985	15 326 907	18 649 101	82.2%	19 711 250	77.8%	2.0%	4	30 325 000
1983	14 927 572	17 929 951	83.3%	19 257 550	77.5%	2.5%	6	29 627 000
1973	12 235 481	14 302 497	85.5%	16 315 200	75.0%	2.6%	4	24 720 000
1965	9 565 574	11 460 766	83.5%	14 417 000	66.3%	4.2%	N/A	22 180 000

[1] *Total votes and registered voters are approximations* [2] *VAP annual growth rate calculated from preceding census years.*
[3] *Total votes include only valid votes.*

Year	Total vote	Registration	Vote/Reg	VAP	Vote/VAP	Invalid	FH	Population
1963	9 717 677	11 353 936	85.6%	13 919 100	69.8%	21.2%	N/A	21 719 000
1962	9 084 512	10 596 321	85.7%	13 704 960	66.3%	3.6%	N/A	21 414 000
1960	8 870 202	10 187 586	87.1%	13 228 160	67.1%	25.2%	N/A	20 669 000
1958	9 088 497	10 002 327	90.9%	12 837 120	70.8%	9.2%	N/A	20 058 000
1954	7 906 858	9 194 157	86.0%	11 994 880	65.9%	2.0%	N/A	18 742 000
1951[1]	7 593 948	8 633 998	88.0%	11 286 400	67.3%	1.6%	N/A	17 635 000
1946	2 839 507	3 405 173	83.4%	10 018 560	28.3%	2.5%	N/A	15 654 000
Armenia		**CIS, Central and Eastern Europe**			**Electoral system: Parallel**			**Voting age: 18**
1999	1 137 133	2 198 544	51.7%	2 500 788	45.5%	5.8%	8	3 738 582
1995	1 183 573	1 195 283	99.0%	2 338 700	50.6%	N/A	8	3 598 000
Aruba		**North America & the Caribbean**			**Electoral system: FPTP**			**Voting age: 18**
1997	44 741	52 166	85.8%	53 174	84.1%	1.3%	3	93 219
1994	39 986	64 848	61.7%	52 560	76.1%	1.0%	3	111 000
1993	40 240	45 680	88.1%	49 680	81.0%	0.9%	3	105 000
Australia		**Pacific**			**Electoral system: AV**			**Voting age: 18**
1998	11 476 609	12 056 625	95.2%	14 039 112	81.7%	3.8%	2	18 750 982
1996	11 182 467	11 668 852	95.8%	13 547 920	82.5%	3.2%	2	18 308 000
1993	10 900 861	11 384 638	95.8%	13 065 440	83.4%	3.0%	2	17 656 000
1990	10 225 800	10 728 435	95.3%	12 457 450	82.1%	3.2%	2	17 065 000
1987	9 715 428	10 353 213	93.8%	11 546 730	84.1%	4.9%	2	16 263 000
1984	9 293 021	9 866 266	94.2%	11 036 240	84.2%	6.8%	2	15 544 000
1983	8 870 174	9 373 580	94.6%	10 919 090	81.2%	2.1%	2	15 379 000
1980	8 513 992	9 014 920	94.4%	10 139 550	84.0%	2.4%	2	14 695 000
1977	8 127 762	8 553 780	95.0%	9 620 530	84.5%	2.5%	2	14 359 000
1975	7 881 873	8 262 413	95.4%	9 308 310	84.7%	1.9%	2	13 893 000
1974	7 535 768	7 898 922	95.4%	8 937 800	84.3%	1.9%	2	13 340 000
1972	6 747 247	7 074 070	95.4%	7 905 600	85.3%	2.2%	2	12 960 000
1969	6 273 611	6 606 873	95.0%	7 478 600	83.9%	2.5%	N/A	12 260 000
1966	5 892 327	6 193 881	95.1%	6 960 000	84.7%	3.1%	N/A	11 600 000
1963	5 575 977	5 824 917	95.7%	6 549 600	85.1%	1.8%	N/A	10 916 000
1961	5 384 350	5 651 561	95.3%	6 409 880	84.0%	2.6%	N/A	10 508 000
1958	5 141 109	5 384 624	95.5%	6 003 620	85.6%	2.9%	N/A	9 842 000
1955	4 525 774	5 172 443	87.5%	5 796 000	78.1%	2.9%	N/A	9 200 000
1954	4 619 571	5 096 468	90.6%	5 661 810	81.6%	1.3%	N/A	8 987 000
1951	4 654 406	4 962 675	93.8%	5 480 150	84.9%	1.9%	N/A	8 431 000
1949	4 697 800	4 895 227	96.0%	5 142 800	91.3%	2.0%	N/A	7 912 000
1946	4 453 941	4 739 853	94.0%	4 852 250	91.8%	2.5%	N/A	7 465 000
Austria		**Western Europe**			**Electoral system: List-PR**			**Voting age: 18**
1999	4 695 192	5 838 373	80.4%	6 463 384	72.6%	1.5%	2	8 156 351
1995	4 959 539	5 768 009	86.0%	6 306 300	78.6%	2.3%	2	8 085 000
1994	4 760 987	5 774 000	82.5%	6 263 129	76.0%	1.7%	2	8 029 717
1991	4 848 741	5 628 912	86.1%	6 025 250	80.5%	3.0%	2	7 825 000
1986	4 940 298	5 461 414	90.5%	5 673 750	87.1%	1.8%	2	7 565 000
1983	4 922 454	5 316 436	92.6%	5 664 000	86.9%	1.4%	2	7 552 000
1979	4 784 173	5 186 735	92.2%	5 510 770	86.8%	1.1%	2	7 549 000
1975	4 662 684	5 019 277	92.9%	5 381 090	86.6%	1.1%	2	7 579 000
1971	4 607 616	4 984 448	92.4%	5 222 000	88.2%	1.1%	2	7 460 000
1970	4 630 851	5 045 841	91.8%	5 173 000	89.5%	0.9%	N/A	7 390 000
1966	4 583 970	4 886 818	93.8%	5 103 000	89.8%	1.1%	N/A	7 290 000
1962	4 506 007	4 805 351	93.8%	4 991 000	90.3%	1.1%	N/A	7 130 000
1959	4 424 658	4 696 603	94.2%	4 934 300	89.7%	1.4%	N/A	7 049 000

[1] *Total votes and registered voters are taken from preliminary estimates*

Parliamentary Elections

Year	Total vote	Registration	Vote/Reg	VAP	Vote/VAP	Invalid	FH	Population
1956	4 427 711	4 614 464	96.0%	4 957 930	89.3%	1.7%	N/A	6 983 000
1953	4 395 519	4 586 870	95.8%	4 937 340	89.0%	1.7%	N/A	6 939 000
1949	4 250 616	4 391 815	96.8%	4 928 820	86.2%	1.3%	N/A	6 942 000
1945	3 253 329	3 449 605	94.3%	4 827 290	67.4%	1.1%	N/A	6 799 000
Azerbaijan		**CIS, Central and Eastern Europe**			**Electoral system: Parallel**		**Voting age: 21**	
2000	2 883 819	4 241 550	68.0%	4 709 852	61.2%	N/A	11	7 623 798
1995	3 556 277	4 132 800	86.1%	4 310 340	82.5%	N/A	12	7 562 000
Bahamas		**North America & the Caribbean**			**Electoral system: FPTP**		**Voting age: 18**	
1997	119 173	129 946	91.7%	175 463	67.9%	0.7%	3	283 005
1992	112 057	122 000	91.9%	163 680	68.5%	N/A	3	264 000
1987	90 280	102 713	87.9%	142 190	63.5%	N/A	5	241 000
1982	75 609	84 235	89.8%	117 720	64.2%	N/A	4	218 000
1977	64 108	71 295	89.9%	104 410	61.4%	N/A	3	197 000
1972	50 216	50 071	100.3%	91 800	54.7%	N/A	N/A	180 000
Bahrain		**Middle East**			**Electoral system: FPTP**		**Voting age: 18**	
1973	19 509	24 883	78.4%	59 800	32.6%	0.3%	11	230 000
Bangladesh		**Asia**			**Electoral system: FPTP**		**Voting age: 18**	
1996	42 880 564	56 716 935	75.6%	66 408 120	64.6%	0.8%	7	122 978 000
1991	34 477 803	62 181 743	55.4%	56 038 800	61.5%	0.6%	5	109 880 000
1988	25 832 858	49 863 829	51.8%	53 311 320	48.5%	N/A	9	104 532 000
1986	28 873 540	47 876 979	60.3%	48 803 040	59.2%	0.8%	9	101 673 000
1979	19 676 124	38 363 858	51.3%	41 588 640	47.3%	1.5%	8	86 643 000
1973	19 329 683	35 205 642	54.9%	35 140 800	55.0%	1.4%	6	73 210 000
Barbados		**North America & the Caribbean**			**Electoral system: FPTP**		**Voting age: 18**	
1999	128 484	203 621	63.1%	187 188	68.6%	N/A	2	269 029
1994	124 121	206 000	60.3%	187 920	66.0%	N/A	2	261 000
1991	121 696	191 000	63.7%	180 600	67.4%	1.1%	2	258 000
1986	135 562	176 739	76.7%	169 510	80.0%	0.7%	2	253 000
1981	119 566	167 029	71.6%	160 000	74.7%	0.9%	2	250 000
1976	99 463	134 241	74.1%	150 060	66.3%	0.9%	2	246 000
1971	94 019	115 189	81.6%	134 400	70.0%	1.3%	N/A	240 000
1966	79 258	99 988	79.3%	137 500	57.6%	0.2%	N/A	250 000
1961	64 090	104 518	61.3%	128 541	49.9%	0.4%	N/A	233 710
1956	62 274	103 290	60.3%	125 950	49.4%	1.2%	N/A	229 000
1951	62 020	95 939	64.6%	116 600	53.2%	1.4%	N/A	212 000
Belarus		**CIS, Central and Eastern Europe**			**Electoral system: TRS**		**Voting age: 18**	
2000*								
1995	4 199 431	7 445 800	56.4%	7 652 340	54.9%	N/A	10	10 341 000
1995	4 821 100	7 445 800	64.7%	7 652 340	63.0%	N/A	10	10 341 000

**Please refer to www.idea.int/turnout*

Year	Total vote	Registration	Vote/Reg	VAP	Vote/VAP	Invalid	FH	Population
Belgium		**Western Europe**			**Electoral system: List-PR**			**Voting age: 18**
1999	6 652 005	7 343 464	90.6%	7 999 572	83.2%	6.6%	2	10 199 967
1995	6 562 149	7 199 440	91.1%	7 887 360	83.2%	7.5%	2	10 122 000
1991	6 623 897	7 144 884	92.7%	7 783 620	85.1%	7.0%	2	9 979 000
1987	6 573 045	7 039 250	93.4%	7 599 900	86.5%	6.6%	2	9 870 000
1985	6 552 234	7 001 297	93.6%	7 590 660	86.3%	7.4%	2	9 858 000
1981	6 504 056	6 878 141	94.6%	6 896 400	94.3%	7.4%	2	9 852 000
1978	6 039 916	6 366 652	94.9%	6 881 000	87.8%	8.4%	2	9 830 000
1977	6 005 195	6 316 292	95.1%	6 678 960	89.9%	7.2%	2	9 822 000
1974	5 711 996	6 322 227	90.3%	6 664 000	85.7%	7.9%	2	9 800 000
1971	5 741 270	6 271 240	91.5%	6 478 900	88.6%	8.0%	N/A	9 670 000
1968	5 554 652	6 170 167	90.0%	6 445 400	86.2%	6.8%	N/A	9 620 000
1965	5 578 876	6 091 534	91.6%	6 338 200	88.0%	7.1%	N/A	9 460 000
1961	5 573 861	6 036 165	92.3%	6 336 960	88.0%	5.5%	N/A	9 184 000
1958	5 575 127	5 954 858	93.6%	6 246 570	89.3%	4.9%	N/A	9 053 000
1954	5 463 130	5 863 092	93.2%	6 173 300	88.5%	5.5%	N/A	8 819 000
1950	5 219 276	5 635 452	92.6%	6 047 300	86.3%	5.3%	N/A	8 639 000
1949	5 320 263	5 635 452	94.4%	6 029 800	88.2%	5.4%	N/A	8 614 000
1946	2 460 796	2 724 796	90.3%	5 856 900	42.0%	3.9%	N/A	8 367 000
Belize		**Latin America**			**Electoral system: FPTP**			**Voting age: 18**
1998	81 090	90 000	90.1%	123 349	65.7%	N/A	2	238 500
1993	70 465	94 470	74.6%	102 500	68.7%	N/A	2	205 000
1989	59 954	82 556	72.6%	89 670	66.9%	1.7%	3	183 000
1984	48 311	64 447	75.0%	73 320	65.9%	1.4%	3	156 000
1979	44 971	50 091	89.8%	65 320	68.8%	1.2%	N/A	142 000
Benin		**Africa**			**Electoral system: List-PR**			**Voting age: 18**
1999	1 776 108	2 533 399	70.1%	2 697 063	65.9%	N/A	5	6 009 635
1995	1 922 553	2 536 234	75.8%	2 610 380	73.7%	2.4%	4	5 554 000
1991	1 069 367	2 069 343	51.7%	2 297 830	46.5%	3.7%	5	4 889 000
Bolivia		**Latin America**			**Electoral system: MMP**			**Voting age: 18**
1997	2 240 000	3 200 000	70.0%	3 596 616	62.3%	N/A	4	7 340 032
1993	1 731 309	2 399 197	72.2%	3 461 850	50.0%	4.8%	5	7 065 000
1989	1 573 790	2 136 587	73.7%	3 086 880	51.0%	10.0%	5	6 431 000
1985	1 728 365	2 108 458	82.0%	2 652 750	65.2%	13.0%	5	5 895 000
1980	1 489 484	2 004 284	74.3%	2 520 000	59.1%	12.1%	12	5 600 000
1979	1 693 233	1 871 070	90.5%	2 452 050	69.1%	13.2%	6	5 449 000
1978	1 971 968	1 921 556	102.6%	2 386 800	82.6%	2.7%	8	5 304 000
1966	1 099 994	1 270 611	86.6%	2 002 500	54.9%	8.2%	N/A	4 450 000
1964	1 297 319	1 411 560	91.9%	1 643 850	78.9%	12.2%	N/A	3 653 000
1962	1 067 877	N/A	N/A	1 597 050	66.9%	2.0%	N/A	3 549 000
1960	987 730	1 300 000	76.0%	1 553 850	63.6%	2.1%	N/A	3 453 000
1958	460 340	N/A	N/A	1 512 000	30.4%	2.6%	N/A	3 360 000
1956	958 016	1 126 528	85.0%	1 503 740	63.7%	2.7%	N/A	3 269 000
Bosnia & Herzegovina		**CIS, Central and Eastern Europe**			**Electoral system: List-PR**			**Voting age: 18**
2000	1 597 805	2 508 349	63.7%	3 053 221	52.3%	N/A	9	4 269 483
1998	1 879 399	2 656 758	70.7%	3 256 197	57.7%	N/A	10	4 022 835
1996[1]	1 335 707	2 900 000	46.1%	2 572 520	51.9%	N/A	10	3 524 000
Botswana		**Africa**			**Electoral system: FPTP**			**Voting age: 18**
1999	354 463	459 662	77.1%	844 338	42.0%	4.9%	5	1 592 528
1994[2]	283375	370 173	76.6%	634 920	44.6%	N/A	5	1 443 000

[1] *Registered voters are approximate*

[2] *Total votes include only valid votes*

Year	Total vote	Registration	Vote/Reg	VAP	Vote/VAP	Invalid	FH	Population
1989	250 487	367 069	68.2%	522 900	47.9%	N/A	3	1 245 000
1984	227 756	293 571	77.6%	420 400	54.2%	N/A	5	1 051 000
1979	134 496	243 483	55.2%	290 033	46.4%	N/A	5	783 873
1974	64 011	205 016	31.2%	244 200	26.2%	N/A	5	660 000
1969	76 858	140 428	54.7%	205 200	37.5%	N/A	N/A	570 000
1965	140 793	N/A	N/A	202 800	69.4%	1.5%	N/A	520 000
Brazil		**Latin America**			**Electoral system: List-PR**			**Voting age: 18**
1998	83 296 067	106 101 067	78.5%	102 802 554	81.0%	N/A	7	161 790 311
1994	77 950 257	94 782 803	82.2%	97 590 050	79.9%	18.8%	6	153 725 000
1990	70 918 635	83 817 593	84.6%	92 622 720	76.6%	40.1%	5	144 723 000
1986	58 791 788	69 166 810	85.0%	83 484 860	70.4%	N/A	4	134 653 000
1982	48 466 898	58 871 378	82.3%	76 084 200	63.7%	15.1%	6	126 807 000
1978	37 629 180	46 030 464	81.7%	67 764 600	55.5%	20.7%	8	112 941 000
1970	22 435 521	28 966 114	77.5%	52 259 200	42.9%	30.3%	N/A	93 320 000
1966	17 285 556	22 387 251	77.2%	45 003 600	38.4%	21.1%	N/A	83 340 000
1962	14 747 221	18 528 847	79.6%	40 011 840	36.9%	17.7%	N/A	74 096 000
1958	12 678 997	12 780 997	99.2%	35 499 600	35.7%	8.4%	N/A	65 740 000
1954	9 890 604	15 104 604	65.5%	31 403 900	31.5%	6.6%	N/A	57 098 000
1950	8 234 906	11 455 149	71.9%	29 106 560	28.3%	7.0%	N/A	51 976 000
1947	2 635 680	6 205 415	42.5%	27 125 280	9.7%	10.8%	N/A	48 438 000
1945	6 122 864	7 499 670	81.6%	25 880 440	23.7%	3.2%	N/A	46 215 000
Bulgaria		**CIS, Central and Eastern Europe**			**Electoral system: List-PR**			**Voting age: 18**
2001	4 608 289	6 916 151	66.6%	6 391 816	72.1%	0.9%	N/A	N/A
1997	4 291 258	4 289 956	58.9%	6 414 519	66.9%	0.8%	5	8 330 544
1994	5 264 614	6 997 954	75.2%	6 501 110	81.0%	1.2%	4	8 443 000
1991	5 694 842	6 790 006	83.9%	6 736 500	84.5%	2.7%	5	8 982 000
Burkina Faso		**Africa**			**Electoral system: List-PR**			**Voting age: 18**
1997	2 220 161	4 985 352	44.5%	5 376 800	41.3%	4.9%	9	10 754 000
1992	1 260 107	3 727 843	33.8%	4 716 500	26.7%	N/A	10	9 433 000
1978	1 161 824	2 887 550	40.2%	2 969 000	39.1%	N/A	5	5 938 000
1970	1 156 697	2 395 226	48.3%	2 497 500	46.3%	3.8%	N/A	5 550 000
Burma		**Asia**			**Electoral system: FPTP**			**Voting age: 18**
1990	15 120 000	20 619 500	73.3%	23 415 280	64.6%	12.3%	14	41 813 000
1956	3 868 242	7 442 770	52.0%	10 920 800	35.4%	N/A	N/A	19 856 000
Burundi		**Africa**			**Electoral system: List-PR**			**Voting age: 18**
1993	2 156 659	2 360 090	91.4%	2 859 840	75.4%	N/A	14	5 958 000
Cambodia		**Asia**			**Electoral system: List-PR**			**Voting age: 18**
1998	5 057 679	5 395 595	93.7%	5 488 029	92.2%	3.1%	12	10 192 000
1993	4 134 631	4 764 430	86.8%	4 654 000	88.8%	3.0%	9	9 308 000
Cameroon		**Africa**			**Electoral system: Parallel**			**Voting age: 18**
1997	2 906 156	3 844 330	75.6%	6 222 978	46.7%	N/A	13	13 829 000
1992	2 435 443	4 019 562	60.6%	5 482 800	44.4%	9.8%	11	12 184 000
1988	3 282 884	3 634 568	90.3%	4 897 350	67.0%	3.1%	12	10 883 000
1960	1 349 739	1 940 438	69.6%	2 350 000	57.4%	N/A	N/A	4 700 000

Year	Total vote	Registration	Vote/Reg	VAP	Vote/VAP	Invalid	FH	Population
Canada		**North America & the Caribbean**			**Electoral system: FPTP**			**Voting age: 18**
2000	12 997 185	21 243 473	61.2%	23 786 167	54.6%	1.1%	2	31 213 580
1997	13 174 698	19 663 478	67.0%	23 088 803	57.1%	N/A	2	30 785 070
1993	13 863 135	19 906 796	69.6%	21 705 750	63.9%	1.4%	2	28 941 000
1988	13 281 191	17 639 001	75.3%	19 433 250	68.3%	0.8%	2	25 911 000
1984	12 638 424	16 775 011	75.3%	18 611 000	67.9%	0.7%	2	25 150 000
1980	11 014 914	15 890 416	69.3%	17 070 530	64.5%	0.6%	2	24 043 000
1979	11 531 000	15 234 997	75.7%	16 860 370	68.4%	0.7%	2	23 747 000
1974	9 671 002	13 620 553	71.0%	15 061 600	64.2%	1.7%	2	22 480 000
1972	9 966 148	12 909 179	77.2%	13 984 000	71.3%	3.0%	2	21 850 000
1968	8 217 916	10 860 888	75.7%	12 023 400	68.3%	1.1%	N/A	20 730 000
1965	7 796 728	10 274 904	75.9%	11 020 800	70.7%	1.1%	N/A	19 680 000
1963	7 958 636	9 910 757	80.3%	10 599 680	75.1%	0.8%	N/A	18 928 000
1962	7 772 656	9 700 325	80.1%	10 602 000	73.3%	1.1%	N/A	18 600 000
1958	7 357 139	9 131 200	80.6%	9 758 400	75.4%	0.9%	N/A	17 120 000
1957	6 680 690	8 902 125	75.0%	9 839 430	67.9%	1.1%	N/A	16 677 000
1953	5 701 963	8 401 691	67.9%	8 720 790	65.4%	1.1%	N/A	14 781 000
1949	5 903 572	7 893 629	74.8%	8 202 670	72.0%	0.9%	N/A	13 447 000
1945	5 305 193	6 952 445	76.3%	7 560 340	70.2%	1.1%	N/A	12 394 000
Cap Verde		**Africa**			**Electoral system: List-PR**			**Voting age: 18**
2001	140 901	260 275	54.1%	213 973	65.8%	3.4%	N/A	436 530
1995	158 901	207 648	76.5%	199 920	79.5%	3.4%	3	392 000
1991	125 564	166 818	75.3%	175 000	71.8%	5.9%	5	350 000
Central African Republic		**Africa**			**Electoral system: TRS**			**Voting age: 18**
1998	834 494	1 427 691	58.5%	1 556 887	53.6%	1.5%	7	3 075 001
1993	809 298	1 191 374	67.9%	1 609 560	50.3%	1.9%	7	3 156 000
Chad		**Africa**			**Electoral system: Parallel**			**Voting age: 18**
1997	881 346	1 757 879	50.1%	3 437 910	25.6%	330.0%	11	6 741 000
Chile		**Latin America**			**Electoral system: List-PR**			**Voting age: 18**
1997	7 046 361	8 069 624	87.3%	9 634 638	73.1%	17.7%	4	14 622 354
1993	7 354 141	8 085 439	91.0%	8 978 450	81.9%	5.5%	4	13 813 000
1989	7 158 646	7 556 613	94.7%	8 295 040	86.3%	5.1%	7	12 961 000
1973	3 687 105	4 510 060	81.8%	5 831 100	63.2%	1.6%	12	10 230 000
1969	2 406 129	3 244 892	74.2%	5 263 500	45.7%	4.1%	N/A	9 570 000
1965	2 353 123	2 920 615	80.6%	4 703 400	50.0%	3.0%	N/A	8 710 000
1961	1 385 676	1 858 980	74.5%	4 321 900	32.1%	3.3%	N/A	7 858 000
1957	878 229	1 284 159	68.4%	3 996 720	22.0%	N/A	N/A	7 137 000
1953	779 174	1 100 027	70.8%	3 400 320	22.9%	N/A	N/A	6 072 000
1949	470 376	591 994	79.5%	3 312 960	14.2%	2.0%	N/A	5 712 000
1945	407 826	624 495	65.3%	3 102 420	13.1%	N/A	N/A	5 349 000
Colombia		**Latin America**			**Electoral system: List-PR**			**Voting age: 18**
1998	9 000 000	20 000 000	45.0%	22 236 403	40.5%	N/A	7	36 453 120
1994	6 145 436	17 003 195	36.1%	21 057 200	29.2%	7.8%	7	34 520 000
1991	4 962 383	15 037 526	33.0%	19 376 190	25.6%	N/A	6	32 841 000
1990	7 631 691	13 793 566	55.3%	19 057 000	40.0%	0.2%	7	32 300 000
1986	6 909 838	15 839 754	43.6%	16 813 440	41.1%	0.4%	5	30 024 000
1982	5 584 037	13 721 607	40.7%	14 410 700	38.7%	0.2%	5	27 190 000
1978	4 180 121	12 519 719	33.4%	13 591 850	30.8%	0.2%	5	25 645 000
1974	5 100 099	8 925 330	57.1%	10 538 000	48.4%	0.3%	4	23 950 000

Year	Total vote	Registration	Vote/Reg	VAP	Vote/VAP	Invalid	FH	Population
1970	3 980 201	7 666 716	51.9%	8 659 200	46.0%	0.3%	N/A	21 120 000
1968	2 496 455	6 696 723	37.3%	8 130 300	30.7%	0.3%	N/A	19 830 000
1966	2 939 222	6 609 639	44.5%	7 634 200	38.5%	0.3%	N/A	18 620 000
1964	2 261 190	6 135 628	36.9%	6 327 940	35.7%	0.4%	N/A	15 434 000
1962	3 090 203	5 338 868	57.9%	6 202 980	49.8%	N/A	N/A	14 769 000
1960	2 542 651	4 397 541	57.8%	5 935 440	42.8%	0.2%	N/A	14 132 000
1958	3 693 939	5 365 191	68.9%	5 679 240	65.0%	0.1%	N/A	13 522 000
1953[1]	1 028 323	N/A	N/A	5 327 520	19.3%	0.3%	N/A	12 108 000
1951	934 580	N/A	N/A	5 310 700	17.6%	0.3%	N/A	11 545 000
1949[1]	1 751 804	2 773 804	63.2%	5 066 900	34.6%	0.3%	N/A	11 015 000
1947[1]	1 472 686	2 613 586	56.3%	4 850 700	30.4%	N/A	N/A	10 545 000
1945	875 856	2 279 510	38.4%	4 645 080	18.9%	N/A	N/A	10 098 000
Comoros Islands		**Africa**			**Electoral system: TRS**		**Voting age: 18**	
1987[2]	221 000	340 000	65.0%[1]	219 600	100.6%	N/A	12	488 000
1978	144 767	191 468	75.6%	167 440	86.5%	0.8%	9	7 364 000
Cook Islands		**Pacific**			**Electoral system: FPTP**		**Voting age: 18**	
1999	9 430	10 600	89.0%	10 808	87.3%	N/A	N/A	17 000
Costa Rica		**Latin America**			**Electoral system: List-PR**		**Voting age: 18**	
1998	1 431 913	2 045 980	70.0%	1 942 346	73.7%	3.0%	3	3 292 112
1994	1 525 624	1 881 348	81.1%	1 811 890	84.2%	3.3%	3	3 071 000
1990	1 383 956	1 692 050	81.8%	1 626 900	85.1%	3.5%	2	2 805 000
1986	1 216 053	1 486 474	81.8%	1 626 900	74.7%	3.5%	2	2 716 000
1982	991 556	1 261 127	78.6%	1 254 960	79.0%	3.6%	2	2 716 000
1978	859 042	1 058 455	81.2%	1 142 100	75.2%	4.6%	2	2 115 000
1974	699 042	875 041	79.9%	979 200	71.4%	4.9%	2	1 730 000
1970	562 678	675 285	83.3%	746 200	75.4%	4.9%	N/A	1 920 000
1966	451 475	554 627	81.4%	646 800	69.8%	8.2%	N/A	1 540 000
1962	391 500	483 980	80.9%	547 600	71.5%	3.7%	N/A	1 274 000
1958	229 507	354 779	64.7%	462 680	49.6%	10.0%	N/A	1 076 000
1953	198 270	293 678	67.5%	396 450	50.0%	11.2%	N/A	881 000
1948	89 010	N/A	N/A	340 200	26.2%	N/A	N/A	756 000
Côte d'Ivoire		**Africa**			**Electoral system: FPTP**		**Voting age: 18**	
2000	1 740 240	5 517 613	31.5%	7 301 400	23.8%	N/A	11	14 786 000
1990	1 872 292	4 408 809	42.5%	4 686 800	39.9%	N/A	10	11 717 000
Croatia		**CIS, Central and Eastern Europe**			**Electoral system: FPTP**		**Voting age: 18**	
2000	2 941 306	4 244 558	69.3%	3 484 951	84.4%	17.1%	5	4 584 831
1995[3]	2 500 000	3 634 233	68.8%	3 464 230	72.2%	3.3%	8	4 499 000
1992	2 690 873	3 558 913	75.6%	3 591 750	74.9%	4.7%	8	4 789 000
Cyprus		**Western Europe**			**Electoral system: List-PR**		**Voting age: 18**	
2001	428 981	467 543	91.8%	552 887	77.6%	4.2%	N/A	776 853
1996	369 521	409 996	90.1%	486 850	75.9%	11.0%	2	749 000
1991	359 640	381 323	94.3%	457 380	78.6%	3.5%	2	639 000
1985	327 821	346 454	94.6%	420 550	78.0%	2.6%	3	647 000
1981	295 602	308 729	95.7%	405 760	72.9%	1.6%	3	634 000
1976[4]	232 764	272 898	85.3%	373 930	62.2%	1.5%	7	613 000
1970	200 141	263 857	75.9%	365 400	54.8%	2.2%	N/A	630 000

[1]Total vote include only valid votes, [2]Registered voters are approximate, [3]Total votes are approximate, [4]The percentage for the winning party is for the coalition between Democratiki Parataci and Edel. Data for one single party was not available.

Year	Total vote	Registration	Vote/Reg	VAP	Vote/VAP	Invalid	FH	Population
Czech Republic		**CIS, Central and Eastern Europe**			**Electoral system: List-PR**		**Voting age: 18**	
1998	6 006 459	8 116 836	74.0%	7 827 723	76.7%	0.4%	3	10 291 000
1996	6 096 404	7 990 770	76.3%	7 859 160	77.6%	0.6%	3	10 341 000
1992[1]	9 750 978	11 515 699	84.7%	11 640 940	83.8%	1.7%	4	15 731 000
1990[1]	10 785 270	11 195 596	96.3%	11 589 140	93.1%	1.4%	4	15 661 000
Democratic Republic of Congo Africa					**Electoral system: TRS**		**Voting age: 18**	
1993	32 948	N/A	N/A	1 172 640	2.8%	N/A	6	2 443 000
1992	874 296	1 232 384	70.9%	1 161 790	75.3%	1.2%	6	2 371 000
Denmark		**Western Europe**			**Electoral system: List-PR**		**Voting age: 18**	
1998	3 431 926	3 993 009	85.9%	4 128 398	83.1%	0.8%	2	5 225 820
1994	3 360 637	3 988 787	84.3%	4 111 950	81.7%	1.0%	2	5 205 000
1990	3 265 420	3 941 499	82.8%	4 060 600	80.4%	0.8%	2	5 140 000
1988	3 352 651	3 991 897	84.0%	4 052 700	82.7%	0.7%	2	5 130 000
1987	3 389 201	3 907 454	86.7%	3 947 790	85.9%	0.8%	2	5 127 000
1984	3 386 733	3 829 600	88.4%	3 936 240	86.0%	0.7%	2	5 112 000
1981	3 314 424	3 776 333	87.8%	3 841 500	86.3%	0.6%	2	5 122 000
1979	3 194 967	3 552 904	89.9%	3 837 750	83.3%	0.7%	2	5 117 000
1977	3 124 967	3 552 904	88.0%	3 561 600	87.7%	0.6%	2	5 088 000
1975	3 068 302	3 477 621	88.2%	3 542 000	86.6%	0.6%	2	5 060 000
1973	3 070 253	3 460 737	88.7%	3 514 000	87.4%	0.6%	2	5 020 000
1971	2 904 096	3 332 044	87.2%	3 326 200	87.3%	0.7%	N/A	4 960 000
1968	2 864 805	3 208 646	89.3%	3 256 200	88.0%	0.4%	N/A	4 860 000
1966	2 802 304	3 162 352	88.6%	3 168 000	88.5%	0.3%	N/A	4 800 000
1964	2 640 856	3 088 269	85.5%	3 115 200	84.8%	0.4%	N/A	4 720 000
1960	2 439 936	2 842 336	85.8%	2 840 220	85.9%	0.3%	N/A	4 581 000
1957	2 321 097	2 772 159	83.7%	2 827 440	82.1%	0.5%	N/A	4 488 000
1953	2 172 036	2 695 554	80.6%	2 752 470	78.9%	0.3%	N/A	4 369 000
1953	2 077 615	2 571 311	80.8%	2 752 470	75.5%	0.3%	N/A	4 639 000
1950	2 059 944	2 516 118	81.9%	2 690 100	76.6%	0.3%	N/A	4 270 000
1947	2 089 015	2 435 306	85.8%	2 611 980	80.0%	0.2%	N/A	4 146 000
1945	2 055 315	2 381 983	86.3%	2 548 350	80.7%	0.3%	N/A	4 045 000
Djibouti		**Africa**			**Electoral system: Block**		**Voting age: 18**	
1997	94 303	165 942	56.8%	316 290	29.8%	1.5%	11	608 000
1992	73 187	151 066	48.4%	278 460	26.3%	1.9%	12	546 000
Dominica		**North America & the Caribbean**			**Electoral system: FPTP**		**Voting age: 18**	
2000	36 264	60 266	60.2%	41 334	87.7%	1.3%	2	74 429
1995[2]	37 563	57 632	65.2%	45 582	82.4%	1.0%	2	71 000
1990[2]	33 693	50 557	66.6%	42 742	78.8%	0.7%	3	71 000
1985[2]	33 565	45 018	74.6%	44 960	74.7%	0.9%	4	80 000
1980[2]	30 842	38 452	80.2%	38 106	80.9%	0.8%	4	73 000
1975[2]	23 107	29 907	77.3%	33 984	68.0%	7.7%	N/A	72 000
1970[2]	21 122	25 899	81.6%	32 480	65.0%	6.4%	N/A	70 000
1966[2]	19 380	24 147	80.3%	32 060	60.4%	6.8%	N/A	70 000
1961[2]	17 571	22 838	76.9%	27 060	64.9%	6.0%	N/A	60 000
1957[2]	17 639	23 348	75.5%	28 544	61.8%	5.7%	N/A	64 000
1954[2]	16 746	23 835	70.3%	24 310	68.9%	6.0%	N/A	55 000
1951[2]	17 680	23 288	75.9%	24 035	73.6%	7.4%	N/A	55 000
Dominican Republic		**North America & the Caribbean**			**Electoral system: List-PR**		**Voting age: 18**	
1998	2 187 528	4 129 554	53.0%	4 795 282	45.6%	4.3%	5	8 313 630

[1] *Figures are for Czechoslovakia,* [2]*Annual VAP calculated from preceding census years.*

Year	Total vote	Registration	Vote/Reg	VAP	Vote/VAP	Invalid	FH	Population
1996	2 946 699	3 750 502	78.6%	4 746 550	62.1%	1.5%	6	8 045 000
1994	1 399 200	3 300 000	42.4%	4 578 400	30.6%	N/A	7	7 760 000
1990	1 840 553	3 275 570	56.2%	4 015 200	45.8%	1.9%	5	7 170 000
1986[1]	2 112 101	3 039 347	69.5%	3 479 450	60.7%	N/A	4	6 565 000
1970[1]	1 238 205	N/A	N/A	1 867 600	66.3%	N/A	N/A	4 060 000
1966[1]	1 345 402	N/A	N/A	1 665 200	80.8%	N/A	N/A	3 620 000
1962[1]	1 054 954	N/A	N/A	1 513 400	69.7%	N/A	N/A	3 220 000
1957	1 265 681	N/A	N/A	1 297 920	97.5%	N/A	N/A	2 704 000
1952	1 098 816	N/A	N/A	1 095 640	100.3%	N/A	N/A	2 236 000
1947	840 340	840 340	100.0%	971 180	86.5%	N/A	N/A	1 982 000

East Timor — Asia — Electoral system: Parallel — Voting age: 17

Year	Total vote	Registration	Vote/Reg	VAP	Vote/VAP	Invalid	FH	Population
2001	384 248	446 666	86.0%	N/A	N/A	5.4%	N/A	N/A

Ecuador — Latin America — Electoral system: Parallel — Voting age: 18

Year	Total vote	Registration	Vote/Reg	VAP	Vote/VAP	Invalid	FH	Population
1998	3 341 902	7 072 496	47.3%	6 892 210	48.5%	N/A	5	12 091 596
1996	4 521 207	6 662 007	67.9%	6 665 580	67.8%	22.1%	6	11 694 000
1994	4 044 433	6 175 991	65.5%	6 100 400	66.3%	15.7%	5	10 900 000
1990	3 651 081	5 259 114	69.4%	5 645 200	64.7%	16.9%	4	10 264 000
1988	3 610 581	4 649 684	77.7%	5 386 700	67.0%	22.5%	4	9 794 000
1986	3 149 690	4 255 346	74.0%	4 851 000	64.9%	30.4%	5	9 330 000
1984	2 656 884	3 734 076	71.2%	4 739 800	56.1%	29.4%	4	9 115 000
1979	1 678 924	2 088 874	80.4%	3 946 500	42.5%	17.1%	4	7 893 000
1962	699 409	N/A	N/A	2 249 590	31.1%	12.1%	N/A	4 591 000
1958	491 359	N/A	N/A	1 991 850	24.7%	2.0%	N/A	4 065 000
1956	599 227	836 955	71.6%	1 950 750	30.7%	N/A	N/A	3 825 000
1954	465 187	569 959	81.6%	1 819 170	25.6%	7.4%	N/A	3 567 000
1952	334 737	N/A	N/A	1 742 000	19.2%	N/A	N/A	3 350 000
1950	276 821	431 794	64.1%	1 641 640	16.9%	7.4%	N/A	3 157 000
1947	199 860	352 550	56.7%	1 508 000	13.3%	6.2%	N/A	2 900 000

Egypt — Africa — Electoral system: TRS — Voting age: 18

Year	Total vote	Registration	Vote/Reg	VAP	Vote/VAP	Invalid	FH	Population
2000[*]								
1995	10 072 017	20 987 453	48.0%	33 115 600	30.4%	2.5%	12	59 135 000
1990	7 253 168	16 326 229	44.4%	28 980 050	25.0%	4.8%	9	52 691 000
1987	7 207 467	14 324 162	50.3%	26 487 000	27.2%	5.5%	13	49 050 000
1984	5 323 086	12 339 418	43.1%	24 654 780	21.6%	3.3%	14	45 657 000
1976	3 803 973	9 564 482	39.8%	20 068 980	19.0%	N/A	13	37 866 000

El Salvador — Latin America — Electoral system: List-PR — Voting age: 18

Year	Total vote	Registration	Vote/Reg	VAP	Vote/VAP	Invalid	FH	Population
2000	1 242 842	3 264 724	38.1%	3 275 328	37.9%	2.6%	5	6 021 403
1997	2 679 055	3 004 174	89.2%	3 258 790	82.2%	N/A	5	6 266 904
1994	1 500 000	2 722 000	55.1%	2 933 320	51.1%	N/A	6	5 641 000
1991	1 153 013	2 180 000	52.9%	2 621 990	44.0%	8.8%	7	5 351 000
1988	1 083 812	1 600 000	67.7%	2 494 100	43.5%	14.1%	6	5 090 000
1985	1 101 606	N/A	N/A	2 282 320	48.3%	12.4%	6	4 856 000
1978[1]	849 208	1 800 000	47.2%	2 046 380	41.5%	N/A	8	4 354 000
1972	634 651	1 119 699	56.7%	1 767 200	35.9%	17.3%	5	3 760 000
1970	622 570	1 494 931	41.6%	1 659 100	37.5%	15.2%	N/A	3 530 000
1968	492 037	1 342 775	36.6%	1 536 900	32.0%	9.3%	N/A	3 270 000
1966[1]	387 155	1 195 823	32.4%	1 428 800	27.1%	N/A	N/A	3 040 000
1964[1]	296 434	1 074 243	27.6%	1 327 280	22.3%	N/A	N/A	2 824 000
1960[1]	420 102	N/A	N/A	1 177 920	35.7%	N/A	N/A	2 454 000
1958[1]	450 000	N/A	N/A	1 114 080	40.4%	N/A	N/A	2 321 000
1956[1]	585 000	N/A	N/A	1 098 000	53.3%	N/A	N/A	2 196 000

[1] *Total vote include only valid votes,*

[*] *Please refer to www.idea.int/turnout*

Year	Total vote	Registration	Vote/Reg	VAP	Vote/VAP	Invalid	FH	Population
1952[1]	700 979	N/A	N/A	1 012 860	69.2%	N/A	N/A	1 986 000
Estonia		**CIS, Central and Eastern Europe**			**Electoral system: List-PR**		**Voting age: 18**	
1999	492 356	857 270	57.4%	1 071 447	46.0%	1.6%	3	1 415 236
1995	545 770	791 957	68.9%	1 117 500	48.8%	N/A	4	1 490 000
1992	467 629	689 319	67.8%	1 142 560	40.9%	1.5%	6	1 544 000
1990	910 000	1 163 683	78.2%	1 162 540	78.3%	N/A	N/A	1 571 000
Ethiopia		**Africa**			**Electoral system: FPTP**		**Voting age: 18**	
2000	18 226 800	20 252 000	90.0%	30 386 448	60.0%	N/A	10	61 679 843
1992	19 148 000	N/A	N/A	24 754 080	77.4%	N/A	10	51 571 000
Fiji		**Pacific**			**Electoral system: AV**		**Voting age: 21**	
2001[*]								
1999	390 877	437 195	89.4%	522 310	74.8%	9.0%	5	832 494
1994	227 046	303 529	74.8%	407 680	55.7%	N/A	7	784 000
1992	238 814	303 172	78.8%	373 000	64.0%	N/A	7	746 000
Finland		**Western Europe**			**Electoral system: List-PR**		**Voting age: 18**	
1999	2 710 095	4 152 430	65.3%	4 155 857	65.2%	1.0%	2	5 180 030
1995	2 803 602	4 088 358	68.6%	3 941 630	71.1%	0.6%	2	5 119 000
1991	2 776 984	4 060 778	68.4%	3 860 780	71.9%	1.8%	2	5 014 000
1987	2 895 488	4 018 248	72.1%	3 748 320	77.2%	0.5%	3	4 932 000
1983	2 992 970	3 951 932	75.7%	3 690 560	81.1%	0.4%	4	7 856 000
1979	2 906 066	3 858 553	75.3%	3 573 750	81.3%	0.4%	4	4 765 000
1975	2 761 223	3 741 460	73.8%	3 439 030	80.3%	0.4%	4	4 711 000
1972	2 587 060	3 178 169	81.4%	3 062 400	84.5%	0.4%	4	4 640 000
1970	2 544 510	3 094 359	82.2%	3 042 600	83.6%	0.3%	N/A	4 610 000
1966	2 378 583	2 800 461	84.9%	2 793 800	85.1%	0.4%	N/A	4 580 000
1962	2 310 090	2 714 838	85.1%	2 703 000	85.5%	0.4%	N/A	4 505 000
1958	1 954 397	2 606 258	75.0%	2 616 000	74.7%	0.5%	N/A	4 360 000
1954	2 019 042	2 526 969	79.9%	2 515 200	80.3%	0.5%	N/A	4 192 000
1951	1 825 779	2 448 239	74.6%	2 468 670	74.0%	0.7%	N/A	4 047 000
1948	1 893 837	2 420 287	78.2%	2 386 320	79.4%	0.7%	N/A	3 912 000
1945	1 710 251	2 284 249	74.9%	2 292 380	74.6%	0.7%	N/A	3 758 000
France		**Western Europe**			**Electoral system: TRS**		**Voting age: 18**	
1997	26 649 818	39 215 743	68.0%	44 521 902	59.9%	4.9%	3	58 581 450
1993	26 860 177	38 968 660	68.9%	43 826 920	61.3%	5.3%	3	57 667 000
1988	24 472 329	36 977 321	66.2%	42 088 500	58.1%	2.0%	3	56 118 000
1986	28 736 080	36 614 738	78.5%	41 104 040	69.9%	4.3%	3	55 546 000
1981	25 182 623	35 536 041	70.9%	39 395 180	63.9%	1.4%	3	53 966 000
1978	24 658 645	34 424 388	71.6%	38 892 210	63.4%	1.9%	3	53 277 000
1973	24 299 210	29 883 738	81.3%	34 405 800	70.6%	2.3%	3	52 130 000
1968	22 500 524	28 178 087	79.9%	32 441 500	69.4%	1.7%	N/A	49 910 000
1967	22 910 839	28 242 549	81.1%	32 207 500	71.1%	2.3%	N/A	49 550 000
1962	18 918 154	27 540 358	68.7%	31 018 680	61.0%	3.1%	N/A	46 998 000
1958	21 026 543	27 244 992	77.2%	29 560 740	71.1%	2.5%	N/A	44 789 000
1956	22 138 046	26 772 255	82.7%	29 813 240	74.3%	2.9%	N/A	43 843 000
1951	19 670 655	24 530 523	80.2%	28 721 840	68.5%	2.8%	N/A	42 238 000
1946	20 215 200	24 696 949	81.9%	27 416 240	73.7%	1.7%	N/A	40 318 000
1945	19 657 603	24 622 862	79.8%	26 588 000	73.9%	2.4%	N/A	39 100 000

[1] *Total vote include only valid votes,* [*] *Please refer to www.idea.int/turnout*

Parliamentary Elections

Year	Total vote	Registration	Vote/Reg	VAP	Vote/VAP	Invalid	FH	Population
Gabon		**Africa**			**Electoral system: TRS**			**Voting age: 18**
1996*								
Gambia		**Africa**			**Electoral system: FPTP**			**Voting age: 18**
1997	307 856	420 507	73.2%	542 850	56.7%	N/A	13	1 155 000
1992[1]	223 200	400 000	55.8%	403 880	55.3%	N/A	3	878 000
1987	200 000	249 376	80.2%	372 140	53.7%	N/A	6	809 000
1982[2]	166 102	N/A	N/A	292 100	56.9%	N/A	6	635 000
1977[2]	177 181	216 234	81.9%	259 910	68.2%	N/A	2	553 000
1972[2]	103 851	136 521	76.1%	235 200	44.2%	N/A	4	490 000
Georgia		**CIS, Central and Eastern Europe**			**Electoral system: Parallel**			**Voting age: 18**
1999	2 539 598	3 990 890	63.6%	3 631 394	69.9%	N/A	7	5 087 215
1995	2 127 946	3 121 075	68.2%	3 929 760	54.1%	N/A	9	5 458 000
1992	2 592 117	3 466 677	74.8%	3 863 820	67.1%	N/A	9	5 442 000
Germany		**Western Europe**			**Electoral system: MMP**			**Voting age: 18**
1998	49 947 087	60 762 751	82.2%	66 313 874	75.3%	1.6%	3	82 172 259
1994	47 737 999	60 452 009	79.0%	65 942 100	72.4%	1.3%	3	81 410 000
1990	46 995 915	60 436 560	77.8%	64 285 650	73.1%	1.1%	3	79 365 000
1987	38 225 294	45 327 982	84.3%	50 954 310	75.0%	0.9%	3	64 499 127
1983	39 279 529	44 088 935	89.1%	48 522 590	81.0%	0.9%	3	61 421 000
1980	38 292 176	43 231 741	88.6%	46 786 360	81.8%	0.9%	3	61 561 000
1976	38 165 753	42 058 015	90.7%	45 519 620	83.8%	0.9%	2	61 513 000
1972	37 761 589	41 446 302	91.1%	42 552 300	88.7%	0.8%	2	61 670 000
1969	33 523 064	38 677 235	86.7%	41 979 600	79.9%	1.7%	N/A	60 840 000
1965	33 416 207	38 510 395	86.8%	41 328 000	80.9%	2.4%	N/A	59 040 000
1961	32 849 624	37 440 715	87.7%	37 820 300	86.9%	4.0%	N/A	54 029 000
1957	31 072 894	35 400 923	87.8%	35 484 630	87.6%	3.8%	N/A	51 427 000
1953	28 479 550	33 120 940	86.0%	35 346 630	80.6%	3.3%	N/A	51 227 000
1949	24 495 614	31 207 620	78.5%	32 035 480	76.5%	3.1%	N/A	47 111 000
Ghana		**Africa**			**Electoral system: FPTP**			**Voting age: 18**
2000	6 546 695	10 698 652	61.2%	10 141 400	64.6%	1.6%	5	20 212 000
1996[3]	5 980 000	9 200 000	65.0%	8 799 420	68.0%	N/A	8	17 958 000
1992[4]	2 059 415	7 336 846	28.1%	6 862 370	30.0%	N/A	10	15 959 000
1979	1 770 379	5 022 092	35.3%	4 770 420	37.1%	N/A	10	11 094 000
1969	1 493 281	2 362 665	63.2%	3 544 800	42.1%	N/A	N/A	8 440 000
1956	697 257	1 392 874	50.1%	2 017 130	34.6%	N/A	N/A	4 691 000
Greece		**Western Europe**			**Electoral system: List-PR**			**Voting age: 18**
2000	7 027 007	9 373 439	75.0%	7 893 346	89.0%	1.6%	4	10 349 420
1996	6 952 938	9 107 766	76.3%	8 289 470	83.9%	2.0%	4	10 493 000
1993	7 019 925	8 462 636	83.0%	8 200 200	85.6%	1.7%	4	10 380 000
1989	6 799 485	8 061 803	84.3%	7 769 300	87.5%	1.5%	3	10 090 000
1989	6 669 228	7 892 904	84.5%	7 769 300	85.8%	2.1%	3	10 090 000
1985	6 421 466	7 661 588	83.8%	7 351 160	87.4%	0.9%	4	9 934 000
1981	5 753 478	7 059 778	81.5%	6 810 300	84.5%	1.4%	3	9 729 000
1977	5 193 891	6 403 738	81.1%	6 302 240	82.4%	1.2%	4	9 268 000
1974	4 966 558	6 241 066	79.6%	6 003 200	82.7%	1.1%	4	8 960 000
1964	4 626 290	5 662 965	81.7%	5 531 500	83.6%	0.6%	N/A	8 510 000
1963	4 702 791	5 662 965	83.0%	5 512 000	85.3%	0.8%	N/A	8 480 000
1961	4 640 512	5 668 298	81.9%	5 374 720	86.3%	0.4%	N/A	8 398 000
1958	3 863 982	5 119 148	75.5%	5 230 720	73.9%	0.4%	N/A	8 173 000
1956	3 379 445	4 507 907	75.0%	4 979 220	67.9%	0.4%	N/A	8 031 000

[1] *Registered voters are approximate,* [2] *Total votes include only valid votes,* [3] *Total votes and registered voters are approximate,* [4] *Total votes and registered voters exclude 23 constituencies with unopposed candidates,* * *Please refer to www.idea.int/turnout*

Year	Total vote	Registration	Vote/Reg	VAP	Vote/VAP	Invalid	FH	Population
1952	1 600 172	2 123 150	75.4%	2 166 080	73.9%	0.5%	N/A	7 736 000
1951	1 717 012	2 224 246	77.2%	2 142 000	80.2%	0.5%	N/A	7 650 000
1950	1 696 146	N/A	N/A	2 117 640	80.1%	0.4%	N/A	7 563 000
1946[1]	1 121 696	N/A	N/A	2 095 240	53.5%	1.2%	N/A	7 483 000
Grenada		**North America & the Caribbean**			**Electoral system: FPTP**		**Voting age: 18**	
1999	41 753	73 682	56.7%	52 117	80.1%	0.5%	3	89 018
1995	44 116	71 412	61.8%	52 532	84.0%	0.5%	3	92 000
1990	39 939	58 374	68.4%	50 596	78.9%	1.2%	4	91 000
1984	41 506	48 158	86.2%	60 368	68.8%	1.1%	8	112 000
1976	41 238	63 193	65.3%	55 212	74.7%	1.0%	6	107 000
1972	34 679	41 539	83.5%	49 500	70.1%	1.3%	5	100 000
1967	29 001	N/A	N/A	49 000	59.2%	N/A	N/A	100 000
1962	21 107	N/A	N/A	43 298	48.7%	N/A	N/A	91 000
1961	20 932	N/A	N/A	42 561	49.2%	N/A	N/A	90 000
1957	24 682	N/A	N/A	41 517	59.5%	N/A	N/A	90 000
1954	22 476	N/A	N/A	37 566	59.8%	N/A	N/A	83 000
1951	20 622	N/A	N/A	34 180	60.3%	N/A	N/A	77 000
Guatemala		**Latin America**			**Electoral system: Parallel**		**Voting age: 18**	
1999	1 800 676	4 458 744	40.4%	5 784 820	31.1%	3.6%	7	11 788 030
1995	1 737 033	3 711 589	46.8%	5 203 310	33.4%	6.4%	9	10 619 000
1994	731 357	3 480 196	21.0%	5 057 780	14.5%	12.0%	9	10 619 000
1990	1 808 718	3 204 955	56.4%	4 415 040	41.0%	14.1%	7	9 198 000
1985	1 904 236	2 753 572	69.2%	3 822 240	49.8%	12.6%	8	7 963 000
1982	1 074 392	2 356 571	45.6%	3 511 200	30.6%	N/A	12	7 315 000
1978[2]	720 000	1 800 000	40.0%	3 140 640	22.9%	N/A	7	6 543 000
1974	727 174	1 568 724	46.4%	2 836 800	25.6%	N/A	7	5 910 000
1970	633 979	1 190 449	53.3%	2 448 000	25.9%	12.5%	N/A	5 100 000
1966	519 393	944 170	55.0%	2 188 800	23.7%	16.0%	N/A	4 560 000
1961	362 064	814 000	44.5%	1 904 140	19.0%	17.5%	N/A	3 886 000
1959	337 496	756 000	44.6%	1 789 480	18.9%	10.1%	N/A	3 652 000
1958	492 274	736 400	66.8%	1 737 540	28.3%	N/A	N/A	3 546 000
1954	485 531	698 985	69.5%	1 494 010	32.5%	N/A	N/A	3 049 000
1950	417 000	583 300	71.5%	1 372 980	30.4%	N/A	N/A	2 802 000
Guinea		**Africa**			**Electoral system: Parallel**		**Voting age: 18**	
1995	1 886 403	3 049 262	61.9%	3 148 530	59.9%	2.5%	11	6 699 000
Guinea Bissau		**Africa**			**Electoral system: List-PR**		**Voting age: 18**	
1999	402 400	503 007	80.0%	550 101	73.2%	N/A	8	1 170 827
1994	178 604	396 938	45.0%	493 194	36.2%	0.2%	7	1 050 000
Guyana		**Latin America**			**Electoral system: List-PR**		**Voting age: 18**	
2001	403 769	440 185	91.7%	556 488	72.6%	1.8%	N/A	867 371
1997	408 057	461 481	88.4%	509 040	80.2%	2.0%	4	848 000
1992	308 852	381 299	81.0%	484 800	63.7%	1.8%	6	808 000
1985[3]	291 175	N/A	N/A	442 400	65.8%	N/A	10	790 000
1980[3]	403 014	430 375	93.6%	441 150	91.4%	N/A	8	865 000
1973	349 587	421 575	82.9%	319 200	109.5%	0.9%	6	760 000
1968	314 246	369 088	85.1%	280 800	111.9%	0.6%	N/A	720 000
1964	240 120	247 604	97.0%	258 710	92.8%	0.7%	N/A	631 000

[1]Population figure is for 1949, [2]Total votes and registered voters are approximate, [3]Total votes include only valid votes.

Year	Total vote	Registration	Vote/Reg	VAP	Vote/VAP	Invalid	FH	Population
Haiti		**North America & the Caribbean**			**Electoral system: TRS**		**Voting age: 18**	
2000	2 547 000	4 245 384	60.0%	4 207 329	60.5%	N/A	11	7 841 574
1995	1 140 523	3 668 049	31.1%	3 448 320	33.1%	N/A	10	7 184 000
1990	1 640 729	3 271 155	50.2%	3 113 750	52.7%	N/A	8	6 625
Honduras		**Latin America**			**Electoral system: Parallel**		**Voting age: 18**	
1997	2 084 411	2 901 743	71.8%	3 066 060	68.0%	N/A	5	6 132 000
1993	1 776 204	2 734 000	65.0%	2 797 500	63.5%	3.7%	6	5 595 000
1989	1 799 146	2 366 448	76.0%	2 376 480	75.7%	2.5%	5	4 951 000
1985	1 597 841	1 901 757	84.0%	2 054 000	77.8%	3.5%	5	4 372 000
1981	1 214 735	1 558 316	78.0%	1 757 000	69.1%	6.3%	6	3 821 000
1980	1 003 680	1 233 756	81.4%	1 697 860	59.1%	4.3%	7	3 691 000
1971	608 342	900 658	67.5%	1 222 000	49.8%	N/A	N/A	2 600 000
1965	613 888	815 261	75.3%	1 024 600	59.9%	1.2%	N/A	2 180 000
1957[1]	331 660	522 359	63.5%	820 260	40.4%	N/A	N/A	1 674 000
1956	512 694	N/A	N/A	796 250	64.4%	N/A	N/A	1 625 000
1954	252 624	411 354	61.4%	787 920	32.1%	N/A	N/A	1 608 000
1948	258 345	300 496	86.0%	662 970	39.0%	N/A	N/A	1 353 000
Hungary		**CIS, Central and Eastern Europe**			**Electoral system: MMP**		**Voting age: 18**	
1998	4 570 400	8 062 700	56.7%	7 742 951	59.0%	N/A	3	10 056 000
1994	5 485 538	7 959 228	68.9%	7 900 970	69.4%	N/A	3	10 261 000
1990	5 901 931	7 822 764	75.4%	7 773 750	75.9%	3.6%	4	10 365 000
Iceland		**Western Europe**			**Electoral system: List-PR**		**Voting age: 18**	
1999	169 431	201 525	84.1%	196 604	86.2%	2.2%	2	276 418
1995	167 751	191 973	87.4%	190 990	87.8%	1.6%	2	269 000
1991	160 142	182 768	87.6%	180 600	88.7%	1.5%	2	258 000
1987	154 438	171 402	90.1%	167 280	92.3%	1.1%	2	246 000
1983	133 764	150 977	88.6%	151 680	88.2%	2.5%	2	237 000
1979	126 929	142 073	89.3%	140 120	90.6%	2.5%	2	226 000
1978	124 377	137 782	90.3%	138 880	89.6%	1.7%	2	224 000
1974	115 575	126 388	91.4%	132 000	87.6%	1.3%	2	220 000
1971	106 975	118 289	90.4%	119 700	89.4%	1.5%	N/A	210 000
1967	97 855	107 101	91.4%	110 000	89.0%	1.8%	N/A	200 000
1963	90 958	99 798	91.1%	101 750	89.4%	1.8%	N/A	185 000
1959	86 426	95 637	90.4%	96 320	89.7%	1.5%	N/A	172 000
1959	86 147	95 050	90.6%	96 320	89.4%	1.6%	N/A	172 000
1956	84 355	91 618	92.1%	91 770	91.9%	2.0%	N/A	161 000
1953	78 754	87 601	89.9%	85 500	92.1%	1.7%	N/A	150 000
1949	73 432	82 481	89.0%	82 600	88.9%	1.7%	N/A	140 000
1946	67 895	77 670	87.4%	77 880	87.2%	1.4%	N/A	132 000
India		**Asia**			**Electoral system: FPTP**		**Voting age: 18**	
1999	370 579 735	620 394 065	59.7%	565 780 483	65.5%	N/A	5	986 856 301
1998	373 678 215	602 340 382	62.0%	556 651 400	67.1%	1.9%	5	970 933 000
1996	343 308 035	592 572 288	57.9%	562 028 100	61.1%	2.5%	8	952 590 000
1991	282 700 000	498 363 801	56.7%	493 963 380	57.2%	N/A	7	851 661 000
1989[1]	290 366 661	498 647 786	58.2%	474 143 040	61.2%	N/A	5	817 488 000
1984	240 846 499	379 116 623	63.5%	373 371 000	64.5%	2.5%	5	746 742 000
1980	201 269 129	354 024 081	56.9%	325 162 040	61.9%	2.4%	5	663 596 000
1977	193 953 183	320 682 598	60.5%	300 392 640	64.6%	2.8%	7	625 818 000
1971	151 296 749	273 832 301	55.3%	264 393 600	57.2%	3.2%	N/A	550 820 000
1967	152 730 000	250 600 000	60.9%	241 996 800	63.1%	N/A	N/A	504 160 000
1962	119 910 000	217 680 000	55.1%	220 324 090	54.4%	N/A	N/A	449 641 000

[1] *Total votes include only valid votes.*

Year	Total vote	Registration	Vote/Reg	VAP	Vote/VAP	Invalid	FH	Population
1957	123 460 000	193 650 000	63.8%	197 090 250	62.6%	N/A	N/A	402 225 000
1952[1]	105 940 000	173 210 000	61.2%	179 830 000	58.9%	N/A	N/A	367 000 000
Indonesia		**Asia**			**Electoral system: List-PR**		**Voting age: 18**	
1999	110 298 176	118 217 393	93.3%	128 717 433	85.7%	3.4%	8	207 152 973
1997	110 938 069	124 740 987	88.9%	119 535 245	92.8%	N/A	12	199 225 408
1992	97 789 534	107 565 697	90.9%	111 625 800	87.6%	N/A	11	186 043 000
1987[2]	85 822 000	94 000 000	91.3%	98 045 700	87.5%	N/A	11	172 010 000
1982	74 930 875	82 132 263	91.2%	84 196 200	89.0%	N/A	10	153 084 000
1977	63 998 344	70 662 155	90.6%	73 780 200	86.7%	N/A	10	136 630 000
1971	54 699 509	58 179 245	94.0%	63 660 600	85.9%	N/A	N/A	117 890 000
Iran		**Middle East**			**Electoral system: TRS**		**Voting age: 18**	
2000[*]								
1996	24 718 661	32 000 000	77.2%	33 824 520	73.1%	N/A	13	62 638 000
1992	18 803 158	N/A	N/A	30 291 090	62.1%	1.7%	12	57 153 000
Ireland		**Western Europe**			**Electoral system: STV**		**Voting age: 18**	
1997	1 788 997	2 707 498	66.1%	2 681 821	66.7%	0.6%	2	3 807 391
1992	1 751 351	2 557 036	68.5%	2 377 830	73.7%	1.5%	2	3 549 000
1989	1 677 592	2 448 810	68.5%	2 355 050	71.2%	1.2%	2	3 515 000
1987	1 793 406	2 445 515	73.3%	2 302 950	77.9%	0.9%	2	3 543 000
1982	1 701 385	2 335 153	72.9%	2 229 120	76.3%	0.7%	2	3 483 000
1981	1 734 379	2 275 450	76.2%	2 201 600	78.8%	0.9%	2	3 440 000
1977	1 616 770	2 118 606	76.3%	1 898 340	85.2%	0.9%	2	3 273 000
1973	1 366 474	1 783 604	76.6%	1 757 400	77.8%	1.2%	3	3 030 000
1969	1 334 963	1 735 388	76.9%	1 728 700	77.2%	1.2%	N/A	2 930 000
1965	1 264 666	1 683 019	75.1%	1 699 200	74.4%	0.9%	N/A	2 880 000
1961	1 179 738	1 670 860	70.6%	1 662 620	71.0%	1.0%	N/A	2 818 000
1957	1 238 559	1 738 278	71.3%	1 759 850	70.4%	0.9%	N/A	2 885 000
1954	1 347 932	1 763 209	76.4%	1 789 130	75.3%	0.9%	N/A	2 933 000
1951	1 343 616	1 785 144	75.3%	1 806 210	74.4%	0.9%	N/A	2 961 000
1948	1 336 628	1 800 210	74.2%	1 820 850	73.4%	1.0%	N/A	2 985 000
Israel		**Middle East**			**Electoral system: List-PR**		**Voting age: 18**	
1999	3 372 952	4 285 428	78.7%	3 994 784	84.4%	5.3%	3	6 089 384
1996	3 119 832	3 933 250	79.3%	3 684 850	84.7%	2.2%	4	5 669 000
1992	2 637 943	3 409 015	77.4%	3 227 490	81.7%	0.8%	4	5 123 000
1988	2 305 576	2 894 267	79.7%	2 798 460	82.4%	1.0%	4	4 442 000
1984	2 091 402	2 654 613	78.8%	2 600 280	80.4%	0.9%	4	4 194 000
1981	1 954 609	2 490 014	78.5%	2 447 760	79.9%	0.9%	4	3 948 000
1977	1 771 726	2 236 293	79.2%	2 203 930	80.4%	1.3%	5	3 613 000
1973	1 601 098	2 037 478	78.6%	1 958 100	81.8%	2.1%	5	3 210 000
1969	1 427 981	1 758 685	81.2%	1 720 200	83.0%	4.2%	N/A	2 820 000
1965	1 244 706	1 449 709	85.9%	1 510 400	82.4%	3.1%	N/A	2 560 000
1961	1 037 030	1 274 880	81.3%	1 289 150	80.4%	2.9%	N/A	2 185 000
1959	994 306	1 218 483	81.6%	1 215 990	81.8%	2.5%	N/A	2 061 000
1955	876 188	1 057 795	82.8%	1 066 280	82.2%	2.6%	N/A	1 748 000
1951	695 007	924 885	75.1%	955 080	72.8%	1.1%	N/A	1 516 000
1949	440 095	506 507	86.9%	671 580	65.5%	1.2%	N/A	1 066 000
Italy		**Western Europe**			**Electoral system: MMP**		**Voting age: 18**	
2001	40 195 500	49 358 947	81.4%	47 332 575	84.9%	7.2%	N/A	57 684 294
1996	40 496 438	48 846 238	82.9%	46 363 590	87.3%	7.8%	3	57 239 000

[1] *Total votes include only valid votes,* [2] *Total votes and registered voters are approximates.* [*] *Please refer to www.idea.int/turnout*

Year	Total vote	Registration	Vote/Reg	VAP	Vote/VAP	Invalid	FH	Population
1994	41 461 260	48 135 041	86.1%	45 641 100	90.8%	5.9%	3	57 049 000
1992	41 479 764	47 435 964	87.4%	44 918 610	92.3%	5.4%	3	56 859 000
1987	40 599 490	45 689 829	88.9%	43 008 750	94.4%	4.9%	2	57 345 000
1983	39 114 321	43 936 534	89.0%	42 627 000	91.8%	5.7%	3	56 836 000
1979	38 112 228	42 181 664	90.4%	41 093 160	92.7%	3.9%	4	56 292 000
1976	37 741 404	40 423 131	93.4%	39 547 710	95.4%	2.7%	3	55 701 000
1972	34 524 106	37 049 654	93.2%	36 454 700	94.7%	3.2%	3	54 410 000
1968	33 003 249	35 566 681	92.8%	35 449 700	93.1%	3.6%	N/A	52 910 000
1963	31 766 058	34 201 660	92.9%	33 328 680	95.3%	3.2%	N/A	50 498 000
1958	30 399 708	32 436 022	93.7%	32 367 060	93.9%	2.8%	N/A	49 041 000
1953	28 410 851	30 267 080	93.9%	31 041 400	91.5%	4.3%	N/A	47 756 000
1948	26 854 203	29 117 554	92.2%	28 794 780	93.3%	2.2%	N/A	45 706 000
1946	24 947 187	28 005 449	89.1%	28 346 220	88.0%	7.7%	N/A	44 994 000

Jamaica		North America & the Caribbean			Electoral system: FPTP		Voting age: 18	
1997	773 425	1 182 292	65.4%	1 585 760	48.8%	0.9%	5	2 170 000
1993	678 572	1 002 571	67.7%	1 518 930	44.7%	1.4%	5	2 411 000
1989	845 485	1 078 760	78.4%	1 434 000	59.0%	1.0%	4	2 390 000
1983[1]	27 043	990 019	2.7%	1 264 480	2.1%	1.8%	5	2 258 000
1980	860 746	990 417	86.9%	1 151 690	74.7%	0.9%	5	2 173 000
1976	742 149	870 972	85.2%	874 860	84.8%	0.8%	4	2 083 000
1972	477 711	605 662	78.9%	834 200	57.3%	0.9%	3	1 940 000
1967	446 815	543 307	82.2%	814 500	54.9%	1.0%	N/A	1 810 000
1962	580 517	796 540	72.9%	788 160	73.7%	0.8%	N/A	1 642 000
1959	563 974	853 539	66.1%	760 320	74.2%	1.1%	N/A	1 584 000
1955	495 682	761 238	65.1%	801 840	61.8%	1.8%	N/A	1 542 000
1949	477 107	732 217	65.2%	714 480	66.8%	2.1%	N/A	1 374 000

Japan		Asia			Electoral system: Parallel		Voting age: 20	
2000[2]	60 882 471	100 433 798	60.6%	103 155 387	59.0%	3.0%	3	126 996 466
1996[3]	57 766 696	97 909 655	59.0%	96 672 730	59.8%	N/A	3	125 549 000
1995	43 307 400	97 320 000	44.5%	96 460 210	44.9%	N/A	3	125 273 000
1993	63 574 819	94 866 020	67.0%	95 955 900	66.3%	1.2%	4	124 670 000
1990	66 215 906	90 322 908	73.3%	88 348 250	74.9%	0.6%	2	124 434 155
1986	61 703 794	96 426 845	64.0%	86 259 320	71.5%	2.0%	2	121 492 000
1983	57 240 830	84 252 608	67.9%	84 673 890	67.6%	0.8%	2	119 259 000
1980	60 338 439	80 925 034	74.6%	80 771 400	74.7%	2.2%	2	117 060 000
1979	54 518 515	80 169 924	68.0%	79 964 100	68.2%	0.9%	3	115 890 000
1976	57 231 993	77 926 588	73.4%	77 814 750	73.5%	1.1%	3	112 775 000
1972	52 929 059	73 769 636	71.7%	71 663 200	73.9%	0.9%	3	106 960 000
1969	47 442 401	69 260 424	68.5%	69 123 900	68.6%	1.0%	N/A	103 170 000
1967	46 599 456	62 992 796	74.0%	63 522 900	73.4%	1.3%	N/A	100 830 000
1963	41 458 946	58 281 678	71.1%	60 416 370	68.6%	1.1%	N/A	95 899 000
1960	39 920 119	54 312 993	73.5%	55 926 000	71.4%	1.0%	N/A	93 210 000
1958	40 042 489	52 013 529	77.0%	54 924 000	72.9%	0.7%	N/A	91 540 000
1955	37 334 338	49 235 375	75.8%	50 730 000	73.6%	0.9%	N/A	89 000 000
1953	34 946 130	47 090 167	74.2%	49 419 000	70.7%	1.0%	N/A	86 700 000
1952	35 749 709	46 772 584	76.4%	46 170 000	77.4%	1.2%	N/A	85 500 000
1949	31 174 957	42 105 300	74.0%	44 161 200	70.6%	1.9%	N/A	81 780 000
1947	27 796 840	40 907 493	68.0%	42 174 540	65.9%	1.6%	N/A	78 101 000
1946	26 582 175	36 878 420	72.1%	40 932 000	64.9%	1.8%	N/A	75 800 000

Jordan		Middle East			Electoral system: SNTV		Voting age: 18	
1997	702 260	1 480 000	47.5%	2 644 116	26.6%	N/A	8	5 508 576
1993	822 294	1 501 279	54.8%	2 369 280	34.7%	N/A	8	4 936 000
1989	541 426	1 020 446	53.1%	1 901 640	28.5%	N/A	10	4 134 000

[1] In 1983 the elections were uncontested in a majority of the constituencies and regular elections were held only in six constituencies, which is the reason for the low turnout figure. [2] Results of single-member constituency. Total votes in proportional representation was 59844601.
[3] Total votes are approximate.

Year	Total vote	Registration	Vote/Reg	VAP	Vote/VAP	Invalid	FH	Population
Kazakhstan		**CIS, Central and Eastern Europe**			**Electoral system: TRS**		**Voting age: 18**	
1995	2 519 733	3 308 897	76.2%	11 125 400	22.6%	0.6%	11	17 116 000
1994*								
Kenya		**Africa**			**Electoral system: FPTP**		**Voting age: 18**	
1997	5 910 580	9 030 092	65.5%	12 664 960	46.7%	1.6%	13	28 784 000
1992	4 622 764	7 855 880	58.8%	11 308 000	40.9%	N/A	9	25 700 000
Kiribati		**Pacific**			**Electoral system: TRS**		**Voting age: 18**	
1998*								
1991[1]	19 285	N/A	N/A	31 080	62.0%	N/A	3	74 000
1983[1]	19 995	25 011	79.9%	25 620	78.0%	N/A	4	61 000
1982[1]	18 826	22 816	82.5%	25 200	74.7%	N/A	4	60 000
1978[1]	15 004	18 523	81.0%	23 520	63.8%	N/A	4	56 000
1974[1]	8 401	12 354	68.0%	25 200	33.3%	N/A	4	60 000[1]
Kuwait		**Middle East**			**Electoral system: Block**		**Voting age: 18**	
1996[2]	85 735	107 169	80.0%	375 120	22.9%	N/A	10	1 563 000
1992[4]	69 224	81 440	85.0%	375 120	18.5%	N/A	10	1 422 000
1985[4]	48 000	56 745	84.6%	567 600	8.5%	N/A	8	1 720 000
1981[4]	37 528	41 698	90.0%	454 460	8.3%	N/A	8	1 466 000
1975[4]	30 863	52 994	58.2%	258 700	11.9%	N/A	7	995 000
Kyrgyzstan		**CIS, Central and Eastern Europe**			**Electoral system: TRS**		**Voting age: 18**	
2000	1 613 855	2 505 763	64.4%	2 638 707	61.2%	N/A	11	4 650 010
1995[3]	1 344 200	2 200 000	61.1%	2 663 610	50.5%	N/A	8	4 673 000
Latvia		**CIS, Central and Eastern Europe**			**Electoral system: List-PR**		**Voting age: 18**	
1998	964 667	1 341 942	71.9%	1 858 210	51.9%	0.5%	3	2 432 841
1995	959 459	1 334 436	71.9%	1 894 500	50.6%	1.5%	4	2 526 000
1993	1 119 432	1 245 530	89.9%	1 939 500	57.7%	1.5%	6	2 586 000
1990	1 600 000	1 970 443	81.2%	1 976 540	80.9%	N/A	N/A	2 671 000
Lebanon		**Middle East**			**Electoral system: Block**		**Voting age: 21**	
2000	1 236 168	2 748 674	45.0%	2 022 400	61.1%	N/A	11	3 282 000
1996[5]	1 112 249	2 577 979	43.1%	1 375 980	80.8%	N/A	11	4 100 000
1992[5]	723 291	2 383 345	30.3%	1 179 000	61.3%	N/A	9	3 800 000
Lesotho		**Africa**			**Electoral system: MMP**		**Voting age: 18**	
1998	617 738	860 000	71.8%	1 001 034	61.7%	N/A	8	2 176 160
1993	532 678	736 930	72.3%	893 780	59.6%	N/A	7	1 943 000
1970	306 529	374 272	81.9%	437 100	70.1%	N/A	N/A	930 000
1965	259 844	416 952	62.3%	394 800	65.8%	N/A	N/A	840 000
Liechtenstein		**Western Europe**			**Electoral system: List-PR**		**Voting age: 18**	
2001	14 178	16 350	86.7%	26 195	54.1%	1.1%	N/A	33 644
1997	12 836	14 765	86.9%	23 840	53.8%	0.5%	2	32 000
1993	12 255	13 999	87.5%	22 050	55.6%	0.9%	2	30 000
1989	12 094	13 307	90.9%	20 300	59.6%	0.7%	2	28 000
1986	11 677	12 512	93.3%	19 373	60.3%	0.2%	N/A	27 000
1982[4]	5 004	5 246	95.4%	8 840	56.6%	1.1%	N/A	26 000
1978[4]	4 670	4 879	95.7%	8 250	56.6%	0.6%	N/A	25 000

*[1] Kiribati population size is calculated on the basis of the 1978 census, [2] Total votes is approximate. VAP include only men, [3] Total votes and registered voters are approximates, [4] VAP includes only men, [5] Registered voters is equal to the number of eligible voters since no registration process took place. * Please refer to www.idea.int/turnout*

Parliamentary Elections

Year	Total vote	Registration	Vote/Reg	VAP	Vote/VAP	Invalid	FH	Population
1974[1]	4 369	4 572	95.6%	7 680	56.9%	0.8%	N/A	24 000
1970[1]	4 091	4 309	94.9%	6 510	62.8%	0.8%	N/A	21 000
1966[1]	3 724	3 892	95.7%	6 000	62.1%	0.3%	N/A	20 000
1962[1]	3 452	3 646	94.7%	5 220	66.1%	0.5%	N/A	18 000
1958[1]	3 419	3 544	96.5%	4 480	76.3%	0.2%	N/A	16 000
1957[1]	3 294	3 525	93.4%	4 440	74.2%	0.3%	N/A	16 000
1953[1]	3 025	3 333	90.8%	4 013	75.4%	3.4%	N/A	15 000
1953[1]	3 173	3 398	93.4%	4 013	79.1%	0.9%	N/A	15 000
1949[2]	3 022	3 285	92.0%	3 605	83.8%	1.5%	N/A	14 000
1945[1]	2 883	3 088	93.4%	2 970	97.1%	1.9%	N/A	12 000
Lithuania		**CIS, Central and Eastern Europe**			**Electoral system: Parallel**		**Voting age: 18**	
2000	1 539 743	2 646 663	58.2%	3 053 037	50.4%	4.4%	3	3 672 338
1996	1 374 612	2 597 530	52.9%	2 751 320	50.0%	4.9%	3	3 718 000
1992	1 918 027	2 549 952	75.2%	2 731 660	70.2%	5.5%	5	3 742 000
Luxembourg		**Western Europe**			**Electoral system: List-PR**		**Voting age: 18**	
1999	191 267	221 103	86.5%	336 027	56.9%	6.5%	2	429 797
1994	191 724	217 131	88.3%	316 790	60.5%	6.5%	2	401 000
1989	191 332	218 940	87.4%	298 620	64.1%	5.5%	2	378 000
1984	191 651	215 792	88.8%	286 770	66.8%	6.5%	2	363 000
1979	188 909	212 614	88.9%	275 880	68.5%	7.3%	2	363 000
1974	185 527	205 817	90.1%	251 600	73.7%	5.8%	3	340 000
1968	170 566	192 601	88.6%	251 600	67.8%	6.4%	N/A	340 000
1964	173 702	191 788	90.6%	239 440	72.5%	6.4%	N/A	328 000
1959	173 836	188 286	92.3%	234 000	74.3%	4.9%	N/A	312 000
1954	170 092	183 590	92.6%	232 560	73.1%	4.9%	N/A	306 000
1951	83 613	92 110	90.8%	224 250	37.3%	4.9%	N/A	299 000
1948	77 865	84 724	91.9%	219 000	35.6%	5.6%	N/A	292 000
1945	159 083	N/A	N/A	212 250	75.0%	N/A	N/A	283 000
Macedonia		**CIS, Central and Eastern Europe**			**Electoral system: Parallel**		**Voting age: 18**	
1998	793 674	1 572 976	50.5%	1 621 599	48.9%	N/A	6	2 008 850
1994	707 210	1 222 899	57.8%	1 477 980	47.8%	3.9%	7	2 142 000
Madagascar		**Africa**			**Electoral system: Parallel**		**Voting age: 18**	
1998	3 147 368	5 234 198	60.1%	7 745 460	40.6%	3.3%	6	16 136 000
1993[3]	3 600 000	6 000 000	60.0%	6 649 920	54.1%	N/A	6	13 854 000
1989	4 283 512	5 741 974	74.6%	5 837 280	73.4%	2.7%	9	12 161 000
1983	3 519 997	4 838 279	72.8%	4 606 000	76.4%	2.5%	11	9 400 000
1970	2 612 656	2 756 978	94.8%	3 037 500	86.0%	0.4%	N/A	6 750 000
Malawi		**Africa**			**Electoral system: FPTP**		**Voting age: 18**	
1999	4 680 262	5 071 822	92.3%	4 419 210	105.9%	4.1%	6	9 692 808
1994	3 021 239	3 775 256	80.0%	4 446 670	67.9%	2.4%	5	9 461 000
Malaysia		**Asia**			**Electoral system: FPTP**		**Voting age: 18**	
1999	6 655 348	9 694 156	68.7%	13 411 519	49.6%	2.2%	10	22 549 627
1995	6 470 882	9 012 370	71.8%	10 175 010	63.6%	N/A	9	19 951 000
1990[3]	5 600 000	8 000 000	70.0%	8 882 000	63.0%	N/A	9	17 764 000
1986	5 052 157	6 791 446	74.4%	7 893 900	64.0%	2.5%	8	16 110 000
1982	4 181 800	5 800 000	72.1%	6 828 160	61.2%	N/A	7	14 528 000
1978	3 473 790	N/A	N/A	6 067 230	57.3%	N/A	6	12 303 000
1974	2 122 927	N/A	N/A	5 265 000	40.3%	N/A	6	11 700 000

[1] *VAP includes only men,* [2] *VAP includes only men, population figure for 1950,* [3] *Registered voters are approximate.*

Year	Total vote	Registration	Vote/Reg	VAP	Vote/VAP	Invalid	FH	Population
Maldives		**Asia**			**Electoral system: Block**		**Voting age: 18**	
1999*								
1994	82 227	109 072	75.4%	100 860	81.5%	1.6%	12	246 000
1989	61 875	90 084	68.7%	87 780	70.5%	7.2%	11	209 000
Mali		**Africa**			**Electoral system: TRS**		**Voting age: 18**	
1997	1 133 769	5 254 299	21.6%	5 282 480	21.5%	1.9%	6	11 239 000
1992	1 008 189	4 780 416	21.1%	4 613 520	21.9%	N/A	5	9 816 000
Malta		**Western Europe**			**Electoral system: STV**		**Voting age: 18**	
1998	268 150	281 078	95.4%	279 515	95.9%	1.4%	2	379 287
1996	264 037	271 746	97.2%	269 370	98.0%	1.1%	2	369 000
1992	249 145	259 423	96.0%	261 360	95.3%	0.8%	2	363 000
1987	236 719	246 292	96.1%	247 680	95.6%	0.7%	3	344 000
1981	225 466	238 237	94.6%	262 080	86.0%	0.6%	5	364 000
1976	206 843	217 724	95.0%	230 300	89.8%	0.7%	3	329 000
1971	168 913	181 768	92.9%	217 800	77.6%	0.5%	N/A	330 000
1966	144 873	161 490	89.7%	188 800	76.7%	1.1%	N/A	320 000
1962	151 533	166 936	90.8%	190 820	79.4%	0.6%	N/A	329 000
1955	121 243	149 380	81.2%	178 980	67.7%	0.5%	N/A	314 000
1953	119 333	148 478	80.4%	180 690	66.0%	0.7%	N/A	317 000
1951	113 366	151 977	74.6%	187 800	60.4%	0.7%	N/A	313 000
1950	106 820	140 516	76.0%	187 200	57.1%	0.6%	N/A	312 000
1947	106 141	140 703	75.4%	180 000	59.0%	0.6%	N/A	300 000
Mauritania		**Africa**			**Electoral system: TRS**		**Voting age: 18**	
1996	541 849	1 040 855	52.1%	1 135 690	47.7%	N/A	12	2 331 248
1992	456 237	1 174 087	38.9%	1 074 570	42.5%	1.2%	13	2 107 000
Mauritius		**Africa**			**Electoral system: Block**		**Voting age: 18**	
2000	630 292	779 433	80.9%	792 125	79.6%	1.1%	3	1 174 772
1995	567 810	712 513	79.7%	736 560	77.1%	1.5%	3	1 116 000
1991	573 419	682 000	84.1%	695 500	82.4%	N/A	3	1 070 000
1987	543 565	639 488	85.0%	642 320	84.6%	N/A	4	1 036 000
1983	470 008	540 000	87.0%	610 080	77.0%	1.2%	4	992 000
1982[1]	486 000	540 000	90.0%	531 360	91.5%	N/A	4	984 000
1976	400 486	N/A	N/A	474 350	84.4%	N/A	4	894 000
Mexico		**Latin America**			**Electoral system: MMP**		**Voting age: 18**	
2000	30 214 419	52 789 209	57.9%	62 684 899	48.2%	2.8%	5	N/A
1997	30 120 221	52 208 966	57.7%	55 406 943	54.4%	N/A	7	95 529 212
1994	35 545 831	45 729 053	77.7%	53 944 640	65.9%	N/A	8	93 008 000
1991	24 149 001	39 517 979	61.1%	48 309 800	50.0%	4.2%	8	87 836 000
1988	18 820 415	38 074 926	49.4%	45 496 550	41.4%	3.3%	7	82 721 000
1985	18 281 851	35 278 369	51.8%	40 527 760	45.1%	5.1%	8	77 938 000
1982	22 866 719	31 516 370	72.6%	35 829 780	63.8%	4.9%	7	73 122 000
1979	13 796 410	27 912 053	49.4%	33 034 820	41.8%	5.0%	6	67 418 000
1976	16 068 911	25 913 066	62.0%	29 046 470	55.3%	5.7%	8	61 801 000
1973	15 009 984	24 890 261	60.3%	23 025 600	65.2%	10.0%	7	56 160 000
1970	13 940 862	21 654 217	64.4%	21 289 800	65.5%	4.2%	N/A	50 690 000
1967	9 938 814	15 821 075	62.8%	18 547 200	53.6%	N/A	N/A	44 160 000
1964	9 051 524	13 589 594	66.6%	16 650 060	54.4%	N/A	N/A	39 643 000
1961	6 845 826	10 004 696	68.4%	15 880 040	43.1%	N/A	N/A	36 091 000
1958	7 332 429	10 443 465	70.2%	14 473 800	50.7%	N/A	N/A	32 895 000

*[1] Total votes and registered voters are approximate. * Please refer to www.idea.int/turnout*

Year	Total vote	Registration	Vote/Reg	VAP	Vote/VAP	Invalid	FH	Population
1955	6 190 376	8 941 020	69.2%	13 506 750	45.8%	N/A	N/A	30 015 000
1952	3 651 483	4 924 293	74.2%	12 416 320	29.4%	N/A	N/A	26 992 000
1949	2 163 582	2 992 084	72.3%	11 423 180	18.9%	N/A	N/A	24 833 000
1946	2 294 928	2 556 949	89.8%	10 478 340	21.9%	N/A	N/A	22 779 000
Micronesia		**Pacific**			**Electoral system: Parallel**		**Voting age: 18**	
1999[1]	17 020	N/A	N/A	57 771	29.5%	N/A	3	116 716
1995	33 686	N/A	N/A	53 500	63.0%	N/A	2	107 000
Moldova		**CIS, Central and Eastern Europe**			**Electoral system: List-PR**		**Voting age: 18**	
2001	1 605 853	2 295 288	70.0%	2 518 141	63.8%	2.5%	N/A	3 657 498
1998	1 680 470	2 431 218	69.1%	2 949 470	57.0%	3.4%	6	4 403 000
1994	1 869 090	2 356 614	79.3%	2 914 500	64.1%	5.0%	8	4 350 000
Monaco		**Western Europe**			**Electoral system: TRS**		**Voting age: 18**	
1998	3 226	4 932	65.4%	27 564	11.7%	2.8%	3	32 580
1993	3 051	4 582	66.6%	25 420	12.0%	3.3%	3	31 000
1988	2 985	4 244	70.3%	23 780	12.6%	5.2%	N/A	29 000
1983	2 930	3 904	75.1%	22 140	13.2%	2.9%	N/A	27 000
1978	2 719	3 647	74.6%	20 500	13.3%	5.5%	N/A	25 000
1973	2 457	3 400	72.3%	16 200	15.2%	2.9%	N/A	20 000
1968	2 388	3 301	72.3%	16 200	14.7%	6.3%	N/A	20 000
Mongolia		**Asia**			**Electoral system: FPTP**		**Voting age: 18**	
2000	1 027 985	1 247 033	82.4%	1 448 576	71.0%	N/A	5	2 501 041
1996	1 014 031	1 147 260	88.4%	1 377 040	73.6%	0.4%	5	2 459 000
1992	1 037 392	1 085 120	95.6%	1 204 690	86.1%	N/A	5	2 273 000
1990	1 006 460	1 027 000	98.0%	1 153 810	87.2%	N/A	8	2 177 000
Morocco		**Africa**			**Electoral system: FPTP**		**Voting age: 18**	
1997	7 456 996	12 790 631	58.3%	14 852 810	50.2%	14.6%	10	28 024 000
1993	7 153 211	11 398 987	62.8%	13 816 570	51.8%	13.0%	10	26 069 000
1984	4 999 646	7 414 846	67.4%	10 510 080	47.6%	11.1%	9	22 848 000
1977	5 369 431	6 519 301	82.4%	7 343 600	73.1%	N/A	7	18 359 000
1970	4 160 016	4 874 598	85.3%	6 363 200	65.4%	1.3%	N/A	15 520 000
Mozambique		**Africa**			**Electoral system: List-PR**		**Voting age: 18**	
1999	4 833 761	7 099 105	68.1%	8 303 686	58.2%	9.6%	7	17 336 171
1994	5 404 199	6 148 842	87.9%	8 140 860	66.4%	11.7%	8	16 614 000
Namibia		**Africa**			**Electoral system: List-PR**		**Voting age: 18**	
1999	541 114	861 848	62.8%	876 828	61.7%	0.9%	5	1 711 793
1994	497 499	654 189	76.0%	780 000	63.8%	1.6%	5	1 500 000
1989	680 688	701 483	97.0%	669 630	101.7%	1.5%	7	1 313 000
Nauru		**Pacific**			**Electoral system: AV**		**Voting age: 20**	
2000	3 400	3 829	88.8%	6 784	50.1%	3.5%	4	12 088
1997[2]	3 139	3 418	91.8%	N/A	N/A	3.0%	4	N/A
1995[2]	2 947	2 952	99.8%	5 940	49.6%	3.1%	4	11 000
1992[2]								
1989[2]	2 358	2 659	88.7%	N/A	N/A	N/A	3	N/A
1987[2]	2 264	2 443	92.7%	4 860	46.6%	2.4%	4	9 000
1983[2]								

[1] *Total votes include only valid votes,* [2] *Population size calculated on the basis of 1966 census.*

Year	Total vote	Registration	Vote/Reg	VAP	Vote/VAP	Invalid	FH	Population
1980[1]	1 587	N/A	N/A	3 780	42.0%	N/A	4	7 000
1977[1]	1 599	N/A	N/A	3 780	42.3%	N/A	4	7 000
1976[1]	1 348	N/A	N/A	3 780	35.7%	N/A	4	7 000
1973[1]	1 148	N/A	N/A	4 860	23.6%	N/A	4	9 000
1971[1]	880	N/A	N/A	4 320	20.4%	N/A	N/A	8 000
Nepal		**Asia**			**Electoral system: FPTP**		**Voting age: 18**	
1999	8 894 566	13 518 839	65.8%	11 738 680	75.8%	2.8%	7	22 341 605
1997	5 725 246	6 496 365	88.1%	11 203 628	51.1%	1.5%	2	21 323 271
1994	5 562 920	6 413 172	86.7%	6 721 260	82.8%	1.7%	2	N/A
1991	5 725 246	6 496 365	88.1%	6 848 400	83.6%	1.5%	2	N/A
1986	5 454 672	9 044 964	60.3%	7 333 480	74.4%	4.7%	7	16 667 000
1981[2]	4 079 400	7 800 000	52.3%	6 759 000	60.4%	N/A	7	15 020 000
1959	1 791 381	4 246 468	42.2%	4 341 120	41.3%	N/A	N/A	9 044 000
Netherlands		**Western Europe**			**Electoral system: List-PR**		**Voting age: 18**	
1998	8 607 787	11 755 132	73.2%	12 275 387	70.1%	1.7%	2	15 661 239
1994	9 021 144	11 455 924	78.7%	11 996 400	75.2%	0.5%	2	15 380 000
1989	8 919 787	11 112 189	80.3%	11 433 730	78.0%	0.3%	2	14 849 000
1986	9 199 621	10 727 701	85.8%	10 923 000	84.2%	0.3%	2	14 564 000
1982	8 273 631	10 216 634	81.0%	10 303 200	80.3%	0.4%	2	14 310 000
1981	8 738 238	10 040 121	87.0%	10 257 120	85.2%	0.5%	2	14 246 000
1977	8 365 829	9 506 318	88.0%	9 697 100	86.3%	0.6%	2	13 853 000
1972	7 445 287	8 916 947	83.5%	8 264 600	90.1%	0.7%	2	13 330 000
1971	6 364 719	8 048 726	79.1%	8 177 800	77.8%	0.7%	N/A	13 190 000
1967	7 076 328	7 452 776	94.9%	7 686 000	92.1%	2.8%	N/A	12 600 000
1963	6 419 964	6 748 611	95.1%	7 299 870	87.9%	2.5%	N/A	11 967 000
1959	6 143 409	6 427 864	95.6%	6 921 060	88.8%	2.3%	N/A	11 346 000
1956	5 849 652	6 125 210	95.5%	6 642 290	88.1%	2.1%	N/A	10 889 000
1952	5 501 728	5 792 679	95.0%	6 333 020	86.9%	3.0%	N/A	10 382 000
1948	5 089 582	5 433 633	93.7%	5 978 000	85.1%	3.1%	N/A	9 800 000
1946	4 913 015	5 275 888	93.1%	5 748 030	85.5%	3.1%	N/A	9 423 000
New Zealand		**Pacific**			**Electoral system: MMP**		**Voting age: 18**	
1999	2 085 381	2 509 872	83.1%	2 794 955	74.6%	1.8%	2	3 829 188
1996	2 135 175	2 418 587	88.3%	2 571 840	83.0%	0.4%	2	3 572 000
1993	1 978 092	2 321 664	85.2%	2 484 720	79.6%	0.6%	2	3 451 000
1990	1 877 115	2 202 157	85.2%	2 387 730	78.6%	0.6%	2	3 363 000
1987	1 883 394	2 114 656	89.1%	2 312 800	81.4%	0.6%	2	3 304 000
1984	1 978 798	2 111 651	93.7%	2 263 100	87.4%	0.4%	2	3 233 000
1981	1 860 564	2 034 747	91.4%	2 093 750	88.9%	0.5%	2	3 125 000
1978	1 721 443	2 027 594	84.9%	2 091 070	82.3%	0.7%	2	3 121 000
1975	1 612 020	1 938 108	83.2%	1 973 120	81.7%	0.5%	2	3 083 000
1972	1 410 240	1 569 937	89.8%	1 653 000	85.3%	0.6%	2	2 900 000
1969	1 351 813	1 503 952	89.9%	1 578 900	85.6%	0.9%	N/A	2 770 000
1966	1 212 127	1 399 720	86.6%	1 527 600	79.3%	0.6%	N/A	2 680 000
1963	1 205 322	1 345 836	89.6%	1 446 660	83.3%	0.6%	N/A	2 538 000
1960	1 176 963	1 303 955	90.3%	1 375 760	85.6%	0.5%	N/A	2 372 000
1957	1 163 061	1 244 748	93.4%	1 359 690	85.5%	0.5%	N/A	2 229 000
1954	1 105 609	1 169 115	94.6%	1 213 940	91.1%	0.8%	N/A	2 093 000
1951	1 074 070	1 116 375	96.2%	1 129 260	95.1%	0.4%	N/A	1 947 000
1949	1 080 543	1 113 852	97.0%	1 085 180	99.6%	0.7%	N/A	1 871 000
1946	1 055 977	1 081 898	97.6%	1 001 080	105.5%	0.8%	N/A	1 726 000

[1] *Population size calculated on the basis of 1966 census,* [2] *Total votes and registered voters are approximates.*

Parliamentary Elections

Year	Total vote	Registration	Vote/Reg	VAP	Vote/VAP	Invalid	FH	Population
Nicaragua		**Latin America**			**Electoral system: List-PR**		**Voting age: 18**	
1996	1 865 833	2 421 067	77.1%	2 447 120	76.2%	5.0%	6	4 706 000
1990	1 419 384	1 752 088	81.0%	1 935 500	73.3%	6.1%	6	3 871 000
1984[1]	1 171 102	1 551 597	75.5%	1 581 000	74.1%	6.7%	10	3 162 000
1974	799 982	1 152 260	69.4%	1 040 000	76.9%	N/A	9	2 080 000
1972[1]	709 068	970 792	73.0%	955 500	74.2%	N/A	7	1 950 000
1967	540 714	N/A	N/A	833 000	64.9%	N/A	N/A	1 700 000
1963	451 064	570 000	79.1%	755 090	59.7%	N/A	N/A	1 541 000
1957	355 178	N/A	N/A	673 920	52.7%	N/A	N/A	1 296 000
1950[1]	202 698	N/A	N/A	572 400	35.4%	N/A	N/A	1 060 000
1947	169 708	N/A	N/A	527 580	32.2%	N/A	N/A	977 000
Niger		**Africa**			**Electoral system: Parallel**		**Voting age: 18**	
1999	4 560 508	4 587 684	99.4%	4 739 028	96.2%	N/A	10	10 318 141
1996[*]								
1995	1 530 198	4 376 021	35.0%	4 114 800	37.2%	5.5%	8	9 144 000
1993	1 282 473	3 878 178	33.1%	3 762 450	34.1%	4.2%	7	8 361 000
Nigeria		**Africa**			**Electoral system: FPTP**		**Voting age: 18**	
1999	49 136 212	57 938 945	84.8%	52 792 781	93.1%	2.4%	7	108 258 359
1983[2]	25 400 000	65 300 000	38.9%	43 620 780	58.2%	N/A	5	89 022 000
1979	15 686 514	48 499 091	32.3%	38 142 090	41.1%	4.0%	N/A	77 841 000
1959	7 185 555	9 036 083	79.5%	16 532 640	43.5%	N/A	N/A	34 443 000
Norway		**Western Europe**			**Electoral system: List-PR**		**Voting age: 18**	
2001	2 517 497	3 358 856	75.0%	3 446 050	73.1%	N/A	N/A	4 494 368
1997	2 583 809	3 311 215	78.0%	3 360 083	76.9%	0.5%	2	4 363 744
1993	2 472 551	3 259 957	75.8%	3 320 240	74.5%	0.4%	2	4 312 000
1989	2 653 173	3 190 311	83.2%	3 254 790	81.5%	0.2%	2	4 227 000
1985	2 605 436	3 100 479	84.0%	3 114 750	83.6%	0.1%	2	4 153 000
1981	2 462 142	3 003 093	82.0%	2 993 000	82.3%	0.1%	2	4 100 000
1977	2 304 496	2 780 190	82.9%	2 910 960	79.2%	0.1%	2	4 043 000
1973	2 155 734	2 686 676	80.2%	2 692 800	80.1%	0.2%	2	3 960 000
1969	2 162 596	2 579 566	83.8%	2 541 000	85.1%	0.2%	N/A	3 850 000
1965	2 056 091	2 406 866	85.4%	2 418 000	85.0%	0.4%	N/A	3 720 000
1961	1 850 548	2 340 495	79.1%	2 382 600	77.7%	0.6%	N/A	3 610 000
1957	1 800 155	2 298 376	78.3%	2 339 640	76.9%	0.5%	N/A	3 492 000
1953	1 790 331	2 256 799	79.3%	2 250 530	79.6%	0.6%	N/A	3 359 000
1949	1 770 897	2 159 005	82.0%	2 198 440	80.6%	0.7%	N/A	3 233 000
1945	1 498 194	1 961 977	76.4%	2 099 840	71.3%	0.9%	N/A	3 088 000
Pakistan		**Asia**			**Electoral system: FPTP**		**Voting age: 18**	
1997	19 058 131	54 189 534	35.2%	60 565 705	31.5%	2.3%	9	137 649 330
1993	20 293 307	50 377 915	40.3%	54 032 880	37.6%	1.3%	8	122 802 000
1990	21 395 479	47 065 330	45.5%	49 301 560	43.4%	1.1%	8	112 049 000
1988	19 903 172	46 206 055	43.1%	46 379 960	42.9%	1.5%	6	105 409 000
1985	17 250 482	32 589 996	52.9%	41 357 400	41.7%	2.4%	9	96 180 000
1977	17 000 000	30 899 152	55.0%	36 213 120	46.9%	N/A	9	75 444 000
Palau		**Pacific**			**Electoral system: FPTP**		**Voting age: 18**	
2000	10 744	13 239	81.2%	13 159	81.6%	0.2%	3	19 092
1996	10 223	12 897	79.3%	N/A	N/A	N/A	3	17 000
1992	9 726	11 658	83.4%	N/A	N/A	0.1%	N/A	N/A
1988	9 195	11 146	82.5%	N/A	N/A	1.0%	N/A	N/A

[1] Data is for constitutional assembly elections. [2] Total votes and registered voters are approximates. [*] Please refer to www.idea.int/turnout

Year	Total vote	Registration	Vote/Reg	VAP	Vote/VAP	Invalid	FH	Population
1984	8 067	9 605	84.0%	N/A	N/A	1.3%	N/A	N/A
1980	6 425	8 032	80.0%	N/A	N/A	2.5%	N/A	N/A
Palestinian Authority		**Middle East**			**Electoral system: Block**		**Voting age: 18**	
1996[1]	780 079	1 035 235	75.4%	1 035 235	75.4%	N/A	11	1 870 000
Panama		**Latin America**			**Electoral system: Parallel**		**Voting age: 18**	
1999	1 326 663	1 746 989	75.9%	1 744 041	76.1%	3.9%	3	2 808 935
1994	1 105 050	1 500 000	73.7%	1 575 630	70.1%	5.3%	5	2 583 000
1984	631 908	917 677	68.9%	1 195 040	52.9%	3.6%	7	2 134 000
1978	658 421	787 251	83.6%	972 550	67.7%	3.8%	10	1 835 000
1960[2]	124 924	N/A	N/A	541 620	23.1%	N/A	N/A	1 062 000
Papua New Guinea		**Pacific**			**Electoral system: FPTP**		**Voting age: 18**	
1997	2 244 531	3 414 072	65.7%	2 272 626	98.8%	N/A	6	4 250 935
1992	1 614 251	1 987 994	81.2%	2 272 626	71.0%	N/A	5	3 847 000
1987	1 355 477	1 843 128	73.5%	1 775 820	76.3%	N/A	4	3 482 000
1982	1 194 114	2 309 621	51.7%	1 577 940	75.7%	1.8%	4	3 094 000
1977	970 172	1 607 635	60.3%	1 460 160	66.4%	N/A	4	2 808 000
1972	829 963	1 386 845	59.8%	1 341 600	61.9%	N/A	6	2 580 000
1968	734 118	1 515 119	48.5%	1 201 200	61.1%	N/A	N/A	2 310 000
1964	743 489	1 028 339	72.3%	1 113 530	66.8%	N/A	N/A	2 101 000
Paraguay		**Latin America**			**Electoral system: List-PR**		**Voting age: 18**	
1998	1 649 419	2 049 449	80.5%	2 777 725	59.4%	N/A	7	5 137 440
1993	1 124 986	1 698 984	66.2%	2 476 980	45.4%	3.6%	6	4 587 000
1989	1 157 781	2 226 061	52.0%	2 161 170	53.6%	1.9%	7	4 089 000
1988	1 333 436	1 446 675	92.2%	2 100 390	63.5%	0.6%	12	3 963 000
1983	1 048 996	1 132 582	92.6%	1 840 690	57.0%	1.1%	10	3 473 000
1978	1 010 299	1 175 351	86.0%	1 514 700	66.7%	1.3%	10	2 970 000
1973	814 610	1 052 652	77.4%	1 308 300	62.3%	1.3%	10	2 670 000
1968	656 414	897 445	73.1%	1 025 800	64.0%	1.0%	N/A	2 230 000
1963	628 615	738 472	85.1%	856 350	73.4%	1.8%	N/A	1 903 000
1958	303 478	N/A	N/A	792 890	38.3%	N/A	N/A	1 687 000
1953	237 049	N/A	N/A	718 080	33.0%	N/A	N/A	1 496 000
Peru		**Latin America**			**Electoral system: List-PR**		**Voting age: 18**	
2001	12 128 969	14 906 233	81.4%	15 429 603	78.6%	11.1%	N/A	26 076 958
2000	11 942 810	14 567 468	82.0%	15 186 617	78.6%	N/A	6	25 666 297
1995	7 874 240	12 421 164	63.4%	13 649 720	57.7%	44.4%	9	23 534 000
1990	6 867 170	10 042 599	68.4%	12 068 000	56.9%	21.1%	7	21 550 000
1985	6 673 218	8 290 846	80.5%	10 291 010	64.8%	12.4%	5	19 417 000
1980	5 217 364	6 485 680	80.4%	8 993 400	58.0%	21.6%	5	17 295 000
1963	1 954 284	2 070 718	94.4%	5 479 000	35.7%	N/A	N/A	10 958 000
1962	1 969 474	2 222 926	88.6%	5 422 320	36.3%	N/A	N/A	10 632 000
1956	1 324 229	1 575 741	84.0%	5 018 520	26.4%	N/A	N/A	9 651 000
Philippines		**Asia**			**Electoral system: Parallel**		**Voting age: 18**	
2001*								
1998	26 902 536	34 163 465	78.7%	40 287 296	66.8%	N/A	5	73 052 254
1995	25 736 505	36 415 154	70.7%	37 652 450	68.4%	N/A	6	68 459 000
1992[3]	22 654 194	32 105 782	70.6%	34 699 860	65.3%	N/A	6	64 259 000
1987[4]	23 760 000	26 400 000	90.0%	30 398 680	78.2%	N/A	4	57 356 000
1978	18 355 862	21 463 094	85.5%	23 354 940	78.6%	N/A	10	45 794 000

[1] Population in West bank and Gaza Strip according to Stateman's Yearbook 1996-1997, [2] Total votes include only valid votes
*[3] Total votes are approximate, [4] Total votes and registered votes are approximate, * Please refer to www.idea.int/turnout*

Parliamentary Elections

Year	Total vote	Registration	Vote/Reg	VAP	Vote/VAP	Invalid	FH	Population
1969	1 969 474	2 222 926	88.6%	14 665 700	13.4%	1.7%	N/A	35 770 000
1967	7 748 900	9 427 532	82.2%	14 495 300	53.5%	N/A	N/A	33 710 000
Poland		**CIS, Central and Eastern Europe**			**Electoral system: List-PR**		**Voting age: 18**	
2001	13 559 412	29 364 455	46.2%	28 469 123	47.6%	4.0%	N/A	N/A
1997	13 616 378	28 409 054	47.9%	27 901 720	48.8%	3.9%	3	38 752 000
1993	14 415 586	27 677 302	52.1%	27 723 600	52.0%	4.3%	4	38 505 000
1991	11 886 984	27 516 166	43.2%	26 771 500	44.4%	5.6%	4	38 245 000
1989	16 994 732	27 362 313	62.1%	26 572 700	64.0%	N/A	7	37 961 000
Portugal		**Western Europe**			**Electoral system: List-PR**		**Voting age: 18**	
1999	5 406 946	8 857 173	61.0%	7 805 152	69.3%	2.0%	2	9 953 648
1995	5 904 854	8 906 608	66.3%	7 463 960	79.1%	1.9%	2	9 821 000
1991	5 674 332	8 322 481	68.2%	7 301 580	77.7%	1.1%	2	9 867 000
1987	5 623 128	7 741 149	72.6%	7 195 680	78.1%	2.2%	3	9 994 000
1985	5 744 321	7 621 504	75.4%	7 207 920	79.7%	2.7%	3	10 011 000
1983	5 629 996	7 159 349	78.6%	7 271 280	77.4%	2.7%	3	10 099 000
1980	5 917 355	6 925 243	85.4%	6 731 320	87.9%	2.4%	4	9 899 000
1979	5 915 168	6 757 152	87.5%	3 702 760	88.2%	2.9%	4	9 857 000
1976	5 393 853	6 477 619	83.3%	6 476 220	83.3%	4.8%	4	9 666 000
1975	5 666 696	6 177 698	91.7%	6 315 420	89.7%	6.9%	8	9 426 000
Republic of Korea		**Asia**			**Electoral system: Parallel**		**Voting age: 20**	
2000	19 156 515	33 482 387	57.2%	34 364 710	55.7%	1.3%	4	47 203 751
1996	20 122 799	31 488 294	63.9%	30 805 360	65.3%	2.3%	4	45 302 000
1992	20 843 482	29 003 828	71.9%	27 944 320	74.6%	1.3%	5	43 663 000
1988	19 840 815	26 198 205	75.7%	26 899 840	73.8%	1.0%	5	42 031 000
1985	20 286 672	23 987 830	84.6%	24 075 540	84.3%	1.5%	9	40 806 000
1981	16 397 845	20 909 120	78.4%	20 910 420	78.4%	1.2%	11	38 723 000
1978	15 025 370	19 489 490	77.1%	19 963 260	75.3%	1.4%	10	36 969 000
1973	11 196 484	15 690 130	71.4%	16 455 000	68.0%	1.8%	11	32 910 000
1971	11 430 202	15 610 258	73.2%	15 278 400	74.8%	2.1%	N/A	31 830 000
1967	11 202 317	14 717 354	76.1%	14 179 200	79.0%	3.1%	N/A	29 540 000
Romania		**CIS, Central and Eastern Europe**			**Electoral system: List-PR**		**Voting age: 18**	
2000	11 559 458	17 699 727	65.3%	18 597 776	62.2%	6.2%	4	22 303 305
1996	13 088 388	17 218 654	76.0%	16 737 320	78.2%	6.5%	5	22 618 000
1992	12 496 430	16 380 663	76.3%	16 408 080	76.2%	12.7%	8	22 789 000
Russia		**CIS, Central and Eastern Europe**			**Electoral system: Parallel**		**Voting age: 18**	
1999	65 370 690	108 073 956	60.5%	109 211 997	59.9%	2.0%	9	157 065 478
1995	69 587 454	107 496 856	64.7%	110 864 250	62.8%	1.9%	7	147 819 000
1993[1]	52 600 000	105 200 000	50.0%	111 390 000	47.2%	N/A	7	148 520 000
San Marino		**Western Europe**			**Electoral system: List-PR**		**Voting age: 18**	
2001	22 648	30 688	73.8%	22 024	102.8%	3.8%	N/A	26 986
1998	22 673	30 117	75.3%	30 117	75.3%	3.8%	2	25 000
1993	22 637	28 191	80.3%	28 191	80.3%	3.8%	2	24 000
1988	21 139	26 052	81.1%	26 052	81.1%	N/A	N/A	23 000
1983	17 204	21 630	79.5%	21 630	79.5%	N/A	N/A	22 000
1978	15 491	19 615	79.0%	19 615	79.0%	2.6%	N/A	21 000
1974	14 086	17 673	79.7%	17 673	79.7%	2.4%	N/A	20 000

[1] *Total votes and registered votes are approximate.*

Year	Total vote	Registration	Vote/Reg	VAP	Vote/VAP	Invalid	FH	Population
Sao Tome e Principe		**Africa**			**Electoral system: List-PR**		**Voting age: 18**	
1998	32 108	49 639	64.7%	63 536	50.5%	9.1%	3	135 000
1994	29 100	55 862	52.1%	58 750	49.5%	12.9%	3	126 000
1991	39 605	51 610	76.7%	56 870	69.6%	6.1%	5	117 000
Senegal		**Africa**			**Electoral system: Parallel**		**Voting age: 18**	
2001	1 888 911	2 808 253	67.3%	4 655 275	40.6%	0.6%	N/A	9 817 462
1998	1 243 026	3 164 827	39.3%	4 513 760	27.5%	1.1%	8	9 212 000
1993[1]	1 070 539	2 650 000	40.4%	3 994 480	26.8%	0.5%	9	8 152 000
1988	1 118 246	1 932 265	57.9%	2 982 420	37.5%	0.4%	7	7 101 000
1983[2]	1 079 824	1 928 257	56.0%	2 715 880	39.8%	4.0%	8	6 316 000
1978	974 826	1 566 250	62.2%	2 320 710	42.0%	N/A	8	5 397 000
1963[2]	1 202 294	N/A	N/A	1 463 440	82.2%	N/A	N/A	3 326 000
Seychelles		**Africa**			**Electoral system: Parallel**		**Voting age: 18**	
1998	47 568	54 847	86.7%	52 729	90.2%	2.5%	6	78 845
1993	43 579	50 370	86.5%	45 360	96.1%	1.6%	7	72 000
Sierra Leone		**Africa**			**Electoral system: List-PR**		**Voting age: 18**	
1996	750 858	1 244 601	60.3%	2 029 720	37.0%	N/A	9	4 613 000
1977	686 810	N/A	N/A	1 443 940	47.6%	N/A	N/A	3 139 000
1968	652 077	N/A	N/A	1 165 600	55.9%	N/A	N/A	2 480 000
Singapore		**Asia**			**Electoral system: Block**		**Voting age: 21**	
2001[3]	638 403	675 306	94.6%	N/A	N/A	2.1	N/A	N/A
1997[4]	734 000	765 332	95.9%	2 076 210	35.4%	2.4%	10	3 009 000
1991	805 573	847 716	95.0%	1 851 210	43.5%	2.7%	8	2 763 000
1988	1 373 064	1 449 838	94.7%	1 741 330	78.9%	2.3%	9	2 599 000
1984	902 980	944 624	95.6%	1 618 560	55.8%	2.9%	9	2 529 000
1980	654 195	685 141	95.5%	1 424 260	45.9%	2.7%	10	2 414 000
1976	815 130	857 130	95.1%	1 192 360	68.4%	2.3%	10	2 293 000
1972	746 219	908 382	82.1%	1 010 500	73.8%	2.0%	10	2 150 000
1968	77 984	82 883	94.1%	944 700	8.3%	2.7%	N/A	2 010 000
Slovakia		**CIS, Central and Eastern Europe**			**Electoral system: List-PR**		**Voting age: 18**	
1998	3 389 346	4 023 191	84.2%	4 297 856	78.9%	1.7%	4	5 274 335
1994	2 923 265	3 876 555	75.4%	3 849 840	75.9%	1.6%	5	5 347 000
1992[5]	9 750 978	11 515 699	84.7%	11 640 940	83.8%	1.7%	4	15 731 000
1990[5]	10 785 270	11 195 596	96.3%	11 589 140	93.1%	1.4%	4	15 661 000
Slovenia		**CIS, Central and Eastern Europe**			**Electoral system: List-PR**		**Voting age: 18**	
2000	1 116 423	1 586 695	70.4%	1 543 425	72.3%	3.3%	3	1 987 985
1996	1 136 211	1 542 218	73.7%	1 499 960	75.7%	5.9%	3	1 948 000
1992	1 280 243	1 490 434	85.9%	1 497 000	85.5%	7.0%	4	1 996 000
Solomon Islands		**Pacific**			**Electoral system: FPTP**		**Voting age: 18**	
1997	137 787	201 584	68.4%	194 824	70.7%	N/A	2	397 600
1993	105 351	165 620	63.6%	173 950	60.6%	N/A	3	355 000
1989	81 239	125 106	64.9%	145 700	55.8%	N/A	2	310 000
1984	65 637	N/A	N/A	123 740	53.0%	N/A	5	269 000
1980	58 136	99 843	58.2%	106 260	54.7%	N/A	4	231 000

[1] *Registered voters are approximate,* [2] *Total votes are approximate,* [3] *Votes from 13 contested constituencies out of 23 electoral districts,* [4] *Votes from 15 contested constituencies out of 24 constituencies,* [5] *Elections are for Czechoslovakia*

Parliamentary Elections

Year	Total vote	Registration	Vote/Reg	VAP	Vote/VAP	Invalid	FH	Population
Somalia		**Africa**			**Electoral system: Parallel**		**Voting age: 18**	
1969	879 554	N/A	N/A	1 010 100	87.1%	11.1%	N/A	2 730 000
South Africa		**Africa**			**Electoral system: List-PR**		**Voting age: 18**	
1999	16 228 462	18 177 000	89.3%	25 411 573	63.9%	1.5%	3	42 424 823
1994[1]	19 726 579	N/A	N/A	23 063 910	85.5%	N/A	5	40 436 000
Spain		**Western Europe**			**Electoral system: List-PR**		**Voting age: 18**	
2000	23 339 490	33 969 640	68.7%	31 631 640	73.8%	0.7%	3	39 394 773
1996	24 985 097	32 007 554	78.1%	31 013 030	80.6%	1.5%	3	39 257 000
1993	23 907 495	31 030 511	77.0%	30 875 570	77.4%	1.3%	3	39 083 000
1989	20 788 160	29 694 055	70.0%	29 166 000	71.3%	1.4%	2	38 888 000
1986	20 489 651	29 117 613	70.4%	27 794 880	73.7%	2.1%	3	38 604 000
1982	21 439 152	26 855 301	79.8%	25 795 580	83.1%	2.4%	3	37 935 000
1979	18 284 948	26 836 500	68.1%	25 284 440	72.3%	1.8%	4	37 183 000
1977	18 175 327	23 616 421	77.0%	22 901 130	79.4%	1.7%	4	36 351 000
Sri Lanka		**Asia**			**Electoral system: List-PR**		**Voting age: 18**	
2000	9 128 823	12 071 062	75.6%	11 110 498	82.2%	N/A	7	19 051 116
1994	8 344 095	10 945 065	76.2%	11 254 950	74.1%	4.8%	9	17 865 000
1989	5 961 815	9 374 880	63.6%	10 263 250	58.1%	6.1%	9	16 825 000
1977	5 780 283	6 667 589	86.7%	7 528 680	76.8%	N/A	5	13 942 000
1970	4 672 656	5 505 028	84.9%	6 505 200	71.8%	N/A	N/A	12 510 000
1965	3 821 918	4 710 887	81.1%	5 803 200	65.9%	N/A	N/A	11 160 000
1960	2 827 075	3 724 507	75.9%	5 142 800	55.0%	N/A	N/A	3 890 000
1960	2 889 282	3 724 507	77.6%	5 142 800	56.2%	N/A	N/A	9 890 000
1956	2 391 538	3 464 159	69.0%	4 643 080	51.5%	N/A	N/A	8 929 000
1952	2 114 615	2 990 912	70.7%	4 279 220	49.4%	N/A	N/A	8 074 000
1947[2]	1 701 150	3 048 145	55.8%	3 714 770	45.8%	N/A	N/A	7 009 000[1]
St. Kitts & Nevis		**North America & the Caribbean**			**Electoral system: FPTP**		**Voting age: 18**	
2000	21 949	34 166	64.2%	25 892	84.8%	0.5%	3	40 976
1995	21 690	31 726	68.4%	31 185	69.6%	N/A	3	42 000
1993	19 256	28 987	66.4%	N/A	N/A	0.3%	2	N/A
1989[3]	17 682	26 481	66.8%	26 775	66.0%	0.5%	2	42 000
1984	18 135	23 328	77.7%	25 300	71.7%	0.4%	2	46 000
1980	14 850	19 921	74.5%	21 120	70.3%	1.0%	5	44 000
1975	12 743	17 685	72.1%	22 560	56.5%	4.0%	N/A	48 000
1971	15 126	17 209	87.9%	32 340	46.8%	3.5%	N/A	70 000
1966	14 774	20 122	73.4%	27 120	54.5%	4.3%	N/A	60 000
1961	12 588	18 310	68.7%	26 078	48.3%	3.8%	N/A	59 000
1957[4]	9 833	N/A	N/A	24 304	40.5%	N/A	N/A	56 000
1952	12 407	12 966	95.7%	21 624	57.4%	2.0%	N/A	51 000
St. Lucia		**North America & the Caribbean**			**Electoral system: FPTP**		**Voting age: 18**	
1997[4]	73 535	111 330	66.1%	82 140	89.5%	2.1%	3	145 077
1992[4]	73 535	97 403	75.5%	79 597	92.4%	3.1%	3	137 000
1987[4]	53 883	83 153	64.8%	74 834	72.0%	2.3%	3	142 000
1987[4]	61 155	83 257	73.5%	74 834	81.7%	2.1%	3	142 000
1982[4]	49 590	75 343	65.8%	75 343	65.8%	2.2%	4	124 000
1979[4]	46 191	67 917	68.0%	67 917	68.0%	2.6%	5	118 000
1974[4]	33 498	39 815	84.1%	42 900	78.1%	3.0%	N/A	110 000
1969[4]	23 892	44 868	53.2%	40 100	59.6%	3.7%	N/A	100 000
1964[4]	19 601	37 748	51.9%	44 900	43.7%	4.5%	N/A	100 000

[1] *No voter registration took place in South Africa in 1994,* [2] *Population figure is calculated from growth rate between 1949-1950,* [3] *Total votes are approximate,* [4] *Annual VAP calculated from preceding census years.*

Year	Total vote	Registration	Vote/Reg	VAP	Vote/VAP	Invalid	FH	Population
1961[1]	19 362	N/A	N/A	46 754	41.4%	N/A	N/A	97 000
1957[1]	22 244	39 147	56.8%	47 320	47.0%	3.0%	N/A	91 000
1954[1]	17 006	34 452	49.4%	47 300	36.0%	7.5%	N/A	86 000
1951[1]	16 786	28 398	59.1%	46 980[2]	35.7%	8.1%	N/A	81 000

St. Vincent & the Grenadines	North America & the Caribbean				Electoral system: FPTP		Voting age: 18	
2001	58 498	84 536	69.2%	63 986	91.4%	0.4%	N/A	114 417
1998	51 513	76 469	67.4%	66 812	77.1%	0.4%	3	114 996
1994	47 212	71 954	65.6%	64 491	73.2%	0.6%	3	111 000
1989	44 218	61 091	72.4%	57 558	76.8%	0.8%	3	106 000
1984	42 507	47 863	88.8%	52 832	80.5%	0.7%	4	104 000
1979	33 276	52 073	63.9%	57 120	58.3%	1.0%	4	119 000
1974	28 574	45 181	63.2%	36 630	78.0%	0.8%	N/A	90 000
1972	32 289	42 707	75.6%	40 600	79.5%	1.1%	N/A	100 000
1967	27 278	33 044	82.6%	36 360	75.0%	1.1%	N/A	90 000
1966	27 787	33 044	84.1%	36 270	76.6%	2.0%	N/A	90 000
1961	23 976	31 086	77.1%	32 882	72.9%	2.7%	N/A	82 000
1957	21 943	30 960	70.9%	32 718	67.1%	10.4%	N/A	82 000
1954	17 465	29 188	59.8%	28 584	61.1%	10.4%	N/A	72 000
1951	19 110	27 409	69.7%	27 324	69.9%	6.8%	N/A	69 000

Sudan	Africa				Electoral system: FPTP		Voting age: 18	
1996[2]	5 525 280	7 652 742	72.2%	15 253 500	36.2%	3.3%	14	30 507 000
1986[4]								
1968	1 825 510	3 049 813	59.9%	6 573 600	27.8%	N/A	N/A	14 940 000

Suriname	Latin America				Electoral system: List-PR		Voting age: 18	
2000	185 064	264 961	69.8%	255 841	72.3%	2.6%	3	416 901
1996	179 416	269 165	66.7%	251 930	71.2%	3.3%	6	427 000
1991[3]	158 809	246 926	64.3%	234 320	67.8%	N/A	8	404 000
1987	177 025	208 356	85.0%	212 850	83.2%	2.0%	8	387 000
1977[3]	123 720	159 082	77.8%	141 180	87.6%	N/A	4	362 000
1973[3]	122 711	161 400	76.0%	156 000	78.7%	N/A	N/A	400 000
1969	204 041	N/A	N/A	140 400	145.3%	N/A	N/A	360 000
1967	207 119	N/A	N/A	143 500	144.3%	N/A	N/A	350 000

Sweden	Western Europe				Electoral system: List-PR		Voting age: 18	
1998	5 374 588	6 603 129	81.4%	6 915 438	77.7%	2.1%	2	8 780 000
1994	5 725 246	6 496 365	88.1%	6 848 400	83.6%	1.5%	2	8 780 000
1991	5 562 920	6 413 172	86.7%	6 721 260	82.8%	1.7%	2	8 617 000
1988	5 441 050	6 330 023	86.0%	6 580 860	82.7%	1.2%	2	8 437 000
1985	5 615 242	6 249 445	89.9%	6 513 000	86.2%	0.9%	2	8 350 000
1982	5 606 603	6 130 993	91.4%	6 327 000	88.6%	0.9%	2	8 325 000
1979	5 480 126	6 040 461	90.7%	6 303 440	86.9%	0.6%	2	8 294 000
1976	5 457 043	5 947 077	91.8%	6 166 500	88.5%	0.4%	2	8 222 000
1973	5 168 996	5 690 333	90.8%	6 023 600	85.8%	0.2%	2	8 140 000
1970	4 984 207	5 645 804	88.3%	5 708 400	87.3%	0.2%	N/A	8 040 000
1968	5 861 901	5 445 333	89.3%	5 616 100	86.6%	0.7%	N/A	7 910 000
1964	4 273 595	5 095 850	83.9%	5 286 090	80.8%	0.7%	N/A	7 661 000
1960	4 271 610	4 972 177	85.9%	5 161 200	82.8%	0.4%	N/A	7 480 000
1958	3 864 963	4 992 421	77.4%	5 112 210	75.6%	0.5%	N/A	7 409 000
1956	3 902 114	4 902 114	79.6%	5 047 350	77.3%	0.6%	N/A	7 315 000
1952	3 801 284	4 805 216	79.1%	4 916 250	77.3%	0.5%	N/A	7 125 000
1948	3 895 161	4 707 783	82.7%	4 749 270	82.0%	0.4%	N/A	6 883 000

[1] Annual VAP calculated from preceding census years, [2] Registered voters are approximate. [3] Total votes include only valid votes, [4] Please refer to www.idea.int/turnout

Parliamentary Elections

Year	Total vote	Registration	Vote/Reg	VAP	Vote/VAP	Invalid	FH	Population
Switzerland		**Western Europe**			**Electoral system: List-PR**		**Voting age: 18**	
1999	2 004 540	4 638 284	43.2%	5 736 298	34.9%	1.0%	2	7 214 950
1995	1 940 646	4 593 772	42.2%	5 442 360	35.7%	2.3%	2	7 068 000
1991	2 076 886	4 510 784	46.0%	5 236 000	39.7%	1.6%	2	6 800 000
1987	1 958 469	4 125 078	47.5%	4 908 750	39.9%	1.2%	2	6 545 000
1983	1 990 012	4 068 532	48.9%	4 878 750	40.8%	1.5%	2	6 505 000
1979	1 856 689	3 863 169	48.1%	4 572 720	40.6%	1.3%	2	6 351 000
1975	1 955 752	3 733 113	52.4%	4 483 500	43.6%	1.2%	2	6 405 000
1971	2 000 135	3 548 860	56.4%	2 055 900	97.3%	1.3%	N/A	6 230 000
1967[1]	1 019 907	1 599 479	63.8%	1 916 800	53.2%	1.8%	N/A	5 990 000
1963[1]	986 997	1 531 164	64.5%	1 846 400	53.5%	1.8%	N/A	5 770 000
1959[1]	1 008 563	1 473 155	68.5%	1 735 470	58.1%	1.9%	N/A	5 259 000
1955[1]	998 881	1 453 807	68.7%	1 643 400	60.8%	1.7%	N/A	4 980 000
1951[1]	986 937	1 414 308	69.8%	1 567 170	63.0%	1.9%	N/A	4 749 000
1947[1]	985 499	1 374 740	71.7%	1 492 920	66.0%	1.9%	N/A	4 524 000
Syria		**Middle East**			**Electoral system: FPTP**		**Voting age: 18**	
1998[*]								
1994	3 693 656	6 037 885	61.2%	6 368 240	58.0%	N/A	14	13 844 000
Taiwan (Republic of China)		**Asia**			**Electoral system: Parallel**		**Voting age: 18**	
1998	10 188 302	14 961 930	68.1%	N/A	N/A	1.5%	4	N/A
1996	10 769 224	14 130 084	76.2%	14 340 580	75.1%	3.2%	6	21 311 000
1995[2]	9 574 388	14 153 424	67.6%	14 273 013	67.1%	1.4%	6	21 258 000
1992	9 666 020	13 421 170	72.0%	13 576 697	71.2%	1.8%	6	20 340 000
1991	8 938 622	13 083 119	68.3%	13 338 634	67.0%	2.0%	6	20 491 000
Tajikistan		**CIS, Central and Eastern Europe**			**Electoral system: TRS**		**Voting age: 18**	
2000	2 683 010	2 873 745	93.4%	3 135 743	85.6%	2.5%	12	6 244 770
1995	2 254 560	2 684 000	84.0%	3 112 530	72.4%	N/A	14	6 103 000
Tanzania		**Africa**			**Electoral system: FPTP**		**Voting age: 18**	
2000	7 341 067	10 088 484	72.8%	16 055 200	45.7%	4.6%	8	33 517 000
1995	6 831 578	8 928 816	76.5%	14 256 000	47.9%	5.5%	10	29 700 000
Thailand		**Asia**			**Electoral system: Block**		**Voting age: 18**	
2001	29 909 271	42 759 001	69.9%	42 663 353	70.1%	N/A	N/A	62 862 098
1996	24 060 744	38 564 836	62.4%	N/A	N/A	1.7%	7	60 652 000
1995	23 462 746	37 817 983	62.0%	36 997 720	63.4%	3.8%	7	60 034 000
1992	19 224 201	32 432 087	59.3%	36 620 740	52.5%	4.3%	7	57 760 000
1988	16 944 931	26 658 637	63.6%	30 923 200	54.8%	3.5%	6	54 326 000
1986[3]	15 104 400	24 600 000	61.4%	27 830 830	54.3%	N/A	6	52 511 000
1983	12 295 339	24 224 470	50.8%	26 213 270	46.9%	4.1%	7	49 459 000
1976	9 084 104	20 791 018	43.7%	18 902 400	48.1%	5.0%	12	42 960 000
1975[4]	8 695 000	18 500 000	47.0%	18 902 400	46.0%	N/A	8	41 896 000
1969	7 285 831	14 820 180	49.2%	15 097 300	48.3%	5.9%	N/A	35 110 000
1957	4 370 789	9 917 417	44.1%	11 108 080	39.3%	N/A	N/A	24 148 000
1957	5 668 566	9 859 039	57.5%	11 108 080	51.0%	N/A	N/A	24 148 000
1952	2 961 291	7 602 591	39.0%	8 828 780	33.5%	N/A	N/A	19 193 000
1948	2 117 464	7 176 891	29.5%	8 191 680	25.8%	N/A	N/A	17 808 000
1946	2 091 827	6 431 827	32.5%	7 838 860	26.7%	N/A	N/A	17 041 000
Togo		**Africa**			**Electoral system: TRS**		**Voting age: 18**	
1999[*]								

[1] VAP includes only men. [2] Figure for population of 15 years of age and over in 1995, [3] Total votes and registered votes are approximate, [4] Registered voters are approximate, [*] Please refer to www.idea.int/turnout

Year	Total vote	Registration	Vote/Reg	VAP	Vote/VAP	Invalid	FH	Population
1997[1]	1 300 000	N/A	N/A	2 065 440	62.9%	N/A	11	4 303 000
1994	1 302 400	2 000 000	65.1%	1 885 440	69.1%	N/A	11	3 928 000
1990[1]	1 300 000	N/A	N/A	1 730 190	75.1%	N/A	12	3 531 000
1985	1 036 975	1 318 979	78.6%	1 483 720	69.9%	N/A	12	3 028 000
Tonga		**Pacific**			**Electoral system: FPTP**		**Voting age: 21**	
1999	27 867	54 912	50.7%	52 065	53.5%	N/A	8	96 829
1996	27 948	49 830	56.1%	66 796	41.8%	0.7%	8	96 020
1993	28 515	48 487	58.8%	N/A	N/A	0.8%	8	N/A
1987	25 253	42 496	59.4%	40 920	61.7%	N/A	8	93 000
Trinidad & Tobago		**North America & the Caribbean**			**Electoral system: FPTP**		**Voting age: 18**	
2000	597 525	947 689	63.1%	853 781	70.0%	0.5%	4	1 289 594
1995	530 311	837 741	63.3%	788 020	67.3%	0.9%	3	1 271 000
1991	522 472	794 486	65.8%	742 200	70.4%	0.5%	2	1 237 000
1986	577 300	882 029	65.5%	717 600	80.4%	0.7%	3	1 196 000
1981	415 416	736 104	56.4%	644 960	64.4%	0.6%	4	1 112 000
1976	315 809	565 646	55.8%	491 520	64.3%	1.2%	4	1 024 000
1971	118 597	357 568	33.2%	463 500	25.6%	0.1%	N/A	1 030 000
1966	302 548	459 839	65.8%	445 500	67.9%	0.1%	N/A	990 000
1961	333 512	378 511	88.1%	398 820	83.6%	0.1%	N/A	867 000
1956	271 534	339 028	80.1%	331 660	81.9%	2.6%	N/A	721 000
1950	198 458	283 150	70.1%	288 420	68.8%	4.3%	N/A	627 000
1946	137 281	259 512	52.9%	256 666	53.5%	6.1%	N/A	557 970
Tunisia		**Africa**			**Electoral system: Parallel**		**Voting age: 18**	
1999	3 100 098	3 387 542	91.5%	5 563 704	55.7%	0.3%	11	9 466 018
1994	2 841 557	2 976 366	95.5%	4 715 820	60.3%	0.3%	11	8 733 000
1989	2 073 925	2 711 925	76.5%	4 113 200	50.4%	1.5%	8	7 910 000
1986	2 175 093	2 622 482	82.9%	3 657 850	59.5%	0.5%	11	7 465 000
1981	1 962 127	2 321 031	84.5%	3 085 550	63.6%	1.0%	10	6 565 000
Turkey		**Western Europe**			**Electoral system: List-PR**		**Voting age: 20**	
1999	32 656 070	37 495 217	87.1%	40 626 996	80.4%	4.5%	9	64 504 287
1995	29 101 469	34 155 981	85.2%	36 812 460	79.1%	3.4%	10	62 394 000
1991	25 157 123	29 979 123	83.9%	31 529 300	79.8%	2.9%	6	57 326 000
1987	24 603 541	26 376 926	93.3%	26 806 110	91.8%	2.6%	6	52 561 000
1983	18 214 104	19 740 500	92.3%	24 112 290	75.5%	4.8%	9	47 279 000
1977	14 785 814[1]	21 000 000	70.4%	22 137 040	66.8%	N/A	5	41 768 000
1973	11 223 843	16 798 164	66.8%	19 800 800	56.7%	4.4%	6	37 360 000
1969	9 516 035	14 788 552	64.3%	16 059 900	59.3%	5.0%	N/A	34 170 000
1961	10 522 716	12 925 395	81.4%	14 014 980	75.1%	3.7%	N/A	28 602 000
1950	7 815 000	8 906 107	87.7%	10 048 800	77.8%	N/A	N/A	20 935 000
Tuvalu		**Pacific**			**Electoral system: FPTP**		**Voting age: 18**	
1998[4]								
1981[2]	2 862	3 368	85.0%	3368	N/A	N/A	4	7 000
1977[2]	2 256	2 862	78.8%	2862	N/A	N/A	4	6 000
Uganda		**Africa**			**Electoral system: FPTP**		**Voting age: 18**	
2001	7 576 144	10 775 836	70.3%	10 206 461	74.2%	2.7%	N/A	22 070 329
1996[3]	5 027 166	8 477 320	59.3%	9 875 250	50.9%	N/A	9	21 945 000
1980	4 179 111	4 899 146	85.3%	6 062 340	68.9%	N/A	10	13 179 000
1962	1 052 534	1 553 233	67.8%	3 297 520	31.9%	N/A	N/A	7 016 000

[1]Total votes are approximate, [2]VAP equals registered voters, [3]Total votes include only valid votes, [4]Please refer to www.idea.int/turnout

Parliamentary Elections

Year	Total vote	Registration	Vote/Reg	VAP	Vote/VAP	Invalid	FH	Population
Ukraine		**CIS, Central and Eastern Europe**			**Electoral system: Parallel**		**Voting age: 18**	
1998	26 521 273	37 540 092	70.6%	38 939 136	68.1%	3.1%	7	51 235 704
1994	28 963 982	38 204 100	75.8%	39 451 600	73.4%	6.3%	7	51 910 000
United Kingdom		**Western Europe**			**Electoral system: FPTP**		**Voting age: 18**	
2001	26 365 192	44 403 238	59.4%	45 804 132	57.6%	N/A	N/A	59 434 645
1997[1]	31 289 097	43 784 559	71.5%	45 093 510	69.4%	N/A	3	58 563 000
1992	33 653 800	43 240 084	77.8%	44 658 460	75.4%	0.1%	3	57 998 000
1987	32 566 523	43 180 573	75.4%	43 326 080	75.2%	0.1%	2	57 008 000
1983	30 722 241	42 192 999	72.8%	42 846 520	71.7%	0.2%	2	56 377 000
1979	31 233 208	41 095 490	76.0%	41 608 720	75.1%	0.4%	2	56 228 000
1974	29 226 810	40 072 970	72.9%	40 298 400	72.5%	0.1%	2	55 970 000
1974	31 382 414	39 753 863	78.9%	40 298 400	77.9%	0.1%	2	55 970 000
1970	28 386 145	39 342 013	72.2%	39 895 200	71.2%	0.1%	N/A	55 410 000
1966	27 314 646	35 957 245	76.0%	37 026 000	73.8%	0.2%	N/A	54 450 000
1964	27 698 221	35 894 054	77.2%	36 864 840	75.1%	0.1%	N/A	54 213 000
1959	27 862 652	35 397 304	78.7%	35 968 320	77.5%	N/A	N/A	52 128 000
1955	26 759 729	34 852 179	76.8%	35 327 310	75.7%	N/A	N/A	51 199 000
1951	28 596 594	34 919 331	81.9%	35 148 400	81.4%	N/A	N/A	50 202 000
1950	28 771 124	34 412 255	83.6%	35 261 100	81.6%	N/A	N/A	50 373 000
1945	24 117 191	33 240 391	72.6%	34 427 400	70.1%	N/A	N/A	49 182 000
United States of America		**North America & the Caribbean**			**Electoral system: FPTP**		**Voting age: 18**	
2000[1]	99 738 383	205 800 000	48.5%	213 954 023	46.6%	N/A	2	284 970 789
1998[1]	73 117 022	141 850 558	51.5%	210 446 120	34.7%	N/A	2	280 298 524
1996[1]	96 456 345	146 211 960	66.0%	196 511 000	49.1%	N/A	2	165 679 000
1994[1]	75 105 860	130 292 822	57.6%	193 650 000	38.8%	N/A	2	262 090 745
1992[1]	104 405 155	133 821 178	78.0%	189 529 000	55.1%	N/A	2	255 407 000
1990[1]	67 859 189	121 105 630	56.0%	185 812 000	36.5%	N/A	2	248 709 873
1988[1]	91 594 693	126 379 628	72.5%	182 778 000	50.1%	N/A	2	245 057 000
1986[1]	64 991 128	118 399 984	54.9%	178 566 000	36.4%	N/A	2	239 529 693
1984[1]	92 652 680	124 150 614	74.6%	174 466 000	53.1%	N/A	2	236 681 000
1982[1]	67 615 576	110 671 225	61.1%	169 938 000	39.8%	N/A	2	233 697 676
1980[1]	86 515 221	113 043 734	76.5%	164 597 000	52.6%	N/A	2	227 738 000
1978[1]	58 917 938	103 291 265	57.0%	158 373 000	37.2%	N/A	2	221 537 514
1976[1]	81 555 789	105 037 989	77.6%	152 309 190	53.5%	N/A	2	218 035 000
1974[1]	55 943 834	96 199 020	58.2%	146 336 000	38.2%	N/A	2	214 305 134
1972[1]	77 718 554	97 328 541	79.9%	140 776 000	55.2%	N/A	2	208 840 000
1970[1]	58 014 338	82 496 747	70.3%	124 498 000	46.6%	N/A	N/A	203 211 926
1968[1]	73 211 875	81 658 180	89.7%	120 328 186	60.8%	N/A	N/A	200 710 000
1966[1]	56 188 046	N/A	N/A	116 132 000	48.4%	N/A	N/A	197 730 744
1964[1]	70 644 592	N/A	N/A	114 090 000	61.9%	N/A	N/A	192 119 000
1962[1]	53 141 227	N/A	N/A	112 423 000	47.3%	N/A	N/A	186 512 143
1960[1]	68 838 204	N/A	N/A	109 159 000	63.1%	N/A	N/A	180 684 000
1958[1]	45 966 070	N/A	N/A	103 221 000	44.5%	N/A	N/A	175 038 232
1956[1]	58 434 811	N/A	N/A	106 408 890	54.9%	N/A	N/A	168 903 000
1954[1]	42 509 905	N/A	N/A	98 527 000	43.1%	N/A	N/A	162 725 667
1952[1]	57 582 333	N/A	N/A	96 466 000	59.7%	N/A	N/A	157 022 000
1950[1]	40 253 267	N/A	N/A	94 403 000	42.6%	N/A	N/A	151 325 798
1948[1]	45 839 622	N/A	N/A	95 310 150	48.1%	N/A	N/A	146 631 000
1946[1]	34 279 158	N/A	N/A	88 388 000	38.8%	N/A	N/A	142 049 065
Uruguay		**Latin America**			**Electoral system: List-PR**		**Voting age: 18**	
1999[1]	2 202 884	2 402 014	91.7%	2 329 231	94.6%	0.4%	3	3 313 283
1994[1]	2 130 618	2 330 154	91.4%	2 216 900	96.1%	4.7%	5	3 167 000
1989[1]	2 056 355	2 319 022	88.7%	2 123 130	96.9%	4.2%	3	3 077 000
1984[1]	1 930 931	2 197 503	87.9%	2 033 200	95.0%	3.2%	9	2 990 000

[1] *Total votes include only valid votes.*

Year	Total vote	Registration	Vote/Reg	VAP	Vote/VAP	Invalid	FH	Population
1971[1]	1 726 049	1 878 132	91.9%	1 956 400	88.2%	2.8%	N/A	2 920 000
1966[1]	1 231 762	1 658 368	74.3%	1 842 500	66.9%	N/A	N/A	2 750 000
1962[1]	1 171 020	1 528 239	76.6%	1 952 380	60.0%	N/A	N/A	2 914 000
1958[1]	1 005 362	1 410 105	71.3%	1 850 540	54.3%	N/A	N/A	2 762 000
1954[1]	879 242	1 295 502	67.9%	1 727 930	50.9%	N/A	N/A	2 579 000
1950[1]	828 403	1 168 206	70.9%	1 612 690	51.4%	N/A	N/A	2 407 000
1946[1]	670 229	993 892	67.4%	1 528 270	43.9%	N/A	N/A	2 281 000
Uzbekistan		**CIS, Central and Eastern Europe**			**Electoral system: TRS**			**Voting age: 18**
1999	11 873 065	12 703 488	93.5%	13 087 167	90.7%	N/A	13	24 305 971
1995	10 511 667	11 248 464	93.4%	12 339 000	85.2%	N/A	14	22 850 000
1994	10 526 654	11 248 464	93.6%	12 068 460	87.2%	6.4%	14	22 349 000
Vanuatu		**Pacific**			**Electoral system: SNTV**			**Voting age: 18**
1998	42 778	107 297	39.9%	89 820	47.6%	0.1%	4	186 277
1995	76 522	105 631	72.4%	97 362	78.6%	0.6%	4	169 000
1991	62 575	87 695	71.4%	88 458	70.7%	N/A	5	153 000
1987[2]	58 100	70 000	83.0%	83 833	69.3%	N/A	6	145 000
1983	44 726	59 712	74.9%	71 692	62.4%	0.1%	6	124 000
Venezuela		**Latin America**			**Electoral system: MMP**			**Voting age: 18**
2000	6 573 663	11 623 547	56.6%	14 131 207	46.5%	N/A	8	24 185 517
1998	5 792 391	11 002 589	52.6%	13 577 150	42.7%	14.5%	5	23 237 250
1993[2]	6 000 000	10 000 000	60.0%	12 012 960	49.9%	N/A	6	20 712 000
1988	7 500 085	9 185 647	81.7%	10 316 320	72.7%	3.8%	3	18 422 000
1983	6 825 180	7 777 892	87.8%	8 852 760	77.1%	3.6%	3	16 394 000
1978	5 449 790	6 223 903	87.6%	7 316 920	74.5%	3.1%	3	14 071 000
1973	4 572 187	4 737 152	96.5%	5 640 000	81.1%	3.8%	4	11 280 000
1968	3 907 823	4 134 928	94.5%	4 617 600	84.6%	5.9%	N/A	9 620 000
1963	3 059 434	3 367 787	90.8%	3 909 120	78.3%	6.5%	N/A	8 144 000
1958	2 684 949	2 913 801	92.1%	3 370 710	79.7%	3.9%	N/A	6 879 000
1947[3]	1 183 764	N/A	N/A	2 274 000	52.1%	N/A	N/A	4 548 000
Western Samoa		**Pacific**			**Electoral system: FPTP**			**Voting age: 18**
2001	76 934	93 213	82.5%	100 416	76.6%	0.6%	N/A	182 574
1996	67 469	78 137	86.3%	64 220	105.1%	0.4%	4	169 000
1991[4]	44 460	57 000	78.0%	57 400	77.5%	N/A	4	164 000
Yugoslavia[6]		**CIS, Central and Eastern Europe**			**Electoral System:List-PR**			**Voting Age: 18**
2000	5 036 478	784 8818	64.2%	N/A	N/A	N/A	8	N/A
1996	4 047 230	7 594 404	53.3%	7 755 520	52.2%	N/A	12	10 624 000
1993	4 983 606	7 394 772	67.4%	7 654 050	65.1%	5.5%	12	10 485 000
1992	4 080 465	7 277 471	56.1%	7 520 400	54.3%	11.0%	11	10 445 000
1953	9 455 980	10 580 648	89.4%	11 214 060	84.3%	N/A	N/A	16 991 000
1950	9 061 780	9 856 501	91.9%	10 559 250	85.8%	N/A	N/A	16 245 000
1945	7 432 469	8 383 455	64.2%	10 158 550	73.2%	N/A	N/A	15 629 000
Yemen		**Middle East**			**Electoral system: FPTP**			**Voting age: 18**
1997	2 792 675	4 600 000	60.7%	7 772 625	35.9%	N/A	11	16 900 000
1993[5]	2 179 942	2 700 000	80.7%	5 781 940	37.7%	N/A	9	12 302 000
Zambia		**Africa**			**Electoral system: FPTP**			**Voting age: 18**
1996	1 779 607	2 267 382	78.5%	4 467 520	39.8%	N/A	9	9 712 000
1991	1 325 038	2 981 895	44.4%	3 869 520	34.2%	3.4%	5	8 412 000

[1] *Total votes include only valid votes,* [2] *Total votes and registered voters are approximations,* [3] *Total votes are approximate,* [4] *Total votes and registered voters are approximates,* [5] *Registered voters are approximate,* [6] *Federal republic of*

Parliamentary Elections

Year	Total vote	Registration	Vote/Reg	VAP	Vote/VAP	Invalid	FH	Population
1968	962 150	2 981 895	32.3%	1 924 800	50.0%	6.6%	N/A	4 010 000

Zimbabwe		Africa			Electoral system: FPTP		Voting age: 18	
2000	2 556 261	5 288 804	48.3%	6 392 195	40.0%	5.4%	11	13 047 482
1995	1 485 660	4 822 289	30.8%	5 718 500	26.0%	5.5%	10	11 437 000
1990	2 235 425	N/A	N/A	4 590 810	47.8%	N/A	10	9 369 000
1985	2 972 146	N/A	N/A	3 938 130	75.5%	1.5%	10	8 379 000
1980	2 702 275	N/A	N/A	3 213 000	84.1%	N/A	7	7 140 000
1979[1]	1 852 772	2 900 000	63.1%	3 118 500	59.4%	3.6%	9	6 930 000

[1] *Registered voters is approximate*

PRESIDENTIAL ELECTIONS

1945-2001

Presidential Elections

Year	Total vote	Registration	Vote/Reg	VAP	Vote/VAP	Invalid	FH	Population
Algeria		**Africa**						
1999	10 652 623	17 488 757	60.9%	16 705 217	63.8%	N/A	11	30 932 382
1995	12 087 281	15 969 904	75.7%	15 090 300	80.1%	3.9%	12	25 533 000
Angola		**Africa**						
1992	4 401 339	4 828 486	91.2%	4 986 230	88.3%	N/A	12	10 609 000
Argentina		**Latin America**						
1999[1]	18 953 456	24 109 306	78.6%	23 877 270	79.4%	N/A	5	36 554 185
1995	17 939 156	22 158 612	81.0%	22 488 050	79.8%	3.7%	5	34 597 000
1989[2]	17 021 951	20 022 072	85.0%	20 552 960	82.8%	2.1%	3	32 114 000
1983	14 927 572	17 929 951	83.3%	19 257 550	77.5%	N/A	6	29 627 000
1973	11 897 443	14 302 497	83.2%	16 315 200	72.9%	N/A	9	24 720 000
1963	9 717 677	11 353 936	85.6%	13 919 100	69.8%	21.3%	N/A	21 719 000
1958	9 088 497	10 002 327	90.9%	12 837 120	70.8%	9.2%	N/A	20 058 000
1951	7 593 948	8 633 998	88.0%	11 286 400	67.3%	1.6%	N/A	17 635 000
1946	2 839 507	3 405 173	83.4%	10 018 560	28.3%	2.5%	N/A	15 654 000
Armenia		**CIS, Central and Eastern Europe**						
1998	1 567 702	2 300 816	68.1%	2 377 830	65.9%	1.6%	8	3 658 200
1996	1 333 204	2 210 189	60.3%	2 366 000	56.3%	4.4%	9	3 640 000
Austria		**Western Europe**						
1998	4 351 272	5 848 584	74.4%	6 344 138	68.6%	4.2%	2	8 087 215
1992	4 592 927	5 676 903	80.9%	6 070 680	75.7%	3.2%	2	7 884 000
1986	4 745 849	5 436 846	87.3%	5 673 750	83.6%	3.7%	2	7 565 000
1980	4 779 054	5 215 875	91.6%	5 510 770	86.7%	7.3%	2	7 549 000
1974	4 733 016	5 031 772	94.1%	5 346 300	88.5%	2.2%	2	7 530 000
1971	4 787 706	5 024 324	95.3%	5 222 000	91.7%	1.6%	N/A	7 460 000
1965	4 679 427	4 874 928	96.0%	5 075 000	92.2%	2.0%	N/A	7 250 000
1963	4 654 657	4 869 928	95.6%	5 020 400	92.7%	3.9%	N/A	7 172 000
1957	4 499 565	4 630 997	97.2%	4 967 870	90.6%	1.8%	N/A	6 997 000
1951	4 373 194	4 513 597	96.9%	4 926 690	88.8%	4.3%	N/A	6 939 000
Azerbaijan		**CIS, Central and Eastern Europe**						
1998	3 359 633	4 255 717	78.9%	4 667 748	72.0%	N/A	10	7 555 645
1993	3 966 327	4 620 000	85.9%	4 213 440	94.1%	N/A	12	7 392 000
Bangladesh		**Asia**						
1986	25 916 291	47 912 443	54.1%	48 803 040	53.1%	N/A	9	101 673 000
1981	21 677 560	38 951 014	55.7%	43 419 360	49.9%	N/A	7	90 457 000
Belarus		**CIS, Central and Eastern Europe**						
2001	6 169 087	7 356 343	83.9%	7 584 762	81.3%	2.2%	N/A	10 112 278
1994	5 032 800	7 200 000	69.9%	7 662 700	65.7%	N/A	8	10 355 000
Benin		**Africa**						
2001*								
1999*								
1996	1 958 855	2 517 970	77.8%	2 686 990	72.9%	2.8%	4	5 717 000
1991	1 315 123	2 052 638	64.1%	2 297 830	57.2%	0.8%	5	4 889 000

[1] *Total votes include only valid votes,* [2] *Total votes and registered votes are taken from preliminary estimates.*
* *Please refer to www.idea.int/turnout*

Year	Total vote	Registration	Vote/Reg	VAP	Vote/VAP	Invalid	FH	Population
Bolivia		**Latin America**						
1997	2 321 117	3 252 501	71.4%	3 596 616	64.5%	N/A	4	7 340 032
1993	1 731 309	2 399 197	72.2%	3 461 850	50.0%	N/A	5	7 065 000
1989	1 563 182	2 136 587	73.2%	3 086 880	50.6%	10.0%	5	6 431 000
1985	1 728 365	2 108 458	82.0%	2 652 750	65.2%	13.0%	5	5 895 000
1980	1 489 484	2 004 284	74.3%	2 520 000	59.1%	12.1%	12	5 600 000
1979	1 693 233	1 871 070	90.5%	2 452 050	69.1%	12.2%	6	5 449 000
1978	1 971 968	1 921 556	102.6%	5 386 800	82.6%	2.7%	8	5 304 000
1966	1 099 994	1 270 611	86.6%	2 002 500	54.9%	8.2%	N/A	4 450 000
1964	1 297 319	1 411 560	91.9%	1 643 850	78.9%	12.2%	N/A	3 653 000
1960	987 730	1 300 000	76.0%	1 553 850	63.6%	2.1%	N/A	3 453 000
1956	958 016	1 126 528	85.0%	1 503 740	63.7%	3.7%	N/A	3 269 000
Bosnia & Herzegovina		**CIS, Central and Eastern Europe**						
1998	1 879 339	2 656 758	70.7%	3 256 197	57.7%	N/A	10	4 022 835
1996	1 333 204	2 210 189	60.3%	2 366 000	56.3%	4.4%	10	3 640 000
Brazil		**Latin America**						
1998	83 297 773	106 101 067	78.5%	102 802 554	81.0%	18.7%	7	161 790 311
1994	77 971 676	91 803 851	84.9%	101 458 500	76.9%	18.8%	6	153 725 000
1989	72 280 909	82 074 718	88.1%	91 075 840	79.4%	6.4%	4	142 306 000
1960	12 586 354	15 543 332	81.0%	37 654 200	33.4%	7.2%	N/A	69 730 000
1955	9 097 014	15 243 246	59.7%	33 100 650	27.5%	5.2%	N/A	60 183 000
1950	8 254 979	11 455 149	72.1%	29 106 560	28.4%	4.3%	N/A	51 976 000
1945	6 200 805	7 459 849	83.1%	25 880 400	24.0%	5.3%	N/A	46 215 000
Bulgaria		**CIS, Central and Eastern Europe**						
1996	3 358 998	6 746 056	49.8%	6 440 280	52.2%	0.6%	4	8 364 000
1992	5 154 973	6 857 942	75.2%	6 405 000	80.5%	N/A	5	8 540 000
Burkina Faso		**Africa**						
1998	2 361 294	4 210 234	56.1%	5 032 586	46.9%	0.1%	9	11 123 673
1991	1 256 381	3 564 501	35.2%	4 595 500	27.3%	3.3%	11	9 191 000
Burundi		**Africa**						
1993	2 291 746	2 355 126	97.3%	2 859 840	80.1%	0.9%	14	5 958 000
Cameroon		**Africa**						
1997*								
1992	3 015 440	4 195 687	71.9%	5 482 800	55.0%	N/A	11	12 184 000
1988*								
Cap Verde		**Africa**						
2001	153 407	260 275	58.9%	213 973	71.7%	1.2%	N/A	436 530
Central African Republic		**Africa**						
1999	1 010 744	1 709 086	59.1%	1 586 468	63.7%	7.4%	7	3 133 426
1993	809 298	1 191 374	67.9%	1 609 560	50.3%	1.9%	7	3 156 000
Chad		**Africa**						
2001	2 487 215	4 069 099	61.1%	3 552 534	70.0%	2.8%	N/A	7 689 365
1996	2 672 358	3 567 913	74.9%	3 345 090	79.9%	N/A	11	6 559 000

* *Please refer to www.idea.int/turnout*

Presidential Elections

Year	Total vote	Registration	Vote/Reg	VAP	Vote/VAP	Invalid	FH	Population
Chile		**Latin America**						
2000	7 326 753	8 084 476	90.6%	10 065 771	72.8%	2.0%	4	15 227 606
1993	7 314 890	8 085 439	90.5%	8 978 450	81.5%	3.6%	4	13 813 000
1989	7 157 725	7 556 613	94.7%	8 295 040	86.3%	2.6%	7	12 961 000
1970	2 954 799	3 539 747	83.5%	5 346 000	55.3%	1.1%	N/A	9 720 000
1964	2 530 697	2 915 121	86.8%	4 585 680	55.2%	0.7%	N/A	8 492 000
1958	1 250 350	1 497 493	83.5%	4 023 800	31.1%	1.2%	N/A	7 316 000
1952	957 102	1 105 029	86.6%	3 439 980	27.8%	0.3%	N/A	5 931 000
1946	479 310	631 257	75.9%	3 149 400	15.2%	0.3%	N/A	5 430 000
Colombia		**Latin America**						
1998	12 310 107	20 857 801	59.0%	22 236 403	55.4%	1.3%	7	36 453 120
1994	7 427 742	17 147 023	43.3%	21 057 200	35.3%	N/A	7	34 520 000
1990	6 047 566	13 903 324	43.5%	19 057 000	31.7%	2.0%	7	32 300 000
1986	7 229 937	15 839 754	45.6%	16 813 440	43.0%	0.7%	5	30 024 000
1982	6 840 362	13 734 093	49.8%	14 410 700	47.5%	0.2%	5	27 190 000
1978	5 075 719	12 580 851	40.3%	13 591 850	37.3%	0.4%	5	25 645 000
1974	5 212 133	8 964 472	58.1%	10 538 000	49.5%	0.2%	4	23 950 000
1970	4 036 458	7 683 785	52.5%	8 659 200	46.6%	1.0%	N/A	21 120 000
1966	2 649 258	6 611 352	40.1%	7 634 200	34.7%	0.6%	N/A	18 620 000
1962	2 634 840	5 404 765	48.8%	6 202 980	42.5%	26.1%	N/A	14 769 000
1958	3 108 567	5 386 981	57.7%	5 679 240	54.7%	0.4%	N/A	13 522 000
1949	1 140 646	2 866 339	39.8%	5 066 900	22.5%	N/A	N/A	11 015 000
1946	1 366 272	2 450 596	55.8%	4 746 280	28.8%	N/A	N/A	10 318 000
Comoros Islands		**Africa**						
1996	179 655	290 000	62.0%	304 200	59.1%	N/A	8	676 000
1990	190 074	315 391	60.3%	244 350	77.8%	1.4%	10	543 000
Costa Rica		**Latin America**						
1998	1 431 913	2 045 980	70.0%	1 942 350	73.7%	3.0%	3	3 292 000
1994	1 525 979	1 881 348	81.1%	1 811 890	84.2%	2.3%	3	3 071 000
1990	1 384 326	1 692 050	81.8%	1 626 900	85.1%	2.6%	2	2 805 000
1986	1 261 300	1 486 474	84.9%	1 548 120	81.5%	2.5%	2	2 716 000
1982	991 679	1 261 127	78.6%	1 254 960	79.0%	2.5%	2	2 324 000
1978	860 206	1 058 455	81.3%	1 142 100	75.3%	3.4%	2	2 115 000
1974	699 340	875 041	79.9%	979 200	71.4%	3.0%	2	1 920 000
1970	562 766	675 285	83.3%	743 900	75.7%	4.0%	N/A	1 730 000
1966	451 490	554 627	81.4%	646 800	69.8%	2.2%	N/A	1 540 000
1962	391 406	483 980	80.9%	547 820	71.4%	2.0%	N/A	1 274 000
1958	229 543	354 779	64.7%	462 680	49.6%	3.5%	N/A	1 076 000
1953	197 489	293 670	67.2%	396 450	49.8%	3.4%	N/A	881 000
1948[1]	99 369	165 564	60.0%	340 200	29.2%	N/A	N/A	756 000
Croatia		**CIS, Central and Eastern Europe**						
2000	2 589 120	4 252 921	60.9%	3 484 951	74.3%	1.1%	5	4 584 831
1997	2 218 448	4 061 479	54.6%	3 450 370	64.3%	1.8%	8	4 481 000
1992	2 677 764	3 575 032	74.9%	3 591 750	74.6%	1.9%	8	4 789 000
Cyprus		**Western Europe**						
1998[1]	417 406	447 046	93.4%	487 702	85.6%	2.5%	2	750 310
1993	367 474	393 993	93.3%	466 700	78.7%	3.2%	2	718 000

[1] *Total votes include only valid votes*

Year	Total vote	Registration	Vote/Reg	VAP	Vote/VAP	Invalid	FH	Population
Djibouti		**Africa**						
1999	96 368	171 232	56.3%	332 151	29.0%	N/A	10	630 122
1993	75 635	150 487	50.3%	289 640	26.1%	N/A	12	557 000
Dominican Republic		**North America & the Carribean**						
2000	3 236 906	4 251 218	76.1%	4 954 832	65.3%	1.3%	4	8 590 243
1996	2 871 487	3 750 502	76.6%	4 743 010	60.5%	0.7%	6	8 039 000
1990	1 958 509	3 275 570	59.8%	4 015 200	48.8%	N/A	5	7 170 000
1986[1]	2 112 101	3 039 347	69.5%	3 479 450	60.7%	N/A	4	6 565 000
1982	1 922 367	2 601 684	73.9%	2 929 440	65.6%	4.8%	3	5 744 000
1978	1 655 807	2 283 784	72.5%	2 634 660	62.8%	N/A	4	5 166 000
1974	1 518 297	2 006 323	75.7%	2 188 800	69.4%	26.7%	6	4 560 000
1970[1]	1 238 205	N/A	N/A	1 867 600	66.3%	N/A	N/A	4 060 000
1966[1]	1 345 404	N/A	N/A	1 665 200	80.8%	0.3%	N/A	3 620 000
1962[1]	1 054 954	N/A	N/A	1 513 400	69.7%	N/A	N/A	3 220 000
1957	1 265 681	N/A	N/A	1 297 920	97.5%	N/A	N/A	2 704 000
1952	1 098 816	N/A	N/A	1 095 640	100.3%	N/A	N/A	2 236 000
1947	840 340	840 340	100.0%	971 180	86.5%	N/A	N/A	1 982 000
Ecuador		**Latin America**						
1998	4 960 075	7 072 496	70.1%	6 892 210	72.0%	N/A	5	12 091 596
1996	4 777 547	6 662 007	71.7%	6 665 580	71.7%	11.3%	6	11 694 000
1992	4 174 097	5 710 363	73.1%	5 907 550	70.7%	N/A	5	10 741 000
1988	3 612 635	4 649 684	77.7%	5 386 700	67.1%	14.7%	4	9 794 000
1984	2 964 298	3 794 149	78.1%	4 739 800	62.5%	10.6%	4	9 115 000
1979	1 681 286	2 088 874	80.5%	3 946 500	42.6%	12.3%	4	7 893 000
1978	1 521 412	2 088 874	72.8%	3 835 500	39.7%	10.5%	8	7 671 000
1968	928 981	1 198 874	77.5%	2 736 000	34.0%	8.8%	N/A	5 700 000
1960	767 105	1 009 280	76.0%	2 116 800	36.2%	N/A	N/A	4 320 000
1956	614 423	836 955	73.4%	1 950 750	31.5%	N/A	N/A	3 825 000
1952	357 654	550 997	64.9%	1 742 000	20.5%	1.0%	N/A	3 350 000
1948	281 713	455 524	61.8%	1 550 640	18.2%	N/A	N/A	2 982 000
El Salvador		**Latin America**						
1999	1 223 215	3 171 224	38.6%	3 209 847	38.1%	N/A	5	5 901 022
1994	1 246 220	2 700 000	46.2%	2 933 320	42.5%	3.9%	6	5 641 000
1989	1 003 153	1 834 000	54.7%	2 544 570	39.4%	6.3%	7	5 193 000
1984	1 524 079	N/A	N/A	2 532 360	60.2%	7.8%	8	5 388 000
1977[1]	1 206 942	N/A	N/A	2 042 400	59.1%	N/A	6	4 255 000
1972	806 357	1 119 699	72.0%	1 767 200	45.6%	4.4%	5	3 760 000
1967[1]	491 894	1 266 587	38.8%	1 480 500	33.2%	N/A	N/A	3 150 000
1962	400 118	N/A	N/A	1 260 960	31.7%	7.8%	N/A	2 627 000
1956[1]	711 931	N/A	N/A	1 098 000	64.8%	N/A	N/A	2 196 000
1950	647 666	N/A	N/A	952 680	68.0%	5.6%	N/A	1 868 000
1945[1]	313 694	N/A	N/A	888 420	35.3%	N/A	N/A	1 742 000
Finland		**Western Europe**						
2000	3 200 580	4 167 204	76.8%	4 166 662	76.8%	N/A	2	5 180 030
1994	3 193 825	4 150 000	77.0%	3 923 150	81.4%	N/A	2	5 095 000
1988	3 141 360	4 036 169	77.8%	3 808 420	82.5%	3.9%	3	4 946 000
1982	3 188 056	3 921 005	81.3%	3 620 250	88.1%	0.3%	4	4 827 000
1978	2 470 339	3 844 279	64.3%	3 564 750	69.3%	0.6%	4	4 753 000
1968	2 048 784	2 930 635	69.9%	3 055 800	67.0%	0.3%	N/A	4 630 000
1962	2 211 441	2 714 883	81.5%	2 703 000	81.8%	0.3%	N/A	4 505 000
1956	1 905 449	2 597 738	73.4%	2 569 200	74.2%	0.3%	N/A	4 282 000
1950	1 585 835	2 487 230	63.8%	2 445 490	64.8%	0.4%	N/A	4 009 000

[1] *Total vote include only valid votes*

Presidential Elections

Year	Total vote	Registration	Vote/Reg	VAP	Vote/VAP	Invalid	FH	Population
France		**Western Europe**						
1995	31 852 695	39 976 944	79.7%	44 080 760	72.3%	6.0%	3	58 007 000
1988[1]	32 164 400	38 200 000	84.2%	42 088 500	76.4%	N/A	3	56 118 000
1981	30 350 568	36 398 762	83.4%	39 395 480	77.0%	2.5%	3	53 966 000
1974[2]	25 100 000	29 800 000	84.2%	34 656 600	72.4%	9.0%	3	52 510 000
1969[2]	22 200 000	28 800 000	77.1%	32 708 000	67.9%	1.0%	N/A	50 320 000
1965[2]	23 744 400	28 200 000	84.2%	31 694 000	74.9%	0.7%	N/A	48 760 000
Gabon		**Africa**						
1998	337 113	626 200	53.8%	614 709	54.8%	1.3%	9	1 159 031
1993	426 594	484 319	88.1%	636 480	67.0%	2.1%	9	1 248 000
Gambia		**Africa**						
1996	394 537	493 171	80.0%	542 850	72.7%	N/A	11	1 155 000
Georgia		**CIS, Central and Eastern Europe**						
2000	2 343 176	3 088 925	75.9%	3 591 086	65.2%	N/A	8	5 030 747
1995	2 121 510	3 106 557	68.3%	3 929 760	54.0%	N/A	9	5 458 000
Ghana		**Africa**						
2000	6 605 084	10 698 652	61.7%	10 141 400	65.1%	1.6%	5	20 212 000
1996	7 257 984	9 279 605	78.2%	8 799 420	82.5%	1.5%	8	17 958 000
1992	4 127 876	8 229 902	50.2%	6 862 370	60.2%	N/A	10	N/A
Guatemala		**Latin America**						
1999	1 800 676	4 458 744	40.4%	5 784 820	31.1%	3.1%	7	11 788 030
1995	1 369 828	3 711 589	36.9%	5 203 310	26.3%	3.8%	9	10 619 000
1991	1 450 603	3 204 955	45.3%	4 544 160	31.9%	5.2%	8	9 467 000
1990	1 808 718	3 204 955	56.4%	4 415 040	41.0%	14.1%	7	9 198 000
1985[2]	1 657 823	2 753 572	60.2%	3 822 240	43.4%	N/A	8	7 963 000
1982	1 079 392	2 355 064	45.8%	3 511 200	30.7%	9.6%	12	7 315 000
1978[2]	652 073	1 785 764	36.5%	3 140 640	20.8%	N/A	7	6 543 000
1974	727 174	1 566 724	46.4%	2 836 800	25.6%	7.8%	7	5 910 000
1970	640 684	1 190 449	53.8%	2 448 000	26.2%	9.6%	N/A	5 100 000
1966	531 270	944 170	56.3%	2 188 800	24.3%	12.1%	N/A	4 560 000
1958	492 274	736 400	66.8%	1 737 540	28.3%	4.9%	N/A	3 546 000
1950	417 570	583 300	71.6%	1 372 980	30.4%	2.4%	N/A	2 802 000
Guinea		**Africa**						
1998	2 650 790	3 796 293	69.8%	3 516 574	75.4%	N/A	11	7 317 331
1993	2 236 406	2 850 403	78.5%	2 963 820	75.5%	6.9%	11	6 306 000
Guinea Bissau		**Africa**						
1999	361 609	503 007	71.9%	311 674	116.0%	3.5%	8	1 170 827
1994	316 861	396 938	79.8%	556 500	56.9%	2.1%	7	1 050 000
Haiti		**North America & the Carribean**						
2000[*]								
1995	994 599	3 668 049	27.1%	3 448 320	28.8%	13.3%	10	7 184 000
1990	1 640 729	3 271 155	50.2%	3 048 420	53.8%	N/A	8	6 486 000
1988	1 063 537	N/A	N/A	2 931 860	36.3%	N/A	12	6 238 000
1957	940 445	N/A	N/A	1 986 450	47.3%	N/A	N/A	3 895 000
1950	527 625	N/A	N/A	1 618 240	32.6%	N/A	N/A	3 112 000

[1]*Total votes and registered voters are approximations,* [2]*Total votes include only valid votes.*
[*]*Please refer to www.idea.int/turnout*

Year	Total vote	Registration	Vote/Reg	VAP	Vote/VAP	Invalid	FH	Population
Honduras		**Latin America**						
1997	2 091 733	2 901 743	72.1%	3 066 060	68.2%	5.7%	5	6 132 000
1993	1 776 204	2 734 000	65.0%	2 797 500	63.5%	1.2%	6	5 595 000
1989	1 799 146	2 366 448	76.0%	2 376 480	75.7%	2.5%	5	4 951 000
1985	1 597 841	1 901 757	84.0%	2 054 000	77.8%	3.5%	5	4 372 000
1981	1 214 735	1 558 316	78.0%	1 757 000	69.1%	2.8%	6	3 821 000
1971	608 342	900 658	67.5%	1 222 000	49.8%	0.3%	N/A	2 600 000
1954	252 624	411 354	61.4%	787 920	32.1%	0.3%	N/A	1 608 000
1948	258 345	300 496	86.0%	662 970	39.0%	1.2%	N/A	1 353 000
Iceland		**Western Europe**						
1996	167 319	194 784	85.9%	192 410	87.0%	1.2%	2	271 000
1988	126 535	173 800	72.8%	175 000	72.3%	0.2%	2	250 000
1980	129 595	143 196	90.5%	141 360	91.7%	0.4%	2	228 000
1968	103 900	112 737	92.2%	114 000	91.1%	0.8%	N/A	200 000
1952	70 457	85 887	82.0%	87 320	80.7%	3.2%	N/A	148 000
Iran		**Middle East**						
2001[*]								
1993	16 796 787	N/A	N/A	31 579 740	53.2%	N/A	13	58 481 000
Ireland		**Western Europe**						
1997	1 279 688	2 739 529	46.7%	2 681 821	47.7%	0.8%	2	N/A
1990	1 584 095	2 471 308	64.1%	N/A	N/A	0.6%	2	N/A
1983[*]								
1976[*]								
1974[*]								
1973	1 279 688	2 688 316	47.6%	2 681 821	47.7%	0.8%	3	3 626 087
1966	1 116 915	1 709 161	65.3%	1 699 200	65.7%	0.6%	N/A	2 880 000
1959	980 167	1 678 450	58.4%	1 679 140	58.4%	1.5%	N/A	2 846 000
1945	1 086 338	1 803 463	60.2%	1 800 720	60.3%	6.2%	N/A	2 952 000
Israel		**Middle East**						
1999	3 373 748	4 285 428	78.7%	3 994 784	84.5%	1.9%	3	6 089 384
1996	3 121 270	3 933 250	79.4%	3 684 850	84.7%	4.8%	4	5 669 000
Ivory Coast		**Africa**						
2000	2 049 018	5 475 143	37.4%	7 301 400	28.1%	12.4%	11	14 786 000
1995[1]	1 722 506	3 800 000	45.3%	5 527 080	31.2%	N/A	11	14 172 000
1990	3 086 166	4 408 809	70.0%	4 686 800	65.8%	N/A	10	11 717 000
Kazakhstan		**CIS, Central and Eastern Europe**						
1999	7 328 970	8 419 283	87.0%	10 155 040	72.2%	N/A	11	15 641 244
Kenya		**Africa**						
1997	4 273 595	5 095 850	83.9%	12 664 960	33.7%	0.7%	13	28 784 000
1992	5 248 596	7 855 880	66.8%	11 308 000	46.4%	N/A	9	25 700 000
Kyrgyzstan		**CIS, Central and Eastern Europe**						
2000	1 960 201	2 537 247	77.3%	2 638 707	74.3%	N/A	11	4 650 010
1995	1 943 077	2 254 348	86.2%	2 663 610	72.9%	1.2%	8	4 673 000

[1] *Total votes include only valid votes. Registered voters are approximates.*
[*] *Please refer to www.idea.int/turnout*

Presidential Elections

Year	Total vote	Registration	Vote/Reg	VAP	Vote/VAP	Invalid	FH	Population
Lithuania		**CIS, Central and Eastern Europe**						
1997	1 937 786	2 630 681	73.7%	2 740 310	70.7%	0.8%	3	3 703 000
1993	2 019 013	2 568 016	78.6%	2 760 200	73.1%	1.7%	4	3 730 000
Macedonia		**CIS, Central and Eastern Europe**						
1999	1 120 087	1 610 340	69.6%	1 438 948	77.8%	1.5%	6	2 020 903
1994	1 058 130	1 360 729	77.8%	1 477 980	71.6%	14.0%	7	2 142 000
Madagascar		**Africa**						
1996	2 167 634	3 557 352	60.9%	7 307 040	29.7%	3.8%	6	15 223 000
1993	4 302 663	6 282 564	68.5%	6 649 920	64.7%	3.6%	6	13 854 000
1992	4 436 351	5 941 427	74.7%	6 649 920	66.7%	2.2%	8	13 854 000
Malawi		**Africa**						
1999	4 755 422	5 071 822	93.8%	4 419 210	107.6%	1.9%	6	9 692 808
1994	3 040 665	3 775 256	80.5%	4 446 670	68.4%	2.0%	5	9 461 000
Maldives		**Asia**						
1998	96 698	126 128	76.7%	130 286	74.2%	0.8%	11	270 597
Mali		**Africa**						
1997	1 542 229	5 428 256	28.4%	5 282 480	29.2%	28.5%	6	11 239 300
Mauritania		**Africa**						
1997	899 444	1 203 668	74.7%	1 203 518	74.7%	0.9%	12	2 349 840
1992	551 356	1 184 372	46.6%	1 074 570	51.3%	0.4%	13	2 107 000
Mexico		**Latin America**						
2000	37 603 923	58 789 209	64.0%	62 684 899	60.0%	2.1%	5	N/A
1994	35 545 831	45 279 053	78.5%	53 944 640	65.9%	2.8%	8	93 008 000
1988[1]	19 091 843	38 074 926	50.1%	45 496 550	42.0%	N/A	7	82 721 000
1982[1]	23 592 888	31 526 386	74.8%	35 829 780	65.8%	4.5%	7	73 122 000
1976[1]	16 727 993	25 913 215	64.6%	29 046 470	57.6%	N/A	8	61 801 000
1970[1]	13 915 963	21 654 217	64.3%	21 289 800	65.4%	N/A	N/A	50 690 000
1964[1]	9 422 185	13 589 594	69.3%	16 650 060	56.6%	N/A	N/A	39 643 000
1958[1]	7 463 403	N/A	N/A	14 473 800	51.6%	N/A	N/A	32 895 000
1952[1]	3 651 483	N/A	N/A	12 416 320	29.4%	N/A	N/A	26 992 000
1946[1]	2 294 728	N/A	N/A	10 479 340	21.9%	N/A	N/A	22 779 000
Moldova		**CIS, Central and Eastern Europe**						
1996	1 748 688	2 441 054	71.6%	2 914 500	60.0%	2.6%	7	4 350 000
Mongolia		**Asia**						
2001[*]								
1997	1 403 204	N/A	N/A	1 403 204	100.0%	N/A	5	2 515 721
1993	1 250 000	1 348 000	92.7%	1 298 080	96.3%	N/A	5	2 318 000
Mozambique		**Africa**						
1999	4 934 352	7 099 105	69.5%	8 303 686	59.4%	2.9%	7	17 336 171
1994	5 412 940	6 148 842	88.0%	8 140 860	66.5%	8.4%	8	16 614 000

[1] *Total votes include valid votes.*

[*] *Please refer to www.idea.int/turnout*

Year	Total vote	Registration	Vote/Reg	VAP	Vote/VAP	Invalid	FH	Population
Namibia		**Africa**						
1999	545 465	878 869	62.1%	876 828	62.2%	1.2%	5	1 711 793
1994	485 295	654 189	74.2%	780 000	62.2%	2.4%	5	1 500 000
Nicaragua		**Latin America**						
1996	1 849 362	2 421 067	76.4%	2 447 120	75.6%	4.9%	6	4 706 000
1990	1 510 838	1 752 088	86.2%	1 935 500	78.1%	6.0%	6	3 871 000
1984	1 170 142	1 551 597	75.4%	1 581 000	74.0%	6.1%	10	3 162 000
1974	799 982	1 152 260	69.4%	1 040 000	76.9%	N/A	9	2 080 000
1967	540 714	N/A	N/A	833 000	64.9%	N/A	N/A	1 700 000
1963	451 064	570 000	79.1%	755 090	59.7%	N/A	N/A	1 541 000
1957	355 178	N/A	N/A	673 920	52.7%	N/A	N/A	1 296 000
1950	202 698	N/A	N/A	527 400	35.4%	N/A	N/A	1 060 000
1947	169 708	N/A	N/A	527 580	32.2%	N/A	N/A	977 000
Niger		**Africa**						
1999	1 815 411	4 608 090	39.4%	4 739 028	38.3%	5.2%	10	10 318 141
1996	2 525 019	3 064 550	82.4%	4 251 600	59.4%	4.3%	8	9 448 000
1993	1 325 152	4 482 096	29.6%	3 762 450	35.2%	2.5%	7	8 361 000
Nigeria		**Africa**						
1999	30 280 052	57 938 945	52.3%	52 792 781	57.4%	1.4%	7	108 258 359
1993	14 039 486	N/A	N/A	50 526 720	27.8%	N/A	12	105 264 000
1979	17 098 267	48 499 091	35.3%	38 142 090	44.8%	2.0%	8	77 841 000
Palau		**Pacific**						
2000	10 744	13 239	81.2%	13 159	81.6%	0.2%	3	19 092
1996	10 223	12 897	79.3%	N/A	N/A	N/A	3	17 000
1992	9 726	11 658	83.4%	N/A	N/A	0.1%	N/A	N/A
1988	9 195	11 146	82.5%	N/A	N/A	1.0%	N/A	N/A
1984	8 067	9 605	84.0%	N/A	N/A	1.3%	N/A	N/A
1980	6 425	8 032	80.0%	N/A	N/A	2.5%	N/A	N/A
Palestinian Authority		**Middle East**						
1996	754 902	1 035 235	72.9%	955 180	79.0%	N/A	11	1 870 000'
Panama		**Latin America**						
1999	1 330 730	1 746 989	76.2%	1 744 041	76.3%	2.7%	3	2 808 935
1994	1 105 388	1 499 848	73.7%	1 575 630	70.2%	3.4%	5	2 583 000
1989	757 797	1 184 320	64.0%	1 363 000	55.6%	12.2%	13	2 350 000
1984	674 075	917 677	73.5%	1 195 040	56.4%	4.8%	7	2 134 000
1968	327 048	544 135	60.1%	675 000	48.5%	1.9%	N/A	1 350 000
1964	326 401	486 420	67.1%	600 500	54.4%	2.8%	N/A	1 201 000
1960	358 039	435 454	82.2%	541 620	66.1%	6.4%	N/A	1 062 000
1956	306 770	386 672	79.3%	495 040	62.0%	15.5%	N/A	952 000
1952	231 848	343 353	67.5%	454 140	51.1%	8.0%	N/A	841 000
1948	216 214	305 123	70.9%	409 320	52.8%	8.3%	N/A	758 000
Paraguay		**Latin America**						
1998	1 650 725	2 049 449	80.5%	2 777 725	59.4%	N/A	7	5 137 440
1993	826 834	N/A	N/A	2 476 980	33.4%	N/A	6	4 587 000
1989	1 202 826	2 226 061	54.0%	2 161 170	55.7%	1.1%	7	4 089 000
1988	1 333 436	1 446 675	92.2%	2 100 390	63.5%	0.6%	12	3 963 000

Year	Total vote	Registration	Vote/Reg	VAP	Vote/VAP	Invalid	FH	Population
1983	1 048 996	1 132 582	92.6%	1 840 690	57.0%	1.1%	10	3 473 000
1978	1 010 299	1 175 351	86.0%	1 514 700	66.7%	1.3%	10	2 970 000
1973	814 610	1 052 652	77.4%	1 308 300	62.3%	1.3%	N/A	2 670 000
1968	656 414	897 445	73.1%	1 025 800	64.0%	1.0%	N/A	2 230 000
1963	628 615	738 472	85.1%	856 350	73.4%	1.8%	N/A	1 903 000
1958	303 478	N/A	N/A	792 890	38.3%	2.7%	N/A	1 687 000
1953	237 049	N/A	N/A	718 080	33.0%	5.2%	N/A	1 496 000
Peru		**Latin America**						
2001	12 128 969	14 906 233	81.4%	15 429 603	78.6%	11.6%	6	26 076 958
1995	9 062 512	12 421 164	73.0%	13 649 720	66.4%	17.7%	9	23 534 000
1990	7 999 978	10 042 599	79.7%	12 068 000	66.3%	9.5%	7	21 550 000
1985	7 557 182	8 290 846	91.2%	10 291 010	73.4%	13.8%	5	19 417 000
1980	5 307 465	6 485 680	81.8%	8 993 400	59.0%	22.3%	5	17 295 000
1963	1 954 284	2 070 718	94.4%	5 479 000	35.7%	7.2%	N/A	10 958 000
1962	1 969 474	2 222 926	88.6%	5 422 320	36.3%	12.2%	N/A	10 632 000
1956	1 324 229	1 575 741	84.0%	5 018 520	26.4%	5.7%	N/A	9 651 000
1950[1]	550 779	776 132	71.0%	4 430 920	12.4%	N/A	N/A	8 521 000
1945[1]	456 310	776 572	58.8%	4 018 040	11.4%	N/A	N/A	7 727 000
Philippines		**Asia**						
1998	27 782 735	34 163 465	81.3%	40 287 296	69.0%	N/A	5	73 052 254
1992[1]	22 654 194	N/A	N/A	34 699 860	65.3%	N/A	6	64 259 000
Poland		**CIS, Central and Eastern Europe**						
2000	17 798 791	29 122 304	61.1%	28 443 524	62.6%	1.1%	3	38 742 748
1995	19 146 496	28 062 205	68.2%	27 790 560	68.9%	2.0%	3	38 598 000
1990	14 703 775	27 535 159	53.4%	26 683 300	55.1%	2.3%	4	38 119 000
Portugal		**Western Europe**						
2001	4 468 442	8 932 106	50.0%	7 812 959	57.2%	2.9%	N/A	9 963 604
1996	5 762 978	8 693 636	66.3%	7 461 680	77.2%	2.5%	2	9 818 000
1991	5 099 092	8 235 151	61.9%	7 301 580	69.8%	3.6%	2	9 867 000
1986	5 939 311	7 600 001	78.1%	7 207 920	82.4%	1.0%	3	10 011 000
1980	5 834 789	6 931 641	84.2%	6 731 320	86.7%	1.1%	4	9 899 000
1976	4 885 624	6 477 484	75.4%	6 476 220	75.4%	1.4%	4	9 666 000
Republic of Korea		**Asia**						
1997	26 041 889	32 290 416	80.6%	28 159 960	92.5%	1.5%	4	46 573 643
1992	23 775 409	N/A	N/A	27 944 320	85.1%	N/A	5	43 663 000
Romania		**CIS, Central and Eastern Europe**						
2000[1]	10 020 870	17 699 727	56.6%	18 597 776	53.9%	N/A	4	22 303 305
1996	13 078 883	17 230 654	75.9%	16 737 320	78.1%	0.8%	5	22 618 000
Russia		**CIS, Central and Eastern Europe**						
2000	75 070 776	109 372 046	68.6%	109 037 258	68.8%	0.9%	10	146 595 254
1996	74 800 449	108 589 050	68.9%	110 642 250	67.6%	1.2%	7	147 523 000
1991	79 498 240	106 484 518	74.7%	108 495 520	73.3%	0.4%	6	148 624 000
Sao Tome e Principe		**Africa**						
2001	47 535	67 374	70.6%	67 504	70.4%	1.5%	N/A	9 817 462
1996	38 841	50 256	77.3%	61 021	63.7%	3.2%	3	130 806
1991	30 966	51 610	60.0%	56 870	54.5%	14.3%	5	121 000

[1] *Total votes include valid votes.*

Year	Total vote	Registration	Vote/Reg	VAP	Vote/VAP	Invalid	FH	Population
Senegal		**Africa**						
2000*								
1996	399 300	N/A	N/A	4 178 230	9.6%	N/A	9	8 527 000
1993	1 313 095	2 549 699	51.5%	3 994 480	32.9%	N/A	9	8 152 000
1988	1 134 239	1 932 265	58.7%	2 982 420	38.0%	N/A	7	7 101 000
1983	1 099 074	1 888 444	58.2%	2 715 880	40.5%	N/A	8	6 316 000
Seychelles		**Africa**						
2001	51 145	54 847	93.3%	52 267	97.9%	1.8%	N/A	80 522
1998	47 550	54 847	86.7%	52 729	90.2%	2.1%	6	78 845
1993	43 584	50 370	86.5%	45 360	96.1%	1.2%	7	72 000
Sierra Leone		**Africa**						
1996	1 028 851	1 500 000	68.6%	2 029 720	50.7%	N/A	11	4 613 000
Singapore		**Asia**						
1993	1 659 482	1 756 517	94.5%	1 983 060	83.7%	2.2%	10	2 874 000
Slovakia		**CIS, Central and Eastern Europe**						
1999	2 981 957	4 038 899	73.8%	3 767 042	79.2%	1.1%	3	1 988 781
Slovenia		**CIS, Central and Eastern Europe**						
1997	1 064 532	1 550 775	68.6%	1 495 460	71.2%	2.1%	3	1 942 000
1992	1 064 446	1 500 000	71.0%	1 497 000	71.1%	N/A	4	1 996 000
1990	1 153 335	N/A	N/A	1 498 500	77.0%	2.3%	N/A	1 998 000
Sri Lanka		**Asia**						
1999	8 635 290	11 779 200	73.3%	11 001 583	78.5%	2.3%	7	18 864 358
1994	7 709 084	10 937 279	70.5%	11 254 950	68.5%	N/A	8	17 865 000
1988	5 186 233	9 375 742	55.3%	10 125 390	51.2%	N/A	7	16 599 000
1982	6 602 617	8 145 015	81.1%	8 809 620	74.9%	1.2%	5	15 189 000
St. Kitts & Nevis		**North America & the Carribean**						
1958	14 738	N/A	N/A	N/A	N/A	N/A	N/A	58 000
Sudan		**Africa**						
1996	5 525 280	7 652 742	72.2%	15 253 500	36.2%	N/A	14	30 507 000
Taiwan (Republic of China)		**Asia**						
2000	12 786 671	15 462 625	82.7%	16 482 816	77.6%	1.0%	3	N/A
1996	10 883 279	14 313 288	76.0%	14 154 000	76.9%	1.1%	6	21 000 000
Tajikistan		**CIS, Central and Eastern Europe**						
1994	2 338 356	2 647 398	88.3%	3 025 830	77.3%	N/A	14	5 933 000
Tanzania		**Africa**						
2000	8 517 648	10 088 484	84.4%	16 055 200	53.1%	4.1%	8	33 517 000
1995	6 846 681	8 929 969	76.7%	14 256 000	48.0%	4.9%	10	29 700 000

* *Please refer to www.idea.int/turnout*

Presidential Elections

Year	Total vote	Registration	Vote/Reg	VAP	Vote/VAP	Invalid	FH	Population
Togo		**Africa**						
1998	1 587 027	2 273 190	69.8%	2 121 207	74.8%	1.8%	11	4 419 181
Tunisia		**Africa**						
1994	2 989 880	3 150 612	94.9%	4 715 820	63.4%	N/A	11	8 733 000
Uganda		**Africa**						
2001	7 576 144	10 775 836	70.3%	10 206 461	74.2%	2.7%	N/A	22 070 329
1996	6 163 678	8 489 915	72.6%	9 875 250	62.4%	N/A	8	21 945 000
Ukraine		**CIS, Central and Eastern Europe**						
1999	28 231 774	37 680 581	74.9%	38 272 306	73.8%	2.5%	7	50 054 276
1994	26 883 642	37 531 666	71.6%	39 451 600	68.1%	N/A	7	51 910 000
U.S.A		**North America & the Carribean**						
2000[1]	105 404 546	205 800 000	51.2%	213 954 023	49.3%	N/A	2	284 970 789
1996	92 712 803	146 211 960	63.4%	196 511 000	47.2%	N/A	2	265 679 000
1992	104 600 366	133 821 178	78.2%	189 529 000	55.2%	N/A	2	255 407 000
1988	91 594 809	126 379 628	72.5%	182 778 000	50.1%	N/A	2	245 057 000
1984	92 652 842	124 150 614	74.6%	174 466 000	53.1%	N/A	2	236 681 000
1980	86 515 211	113 043 734	76.5%	164 597 000	52.6%	N/A	2	227 738 000
1976	81 555 889	105 037 986	77.6%	152 309 190	53.5%	N/A	2	218 035 000
1972	77 718 554	97 328 541	79.9%	140 776 000	55.2%	N/A	2	208 840 000
1968	73 211 875	81 658 180	89.7%	120 328 186	60.8%	N/A	N/A	200 910 000
1964	70 644 592	73 715 818	95.8%	114 090 000	61.9%	N/A	N/A	192 119 000
1960	68 838 219	N/A	N/A	109 159 000	63.1%	N/A	N/A	180 684 000
1956	62 026 908	N/A	N/A	106 408 890	58.3%	N/A	N/A	168 903 000
1952	61 551 118	N/A	N/A	102 064 300	60.3%	N/A	N/A	157 022 000
1948	48 692 442	N/A	N/A	95 310 150	51.1%	N/A	N/A	146 631 000
Uruguay		**Latin America**						
1999	2 206 112	2 402 135	91.8%	2 329 231	94.7%	N/A	3	3 313 283
1994	2 130 618	2 330 154	91.4%	2 216 900	96.1%	N/A	4	3 167 000
1989	1 970 586	2 319 022	85.0%	2 123 130	92.8%	N/A	3	3 077 000
1984	1 886 756	2 200 086	85.8%	2 033 200	92.8%	N/A	9	2 990 000
1971	1 664 119	1 878 132	88.6%	1 956 400	85.1%	N/A	N/A	2 920 000
1966	1 231 762	1 658 368	74.3%	1 842 500	66.9%	N/A	N/A	2 750 000
1962	1 171 020	1 528 239	76.6%	1 952 380	60.0%	N/A	N/A	2 914 000
1958	1 005 362	1 410 105	71.3%	1 850 540	54.3%	N/A	N/A	2 762 000
1954	879 242	1 295 502	67.9%	1 727 930	50.9%	N/A	N/A	2 579 000
1950	823 829	1 168 206	70.5%	1 612 690	51.1%	N/A	N/A	2 407 000
1946	649 405	993 892	65.3%	1 528 270	42.5%	N/A	N/A	2 281 000
Uzbekistan		**CIS, Central and Eastern Europe**						
2000*								
1991	9 870 000	10 500 000	94.0%	11 074 880	89.1%	N/A	11	20 896 000
Venezuela		**Latin America**						
2000	6 600 196	11 681 645	56.5%	14 131 207	46.7%	N/A	8	24 185 517
1993	5 829 216	10 000 000	58.3%	12 012 960	48.5%	3.6%	6	20 712 000
1988	7 518 663	9 185 647	81.9%	10 316 320	72.9%	2.5%	3	18 422 000
1983	6 792 208	7 777 892	87.3%	8 852 760	76.7%	4.9%	3	16 394 000
1978	5 448 801	6 223 903	87.5%	7 316 920	74.5%	3.1%	3	14 071 000

[1] *The number of registered voters is an approximate figure.*

* *Please refer to www.idea.int/turnout*

Year	Total vote	Registration	Vote/Reg	VAP	Vote/VAP	Invalid	FH	Population
1973	4 571 561	4 737 152	96.5%	5 640 000	81.1%	4.3%	4	11 280 000
1968	3 999 617	4 134 928	96.7%	4 617 600	86.6%	7.0%	N/A	9 620 000
1963	3 107 563	3 367 787	92.3%	3 909 120	79.5%	6.1%	N/A	8 144 000
1958	2 722 053	2 913 801	93.4%	3 370 710	80.8%	4.1%	N/A	6 879 000
1947[1]	1 172 543	N/A	N/A	2 274 000	51.6%	N/A	N/A	4 548 000
Zambia		**Africa**						
1996	1 258 805	2 267 382	55.5%	4 467 520	28.2%	5.3%	9	9 712 000
1991	1 325 155	2 981 895	44.4%	3 869 520	34.2%	N/A	5	8 412 000
Zimbabwe		**Africa**						
1996	1 557 558	4 822 289	32.3%	5 839 000	26.7%	3.0%	10	11 678 000
1990	2 587 204	N/A	N/A	4 590 810	56.4%	5.7%	10	9 369 000

[1] *Total votes include only valid votes.*

Contributors

Jamal Adimi a lawyer by profession and has been teaching law at various institutes in Yemen as well as conducting research on law and electoral law in the Middle East. He is Secretary-General of the Forum for Civil Society (FCS) in Yemen, manager of the Jamal Adimi Law office, and a consultant to Yemeni companies and international organizations. He is a Yemeni national and currently lives and works in Sana'a, Yemen.

Julie Ballington joined International IDEA as Assistant Programme Officer in the Normative Division in 2001. She previously worked as a researcher at the Electoral Institute of Southern Africa based in Johannesburg, South Africa. Her interest is in gender and electoral politics, and she has written about these issues in the southern African context. She holds a Master of Arts in political studies from the University of the Witwatersrand where she is presently a Ph.D. candidate.

Craig Brians is an Assistant Professor in the Department of Political Science at Virginia Tech. His teaching and research interests focus on elections, particularly the impact of institutions, social settings, mass media information and personal characteristics on political participation. Brians has a Ph.D. in Political Science and a Masters in Social Science from the University of California, Irvine. His published research has appeared in a wide range of journals, including the American Political Science Review, the American Journal of Political Science, Social Science Quarterly and Public Choice.

Maria Gratschew is a graduate of the University of Uppsala, Sweden. She joined International IDEA in 1999 as project officer responsible for International IDEA's Voter Turnout Project, which is available at www.idea.int/turnout. She works mainly on voter turnout, voter registration and compulsory voting issues.

Rafael López Pintor is Professor of Sociology and Political Science at the Universidad Autónoma in Madrid, Spain, and is an international political consultant to the United Nations, the European Union and International IDEA among other organisations. He has published a number of books and articles in the field of public opinion and elections in a variety of languages. His most recent studies are *Electoral Management Bodies as Institutions of Governance* (New York: UNDP, 2000), and *Votos contra Balas* (Barcelona: Planeta, 1999).

Contributors

Sergei Lounev is a Leading Research Fellow at the Institute of World Economy and International Relations, Russian Academy of Sciences, and Professor at Moscow State University and the Moscow Academy for Humanitarian and Social Studies. He has published more that 100 works, including several monographs. His most recent monographs are *The Challenges to the Southern Borders of Russia* (Moscow Public Science Foundation, 1999), *Transformation of the World System: the Role of the Largest States of Eurasia* (Academia, 2001) and *Central Asia and Russia* (Institute of Oriental Studies, RAS, 2001). He is the editor of *The Vitality of Russia* (forthcoming).

Dieter Nohlen has been Professor of Political Science at Heidelberg University since 1974 and is also Scientific Director of the Heidelberg Center for Latin America at the University of Heidelberg in Santiago de Chile. His main fields of interest and research include comparative government, electoral studies, Spanish and Latin American politics, development studies and theory. Among his publications are *Elections in Germany, Parliamentarism in Spain, Socialist Revolution in Chile* and *Electoral Systems in Comparative Perspective*. He is also the editor of *Elections in Africa: A Data Handbook* (Oxford University Press, 1999).

Pippa Norris is Associate Director (Research) at the Shorenstein Center on the Press, Politics and Public Policy and Lecturer at the John F. Kennedy School of Government, Harvard University. She has published two dozen books comparing gender politics, elections and voting behaviour, and political communications. Her most recent studies are *A Virtuous Circle: Political Communications in Post-Industrial Societies* (Cambridge University Press, 2000) and *Digital Divide: Civic Engagement, Social Equality and the Internet Worldwide* (Cambridge University Press, 2001).

Smita Notosusanto is currently the Executive Director of the Centre for Electoral Reform, based in Jakarta. She is also a lecturer at the Department of International Relations as well as the Women's Studies Program of the University of Indonesia in Jakarta.

Kate Sullivan joined International IDEA's elections team in 2000. She was previously Assistant Director, Government and Legal, at the Australian Electoral Commission in Canberra. A graduate of the Australian National University, she is involved in International IDEA's work on electoral structures and administration.

Edmundo Urrutia, a Guatemalan national, studied philosophy and political science in Guatemala and Mexico (FLACSO) and later in the United States (University of New Mexico, Albuquerque). He is a consultant at ASIES, Asociación de Investigación y Estudios Sociales, and Professor of Political Science at Landivar University, Guatemala. He is also a columnist in El Periodico, a Guatemalan newspaper, and wrote a novel in 1998, *El Naufragio de las Palabras.*

General Sources

The Administration and Cost of Elections Project (ACE project), 1999, joint project between International IDEA, United Nations and International Foundation for Election Systems, www.aceproject.org.

US Central Intelligence Agency, 2000. The World Factbook. Washington, D.C.

US Central Intelligence Agency, 2001. The World Factbook. Washington, D.C.

Freedom in the World: The Annual Survey of Political Rights and Civil Liberties 1972–1973 to 2000–2001. New York: Freedom House, www.freedomhouse.org.

International Foundation for Electoral Systems (IFES), Washington, D.C, United States, www.ifes.org.

International IDEA. 1997. Voter Turnout from 1945 to 1997: a Global Report on Political Participation, 2nd ed. Stockholm: International IDEA. www.idea.int/turnout.

Nohlen D, Grotz F and Hartmann C (eds), 2001, Elections in Asia & the Pacific – A Data Handbook, London ,Oxford University Press.

Nohlen D, Kreenerich M, Thibaut B, (eds), 1999. Elections in Africa – A Data Handbook, London, Oxford University Press.

Inter-Parliamentary Union (IPU), Geneva, Switzerland, www.ipu.org.

Reynolds, A. and B. Reilly. 1997. The International IDEA Handbook on Electoral System Design. Stockholm: International IDEA.

The Electoral Process Information Collection Project (EPIC project) joint project between International IDEA, UNDP and IFES, www.epicproject.org.

United Nations. 2000. 1998 Demographic Yearbook. New York.

United Nations. 1998. 1996 Demographic Yearbook. New York.

United Nations. 1999. World Population Prospects: The 1998 Revision (Volume I: Comprehensive Tables and Volume II: The Sex and Age Distribution of the World Population). New York.

UN Development Programme. 1999. Human Development Report. New York.

Country-specific Sources

ALBANIA
The International Foundation for Election Systems (IFES) field office, Albania.

ALGERIA
Embassy of Sweden, Algeria.

ANDORRA
Consell General del Principat d'Andorra, Andorra.

ANGUILLA
Electoral Office, Anguilla.

ANTIGUA AND BARBUDA
Electoral Office, Antigua & Barbuda.

ARGENTINA
Camara Nacional Electoral, Argentina
www.pjn.gov.ar/cne

ARMENIA
Central Electoral Committee, Armenia.
www.am.elections.am

ARUBA
Electoral Council of Aruba, Aruba.

AUSTRALIA
Australian Electoral Commission (AEC), Australia.
www.aec.gov.au

AUSTRIA
Wahlanbelägenheiten, Bundesministerium fur Inneres, Austria.
http://ln-inter11.bmi.gv.at/web/bmiwebp.nsf/AllPages/WA991217000011

AZERBAIJAN
Central Election Commission, Azerbaijan.
www.cec.gov.az

BAHAMAS
Parliamentary Registration Department, Ministry of National Security, Bahamas.

BANGLADESH
Bangladesh Election Commission, Bangladesh.
www.bd-ec.org/index.php3

BARBADOS
Electoral and Boundaries Commission, Barbados.
www.bgis.gov.bb

BELARUS
Central Electoral Commission of Belarus, Belarus.
www.rec.gov.by

BELGIUM
Ministry of Interior, Belgium.
www.belgium.fgov.be

BELIZE
Elections and Boundaries Department, Ministry of the Public Service, Labour and Civil Society, Belize.
www.belize-elections.org

BENIN
Commission Electorale Nationale Autonome (CENA), Benin.

BOLIVIA
Corte Nacional Electoral, Bolivia.
www.bolivian.com/cne

BOSNIA AND HERZEGOVINA
University of Essex, Department of Government, United Kingdom.

www.essex.ac.uk/elections

OSCE Mission to Bosnia and Herzegovina.
www.oscebih.org/elections/eng/elections.htm

BOTSWANA
Independent Electoral Commission of Botswana.

www.gov.bw/elections

BRAZIL
Tribunal Superior Electoral, Brazil.

www.tse.gov.br

BULGARIA
Central Electoral Commission, Bulgaria.

www.parliament.bg

BURKINA FASO
Comission Electorale Nationale Independante, Burkina Faso.

www.ceni.bf

CAMBODIA
Electoral Commission, Pohnpei State Government, Cambodia.

The Asia Foundation, Cambodia.

CAMEROON
Prime Minister's Cabinet, Cameroon.

CANADA
Elections Canada, Canada.

www.elections.ca

CAPE VERDE
National Electoral Commission, Cape Verde.

CENTRAL AFRICAN REPUBLIC
United Nations Development Programme.

www.undp.org

CHAD
United Nations Development Programme (UNDP), Chad.

CHILE
Servicio Electoral de Chile, Chile.

www.servel.cl

COLOMBIA
Consejo Nacional Electoral, Colombia.

COOK ISLANDS
Electoral Office, Cook Islands.

COSTA RICA
Tribunal Supremo de Elecciones, Costa Rica.

www.tse.go.cr

CÔTE D'IVOIRE
The United Nations Development Programme.

www.undp.org

CROATIA
Election Commission of Croatia, Croatia.

www.izbori.hr

CYPRUS
Cyprus Central Electoral Service, Ministry of Interior, Cyprus.

CZECH REPUBLIC
Department of the General Administration, Ministry of Interior, Czech Republic.

www.volby.cz

DENMARK
Ministry of the Interior, Denmark.

www.inm.dk

DJIBOUTI
International Foundation for Election Systems (IFES), United States.

www.ifes.org

DOMINICA
Office of the Clerk, House of Assembly, Dominica.

DOMINICAN REPUBLIC
Central Electoral Board, Dominican Republic.

www.jce.do

ECUADOR
Embassy of Ecuador, Stockholm.

EGYPT
Embassy of Egypt, Sweden.

Country-specific Sources

EL SALVADOR
Tribunal Supremo Electoral, El Salvador.
www.tse.gob.sv

EQUATORIAL GUINEA
United Nations Development Programme (UNDP).
www.undp.org

ESTONIA
Riigikogu Valimine, Estonia.
www.vvk.ee

FEDERAL REPUBLIC OF YUGOSLAVIA
University of Essex, Department of Government, United Kingdom.
www.essex.ac.uk/elections

FIJI
Office of the Supervisor of Elections, Fiji.

FINLAND
Ministry of Justice, Finland.
www.om.fi

FRANCE
Conseil Constitutionnel, France.

GEORGIA
Central Electoral Commission, Georgia.
www.cec.gov.ge

GERMANY
Der Bundeswahlleiter, Germany.
www.destatis.de/wahlen

GHANA
Electoral Commission of Ghana, Ghana.

GREECE
Embassy of the Hellenic Republic, Sweden. Ministry of Interior, Greece.

GRENADA
Parliamentary Elections Office, Grenada.
www.spiceisle.com/elections99/electora

GUATEMALA
Tribunal Supremo Electoral, Guatemala.
www.tse.org.gt

GUINEA
United Nations Development Programme, (UNDP).
www.undp.org

GUINEA BISSAU
United Nations Development Programme, (UNDP)
www.undp.org

GUYANA
United Nations Development Programme (UNDP), Guyana.
www.undp.org

HAITI
Organisation of American States (OAS), United States.
www.oas.org

HONDURAS
Tribunal Nacional de Elecciones, Honduras.

HUNGARY
Secretariat for the Association for Central and Eastern European Electoral Officials (ACEEEO)
Central Data Processing, Registration and Election Office, Ministry of Interior, Hungary.
www.aceeeo.com
www.election.hu

ICELAND
Ministry of Justice, Iceland.
www.brunnur.stjr.is/interpro/dkm/dkm.nsf/pages/english

INDIA
Election Commission of India, India.
www.eci.gov.in

INDONESIA
Indonesian Electoral Commission (KPU), Indonesia.

IRELAND
Ministry of Environment and Local Governance, Ireland.
www.environ.ie

ISRAEL
The editors of the Knesset Website, Israel.
www.knesset.gov.il/elections01/eindex.html

ITALY
Department for Political Science and Sociology, University of Florence (DISPO), Florence

www.unifi.it

JAMAICA
Electoral Office, Jamaica.

www.eoj.com.jm

JAPAN
International Affairs Division for Local Authorities, Ministry of Public Management, Home Affairs, Posts and Telecommunications, Japan.

KAZAKHSTAN
International Foundation for Election Systems (IFES), United States.

www.ifes.org

KENYA
Electoral Commission of Kenya, Kenya.

www.kenyaweb.com/politics/electoral.html

KIRIBATI
Electoral Office, Ministry of Home Affairs and Rural Development, Kiribati.

KYRGYZSTAN
Central Election Commission, Kyrgyzstan.

www.cec.bishkek.su

LATVIA
Central Electoral Commission, Latvia.

www.saeima.lanet.lv/cvsetv

LEBANON
Lebanese Center for Policy Studies, Lebanon.

www.lcps-lebanon.org/resc/democ

LESOTHO
Independent Electoral Commission of Lesotho.

LIECHTENSTEIN
Ministry of Justice, Liechtenstein.

LITHUANIA
Central Election Committee, Lithuania
Inter-Parliamentary Union, Geneva.

www.lrs.lt/rinkimai
www.ipu.org

LUXEMBOURG
Chambre des Deputes, Luxembourg.

MALAWI
Electoral Commission, Malawi.

MALAYSIA
Electoral Commission of Malaysia, Malaysia.

www.spr.gov.my

MALDIVES
Office of the Commissioner of Elections, Maldives.

MALI
Ministère de l'administration Territoriale et des Collectivités Locales, Mali.

MALTA
Electoral Office, Malta.

MAURITIUS
Elections Commission, Mauritius.

www.ncb.intnet.mu/pmo

MEXICO
Federal Electoral Institute, Mexico.

MICRONESIA (FEDERATED STATES OF)
National Electoral Commission, Federated States of Micronesia.

MONACO
Parliament of Monaco, Monaco.

MONGOLIA
Parliament of Mongolia, Mongolia.

www.parl.gov.mn
Inter-Parliamentary Union, Geneva.

www.ipu.org
Embassy of Mongolia to the United Kingdom, UK.

MOROCCO
National Democratic Institute, Morocco.

www.ndi.org/worldwide/mena/morocco/morocco.asp

MOZAMBIQUE
Secretariado Técnico de Administracão Eleitoral (STAE), Mozambique.

Country-specific Sources

NAMIBIA
Electoral Commission of Namibia, Namibia.

NAURU
Returning Officer of Nauru & Secretary of State, Government of Nauru, Nauru.

NEPAL
Election Commission of Nepal, Nepal.
www.election-commission.org.np/

NETHERLANDS
National Election Board, Netherlands.

NEW ZEALAND
Electoral Commission, New Zealand.
www.elections.org.nz/elections

NICARAGUA
Consejo Supremo Electoral, Nicaragua.
www.cse.gob.ni

NIGER
Inter-Parliamentary Union, Geneva
www.ipu.org

NIGERIA
Independent National Electoral Commission (INEC), Nigeria.

NORWAY
Ministry of Local Government and Regional Development, Norway.
www.stortinget.no

PAKISTAN
Election Commission of Pakistan, Pakistan.

PALAU
Office of the Election Commission, Palau.

PANAMA
Tribunal Electoral, Panama.
www.tribunal-electoral.gob.pa

PAPUA NEW GUINEA
Electoral Commission, Papua New Guinea.

PARAGUAY
Tribunal Superior de Justicia Electoral.
www.tsje.gov.py

PERU
Transparencia, Peru.
www.transparencia.org

PHILIPPINES
Commission on Elections, Philippines.
www.codewan.com.ph/peoplespower/comelec

POLAND
National Electoral Office, Poland.

PORTUGAL
Secretariado Tecnico para Assuntos para o Processo Eleitoral (STAPE), Portugal.
www.stape.pt

ROMANIA
Central Electoral Bureau, Romania.
www.kappa.ro/guv/bec/ceb96.html

RUSSIA
Section for International Cooperation, Central Election Commission, Russia.
www.fci.ru

RWANDA
Commission Electorale Nationale, Rwanda.

SAN MARINO
Ufficio Comunicazione Istituzionale e Relazioni con il Pubblico (U.C.I.R.P.), State Office for Elections, Ministry for Internal Affairs, San Marino
www.elezioni.sm

SÃO TOMÉ AND PRINCIPE
United Nations Development Programme (UNDP), São Tomé & Principe.

SENEGAL
Interview with Mr. Momar Diop, Senior Programme Officer at the Capacity-Building Programme, International IDEA.

SEYCHELLES
Electoral Commission, Seychelles.

SIERRA LEONE
National Electoral Commission, Sierra Leone.

Report on the Work of the Interim National Electoral Commission.

(INEC) 1994 - 1996. Freetown, December, 1996..

SINGAPORE
Elections Department, Government of Singapore, Singapore.

www.gov.sg/pmo/elections/index.html

SLOVAKIA
Parliamentary Institute, Chancellery of the National Council of the Slovak Republic, Slovakia.

www.nrsr.sk

SLOVENIA
Inter-Parliamentary Union, Switzerland.

www.ipu.org

SOLOMON ISLANDS
Electoral Commission, Solomon Islands.

SOUTH AFRICA
Independent Electoral Commission, South Africa.

www.elections.org.za

SPAIN
Ministry of Interior, Spain.

www.mir.es

SRI LANKA
Department of Elections, Elections Secretariat, Sri Lanka.

ST. KITTS AND NEVIS
Electoral Office, St. Kitts and Nevis.

ST. LUCIA
Electoral Department, Government of St. Lucia.

ST. VINCENT AND THE GRENADINES
Electoral Office, St. Vincent & the Grenadines.

SURINAME
Technical State Commission Election 2000, Suriname.

SWEDEN
Electoral Unit at the Swedish Taxboard (from July 2001 the Election Commission of Sweden) Sweden.

www.val.se

SWITZERLAND
Section of Political Rights, Swiss Federal Chancery, Switzerland.

www.admin.ch/ch/d/pore/index

TAIWAN (REPUBLIC OF CHINA)
Central Election Commission, Taipei, Taiwan.

www.cec.gov.tw

TAJIKISTAN
Inter-Parliamentary Union, Switzerland.

www.ipu.org

TANZANIA
United Nations Development Programme (UNDP), Tanzania.

www.undp.org

THAILAND
Inter-Parliamentary Union, Geneva.

www.ipu.org

TONGA
The Supervisor of Elections, Prime Minister's Office, Tonga.

TRINIDAD AND TOBAGO
Electoral Office, Trinidad & Tobago.

TUNISIA
Embassy of Tunisia, Sweden.

Embassy of Tunisia, Algeria.

TURKEY
Inter-Parliamentary Union, Switzerland.

www.ipu.org

TUVALU
Electoral Office, Tuvalu.

UGANDA
Election Commission of Uganda, Uganda.

UKRAINE
Central Electoral Commission and Committee of Voters, Ukraine.

www.cvk.ukrpack.net

UNITED KINGDOM
UK Independent Electoral Commission.

www.electoralcommission.co.uk

URUGUAY
Corte Electoral, Uruguay.

USA
Federal Election Commission.
www.fec.gov

UZBEKISTAN
International Foundation for Election Systems (IFES), United States.
www.ifes.org

VANUATU
Vanuatu Electoral Commission, Vanuatu.

VENEZUELA
Consejo Nacional Electoral, Venezuela.
www.cne.gov.ve

WESTERN SAMOA
Office of the Clerk of the Legislative Assembly, Samoa.

YEMEN
Transparency Yemen, Yemen.
www.TransparencyYemen.org.ye

ZAMBIA
Electoral Commission of Zambia, Zambia.

ZIMBABWE
Zimbabwe Election Support Network, Zimbabwe.
www.zesn.org.zw

The work of this publication builds on the first and second editions of the Voter Turnout Reports. Please refer to these two editions for an additional list of general as well as country-specific sources.
This list is also available on our website at www.idea.int/voter_turnout/intro_sources_and_definitions.html